# Jane's Fame

# Jane's Fame

## HOW JANE AUSTEN CONQUERED

## THE WORLD

## CLAIRE HARMAN

A JOHN MACRAE BOOK

HENRY HOLT AND COMPANY

NEW YORK

Henry Holt and Company, LLC
*Publishers since 1866*
175 Fifth Avenue
New York, New York 10010
www.henryholt.com

Henry Holt® and 🏛® are registered trademarks of Henry Holt and Company, LLC.

Originally published in Great Britain in 2009 by Canongate Books Ltd

Library of Congress Cataloging-in-Publication Data

Harman, Claire.
Jane's fame: how Jane Austen conquered the world / Claire Harman.—1st U.S. ed.
  p. cm.
Originally published : Edinburgh : Canongate, 2009.
Includes bibliographical references and index.
ISBN-13: 978-0-8050-8258-6
  1. Austen, Jane, 1775–1817—Appreciation.   2. Austen, Jane, 1775–1817—Influence.
3. Novelists, English—19th century—Biography.   I. Title.
PR4036.H37 2010
823.7—dc22
  [B]                                                                     2009022291

Henry Holt books are available for special promotions and premiums.
For details contact: Director, Special Markets.

First U.S. Edition 2010

Designed by Meryl Sussman Levavi

Printed in the United States of America

1   3   5   7   9   10   8   6   4   2

*For Paul*

# Contents

ILLUSTRATION CREDITS xi

PREFACE xv

1. "AUTHORS TOO OURSELVES" 1

2. PRAISE AND PEWTER 27

3. MOULDERING IN THE GRAVE 61

4. A VEXED QUESTION 94

5. DIVINE JANE 123

6. CANON AND CANONIZATION 160

7. JANE AUSTEN™ 197

ABBREVIATIONS 231

NOTES 233

MANUSCRIPT SOURCES 249

SELECTED BIBLIOGRAPHY 251

ACKNOWLEDGMENTS 259

INDEX 263

# *Illustration Credits*

⟋⟍

1. Manuscript of "Sir Charles Grandison" by Jane Austen (kind permission of Chawton House Library, Hampshire, http://www.chawtonhouse.org).

2. The Reverend George Austen (1731–1805).

3. Letter from Rev. George Austen to Thomas Cadell, November 1, 1797 (by kind permission of the president and scholars of Saint John Baptist College in the University of Oxford).

4. John Murray II, mezzotint after unknown artist, early 1800s (© National Portrait Gallery, London).

5. Royalty check from the firm of John Murray to Jane Austen, 1816 (John Murray Archive © Trustees of the National Library of Scotland).

6. Portrait of a man said to be the Reverend James Stanier Clarke, LLD, FRS (1765–1834) by John Russell (1745–1806), ca. 1790 (© V&A Images / Victoria and Albert Museum).

7. Henry Austen (1771–1850), miniature, ca. 1820 (in family possession).

8. Silhouette of Cassandra Austen (1773–1845), undated (Jane Austen Memorial Trust).

9. Jane Austen's gravestone in Winchester Cathedral (© The Dean and Chapter of Winchester).

10. Richard Bentley, lithograph by Charles Baugniet, 1844 (© National Portrait Gallery, London).

11. Engraved title page of *Sense and Sensibility*, published by Richard Bentley & Co. in 1833.

12. James Edward Austen-Leigh (1798–1874), artist unknown (Jane Austen Memorial Trust).

13. Robert William Chapman, bromide print by Walter Stoneman, 1949 (© National Portrait Gallery, London).

14. Chawton Cottage, photographed for the *Bookman*, January 1902 (The Bodleian Library, University of Oxford, Per 25805 c.2).

15. Dorothy Darnell and T. Edward Carpenter at Chawton Cottage, late 1940s (Jane Austen Memorial Trust).

16. Jane Austen, pencil and watercolor drawing by Cassandra Austen, ca. 1810 (© National Portrait Gallery, London).

17. Watercolor painting by James Andrews after Cassandra Austen, 1869 (private family collection).

18. Engraving after Cassandra Austen; the frontispiece to James Edward Austen-Leigh's *Memoir of Jane Austen*, 1870 (© Bettman/Corbis).

19. Steel engraving from Evert A. Duyckinck's *Portrait Gallery of Eminent Men and Women*, 1873, artist unknown.

20. Silhouette, said to be of Jane Austen, artist unknown (Patrick O'Connor Collection).

21. "Mr. and Mrs. Bennet" from *Pride and Prejudice*, Allen and Macmillan, 1894; illustration by Hugh Thomson.

22. Jane Austen, woodcut by Félix Vallotton, from *La Revue Blanche*, January–April 1898.

23. Lithograph portrait of Félix Fénéon by Maximilien Luce, from *Mazas*, 1894 (© ADAGP, Paris, and DACS, London, 2009).

24. Cover of *The Story-Teller*, May 1924 (The Bodleian Library, University of Oxford, Per 2561 d.46).

25. Cartoon from "Real Life Stories: Jane Austen," *Girl*, October 20, 1954, drawn by Eric Dadswell (© IPC Magazines).

26. Royal Mail commemorative stamps, 1975, designed by Barbara Brown.

27. Greer Garson and Laurence Olivier in Robert Z. Leonard's *Pride and Prejudice*, 1940 (© Turner Entertainment Co., A Warner Bros. Entertainment Company. All rights reserved).

28. James McAvoy and Anne Hathaway in *Becoming Jane*, 2007 (BFI).

29. *Jane Austen*, 1995 (© Theo Westenberger/Corbis).

# *Preface*

*What is all this about Jane Austen? What is there in her?*
*What is it all about?*

JOSEPH CONRAD TO H. G. WELLS, 1901

WHEN JANE AUSTEN'S BROTHER HENRY WROTE THE FIRST "Biographical Notice" about the author for the posthumous publication of *Northanger Abbey* and *Persuasion* in 1818, he clearly thought his would be the last words on the subject. "Short and easy will be the task of the mere biographer," he wrote. "A life of usefulness, literature and religion was not by any means a life of event." As far as Henry and his siblings were concerned, the story of their sister's authorship was over. A few of her remaining letters were bequeathed as keepsakes to nephews and nieces; others were destroyed or forgotten. The books went out of print, and Jane's generation of Austens aged and died secure in the belief that the public's curiosity about their sister—such as it was—had been satisfied.

But almost two hundred years and tens of thousands of books on Austen later, her fame and readership worldwide continue to grow. Her six completed novels are among the best-known, best-loved, most-read works in the English language. Practically overlooked for thirty or forty years after her death, the "tide of her fame" that Henry James imagined had already "passed the high-water" at the end of the nineteenth century has swollen and burst its banks. She is now a truly global phenomenon, known as much through film and television adaptations of her stories as through the books themselves, revered by non-readers and scholars alike. Her influence reaches from the decoration of tea towels to a defense of extreme pornography, and her fans have included Queen Victoria, E. M. Forster, B. B. King ("Jane Austen! I *love* Jane Austen!")[1] and the editor of the men's magazine *Nuts*. As the title of one Austen blog has it, "Jane Austen—She's Everywhere!" endlessly referenced and name-dropped and part of today's multinational, multilingual, multicultural single currency.

The use of Austen's name knows no generic boundaries. Who else is cited with equal approval by feminists and misogynists, can be linked to nineteenth-century anarchism, twenty-first-century terrorism, and the National Trust, and forms part of the inspiration behind works as diverse as *Eugene Onegin* and *Bridget Jones's Diary*? During the 2006 World Cup Final, some viewers may have been momentarily distracted from the foot- and headwork of Zinedine Zidane by the Phillips advertisement behind the French goal announcing *Sense and Simplicity*, while a recent article about possible infiltration of U.S. educational programs by terrorists was titled "Osama Bin Laden a Huge Jane Austen Fan." The phrase "Pride and Prejudice" itself, sonorous, moralistic, and nicely alliterative, has provided headline writers with one of their readiest formulas, though, of course, Austen's novel is rarely the subject of whatever follows; it could be cricket match coverage, the stalemate in a steel strike, the fallout from an anti-Islamic newspaper article, or the description of Bob Woodward's latest book about the Bush administration's Iraq strategy: "A Heady Mix of Pride and Prejudice Led to War." There is a long tradition of linking the phrase with public affairs; in 1900 the *New York Times* ran a letter about the conduct of the British in the Boer War under that title, as the writer had claimed, "Pride has made them believe themselves perfect; prejudice against things foreign has so isolated their army that it is now actually antiquated and worthy of the days of George III."[2] In the spring of 2007, it turned up in a headline about the birth of a child to the American vice president's lesbian daughter, Mary: "Pride and Prejudice: Dick Cheney's family values."[3]

If *Pride and Prejudice* is the representative Austen title, its opening sentence is one of the most frequently abused quotes in the language, second only to "to be or not to be." Marjorie Garber has called it a "cultural bromide" and cited its forced use in articles on subjects as diverse as grape allergies, opera stars, and restaurant services, as well as pieces about Austen and her books, of course.[4] The mathematical neatness of the sentence lends itself to appropriation: "It is a truth universally acknowledged that a [blank] in possession of a [blank] must be in want of a [blank]." Almost every day of the week, you'll find it in a paper or on a Web site somewhere: "It is a truth universally acknowledged that an unemployed believer in possession of a missile-launcher must be in want of a jihad" or "It is a truth universally acknowledged that the acquisition and enhancement of literacy skills is a fundamental educational goal."[5]

Austen's success as an infinitely exploitable global brand, or conceptual product, has everything to do with recognition and little to do with reading. The Victorian novelist Margaret Oliphant understood this at the very dawn of Janeism: " 'The best judges' have here, for once, done the office of an Academy," she wrote in March 1870, suspicious of the fuss around the first biography. "[They have] laureated a writer whom the populace would not have been likely to laureate, but whom it has learned to recognise." The "universality of applause" that Austen had already excited seemed to Oliphant "half-real half-fictitious,"[6] the result of wishful thinking on the part of readers and exploitation by what Henry James later identified as "bookselling spirits" and "the stiff breeze of the commercial." If this was true in 1870, how much more so is it today, when Austen's name bears such a weight of signification as to mean almost nothing at all? To many people, *Pride and Prejudice*, and even "Jane Austen," simply evoke the actor Colin Firth in a wet shirt, and for all her consistent topping of "Nation's Favorite" list (in 2007 *Pride and Prejudice* was voted "the book the United Kingdom can't do without"; the Bible was sixth), Austen's texts remain unfamiliar to many readers. In 2007, the director of the Jane Austen Festival in Bath, an unpublished novelist, tested the alertness of eighteen contemporary British publishers by sending them the first chapters of *Pride and Prejudice*, with proper nouns slightly adjusted, under the title " 'First Impressions,' by Alison Laydee." It was rejected by all of them, but more surprisingly, only one editor seems to have recognized the manuscript's origins and the presence of a hoax.[7]

But unlike many candidates for global celebrity, Austen is a genuinely great artist as well as a popular one, "an example of high culture in its least challenging form . . . at once formidable and nonthreatening," as the critic Claudia Johnson has said.[8] Her "monoplot," once described as "Boy meets Girl—Girl gets Boy,"[9] fulfills every requirement of romance and erotic fantasy literature but also contains matter for a lifetime's rumination on relations between the sexes. Her clear prose style is extraordinarily accessible, while her irony allows illimitable interpretation.

Austen's appeal has been powerful enough to threaten the jurisdiction of critics and certainly of literary critics. She is one of few writers who inspire personal love and strong feelings of proprietorship. Virginia Woolf observed that Austen's characters are so rounded and substantial that readers treat them "as if they were living people,"[10] while more recently, Austen's biographer Claire Tomalin has remarked how "many readers feel strongly that she is their personal property, not to be tampered with or subjected to questions and theories."[11] The Web-connected world allows full indulgence of readers' identification with the author and her works; there are hundreds of Austen blogs and sites, including Austen Addicts, Lost in Austen, Austen-Prose ("A daily celebration of the brilliance of Jane Austen's writing"), and the Republic of Pemberley, a heavily ironized zone that promises, rather unnecessarily, to be "your haven in a world programmed to misunderstand all things Austen." In the blogosphere, Austen's novels are valued as self-help literature and dating aids (a popular interactive quiz is "Which Austen Heroine Are You?"), and it is easy to imagine that there are plenty of contented readers doing what the characters in Karen Joy Fowler's hit novel *The Jane Austen Book Club* intend to do: read "all Jane Austen all of the time." Austen seems to proffer not just a read, but a creed: a whole way of life. An ardent Indian blogger with a tribute middle name, Mayank Austen Soofi, has imagined what it would be like if his dream of establishing a Jane Austen Society in Delhi came true:

Each Sunday evening, after completing their purchases in Darya-ganj's Sunday Book Bazaar, Austen admirers would gather in front of Urdu Bazaar and sit on the Jama Masjid stairs. Over *doodh-waali* chai and *biskut*, they would enjoy and appreciate Austen's novels. There would also be a guest of honour at each meet. For instance, *firangi* backpackers from the unsanitary bowels of Pahar-ganj would be invited to share how Delhi belly keeps them "in a continual state of inelegance" while residents of North Delhi would complain of snobbish south Delhi's myopic belief that their Delhi is the only Delhi (ah, "one half of the world cannot understand the pleasures of the other"). . . . The society would also occasionally conduct walking tours in the city where you might pretend as if you are strolling the grassy verdant grounds of England, and not the sunny smoggy steamy lanes of Delhi. You can also hop by landmarks like Ghalib's haveli in Ballimaran and recite his verses as passionately as Marianne Dashwood recited Shakespeare's in *Sense and Sensibility*.[12]

THE HISTORY OF AUSTEN's fame is one of changing public tastes and critical practices. Edmund Wilson was wrong to say that "there have been several revolutions of taste during the last century and a quarter of English Literature, and through them all perhaps only two reputations have never been affected by the shifts of fashion: Shakespeare's and Jane Austen's."[13] While not experiencing *revolutions* of taste, public awareness and appreciation of Austen have varied hugely. The early editions of her books were small, sold only just well enough not to be an embarrassment, and were remaindered or pulped soon after her death. For most of the 1820s, she was out of print—her family thought forever. In the mid-nineteenth century—heyday of the Victorian triple-decker novel—Austen's restrained Regency romances looked old-fashioned and irrelevant and met with very mixed critical responses. G. H. Lewes was an ardent advocate, but Charlotte Brontë thought her second-rate; Thomas Babington Macaulay compared her with Shakespeare and pressed for a public monument, while Thomas Carlyle reviled the novels as "dismal trash" and "dishwashings." But by the end of the century, the journalist Thomas E. Kebbel announced that "all the reading world is now at Miss Austen's feet,"[14] and a hundred years on, Austen is the only writer who is instantly recognizable by her first name.

There have been two big surges of "Austen mania": one after the publication of the first biography, James Edward Austen-Leigh's myth-mongering *Memoir of Jane Austen* in 1870; the other after the burst of film and television versions of Austen novels in the mid-1990s (starting with the BBC's stupendously successful *Pride and Prejudice*). The first led to the late-Victorian cult of "Divine Jane," the most camp and breathless literary phenomenon the world had known since "Bardolatry"; the second has taken Austen to the farthest corners of the world and to the heart of contemporary debate about marriage, morals, and female empowerment. She is now a pivotal figure not simply in literature of all sorts (including romance fiction, chick-lit, and style magazines) but in the heritage industry and multimedia.

Almost every major writer in the past hundred and fifty years has recorded an opinion of Jane Austen and, as Lionel Trilling remarked, "It is possible to say of . . . Austen, as probably we can say of no other writer, that the opinions which are held of her work are almost as interesting, and almost as important to think about, as the work itself."[15] Jane Austen will not just come out first, second, or third (as Virginia Woolf said) in any arrangement of the greatest novelists but has attained iconic status. How did she get to be this special, this useful to the culture, this important to a nation? How did a young woman who was happy to limit her scope to "3 or 4 Families in a Country Village" conquer the world?

This book charts the growth of Austen's fame and the changing status of her work and what it has stood for—or been made to stand for—in English culture over the past two hundred years. In the foreground is the story of Austen's authorship, one of persistence, accident, advocacy, and sometimes surprising neglect. Not only did Austen publish her books anonymously and enjoy very little success during her lifetime, but publication itself came only very late, after twenty years of unrewarded labor. I have sought to reconstruct these prefame years in the spirit of uncertainty through which Austen lived them. Her prized irony and famous manipulation of tone I believe owes much to it; part of the reason why she pleases us so much now is that she was, for years, pleasing only herself.

# Jane's Fame

# CHAPTER I

# *"Authors Too Ourselves"*

In 1869, Jane Austen's first biographer, James Edward Austen-Leigh, expressed surprise at how his aunt had managed to write so much in the last five years of her life, living in the close quarters of Chawton Cottage with her mother, sister, friend Martha Lloyd, and a couple of servants. "She had no separate study to retire to," said James Edward, with evident pity, "and most of the work must have been done in the general sitting-room, subject to all sorts of casual interruptions." He described how, careful to conceal her occupation from "servants, or visitors, or any persons beyond her own family party,"[1] she wrote "upon small sheets of paper which could easily be put away, or covered with a piece of blotting paper." A squeaking swing door elsewhere in the cottage gave her warning whenever someone was approaching and time to hide the latest sheet of *Mansfield Park*, *Emma*, *Persuasion*, or "Sanditon."

Quite where this famous story originated is a puzzle, as James Edward goes on to say that neither he nor his sisters (the main sources of all anecdotage about Austen) were ever aware of disturbing their aunt at her writing, and he makes it clear that there was no attempt at concealment "within her own family party." But secrecy about her work became a cornerstone of the Austen myth; the image conjured up was of the endlessly patient genius putting the demands of family life, however petty, before her work, writing, when she could, in guarded but modest isolation in a corner of a shared sitting room.

The truth is that Jane Austen never exhibited self-consciousness or shame about her writing and never needed to. Unlike many women writers of her generation—or stories about them—she had no struggle for permission to write, no lack of access to books, paper, and ink; no frowning paterfamilias to face down or from whom to conceal her scribbling. Her ease and pleasure in writing as an occupation are evident from the very beginning, as is the full encouragement of her family, and if there was little space in her various homes, that was more a simple fact of life and square footage in relatively cramped households than a metaphor for creative limitations.

What James Edward Austen-Leigh's testimony really reveals is not the author's lack of vanity but how much her writing was accepted, and even overlooked, within her family. Austen is now such a towering figure in literature and myth that it is hard to reinsert her in her home environment and not still see a genius; even James Edward was blinded by the awe factor by the time he came to write her biography, fifty years after his aunt's death. A generation younger than her, he was one of the last to find out that Aunt Jane was the anonymous "Author of 'Sense & Sensibility', 'Pride & Prejudice' etc." His surprise at this news, and his subsequent interest in his aunt, mark him out as not of the inner circle. *They* were not so susceptible to awe.

This is not to say that Austen's closest family members were indifferent to her ambitions and achievements as a writer or callously withholding of praise, but that the home context of genius is, by definition, utterly unlike any other. According to the theorist Leo Braudy, fame can be thought of as having four elements: a person, an accomplishment, their immediate publicity, and what posterity makes of them.[2] The "immediate publicity" of Jane Austen's fame is interesting not so much in how and where her books were reviewed or what her contemporaries thought of them, but in how she was treated in her own circle and what sort of climate that provided. And the reason that Jane Austen did not require, or receive, any special treatment within her family was that she was by no means the only writer among them.

JANE WAS THE SECOND youngest of the Austen children, ten years younger than her eldest brother, James, and two years younger than her only sister, Cassandra. She was born and lived the first twenty-six years of her life at Steventon, on the northeasterly edges of Hampshire. Her father, the Reverend George Austen, was a clever, gentle man; her mother, Cassandra Leigh, a highly articulate woman with aristocratic ancestors, the niece of a famous Oxford scholar and wit. The family was only modestly well-off, and Jane's lively, good-looking, and accomplished brothers had to make their own ways in the world; James and Henry, both Oxford graduates, joined the church and the army, Francis and Charles joined the navy, and lucky Edward was adopted by childless relatives, Mr. and Mrs. Thomas Knight of Godmersham, sent on the grand tour, and made heir to their estates in Kent and Hampshire. Only George, the second son, did not share the family's health and success; disabled in some way, he spent his life being cared for elsewhere and hardly appears in the family records at all.

Jane and her beloved elder sister Cassandra grew up surrounded by boys, for the Reverend Austen supplemented his clerical income by taking in pupils, running, in effect, a small school for the sons of the local gentry. Though the girls were later sent away to school briefly in Oxford, Reading, and Southampton, they spent most of their childhood in the more challenging intellectual atmosphere of their own home. At the rectory, there was a well-stocked library that included works of history, poetry, topography, the great essayists of the century, and plenty of fiction, for the Austens were "great Novel readers & not ashamed of being so"[3] and subscribed to the local circulating library, which held copies of all the recent best sellers. Jane was a fan of Fanny Burney and Maria Edgeworth, Charlotte Smith, Ann Radcliffe, Elizabeth Inchbald, and a host of less memorable eighteenth-century romancers, lapping up their stories and lampooning their more absurd conventions with equal glee. "From an early age," the critic Isobel Grundy has noted, "she read like a potential author. She looked for what she could use—not by quietly absorbing and reflecting it, but by actively engaging, rewriting, often mocking it."[4]

Like the eponymous heroine of her early work, "Catharine, or The Bower," the teenage Jane was "well-read in Modern History" and left more than a hundred marginal notes in a schoolroom copy of Oliver Goldsmith's 1771 *History of England*, still in the possession of the Austen family. Her cheeky ripostes, mostly in defense of her favorites, the Stuarts, give a strong impression of her intellectual confidence, as well as of her pleasure in acting as the classroom wit. In the same irreverent spirit, Austen wrote her own pro-Stuart "History of England" in 1791, for recital and circulation among the family. Her section on Henry VIII begins like this: "It would be an affront to my Readers were I to suppose that they were not as well acquainted with the particulars of this King's reign as I am myself. It will therefore be saving *them* the task of reading again what they have read before, and *myself* the trouble of writing what I do not perfectly recollect, by giving only a slight sketch of the principal Events which marked his reign."[5]

When "The History of England" was eventually published, in 1922, Virginia Woolf characterized the girlish author as "laughing, in her corner, at the world," but the writer of such a brilliant comic party piece was hardly the shrinking (or smirking) violet Woolf imagines, but a quick-witted, praise-hungry teenager, competing for attention in a close, loving, intellectually competitive household. With people outside her immediate circle, whose approval she didn't seek or value, Austen was likely to fall silent; hence her cousin Philadelphia's description of Jane in 1788 as "whimsical & affected . . . not at all pretty & very prim, unlike a girl of twelve."[6] The family, especially those she was closest to—Cassandra, Henry, Frank, Charles, and her father—would have known very well how "unlike a girl of twelve" Jane was, how fanciful, and how funny. But she didn't always choose to perform.

In the years between 1788 and 1792, that is, between the ages of twelve and sixteen, Jane copied out her skits, plays, and stories into three notebooks titled humorously "Volume the First," "Volume the Second," and "Volume the Third," named as if they were installments of a conventional three-part novel. There was a habit among the Austens of using high-quality quarto notebooks (and one's best handwriting) to make, in effect, manuscript *books* to be passed around and enjoyed in the family; editions of one, but still editions. Much later, in 1812, Jane made a reference in a letter to a comic quatrain she had written and sent to her brother James for his comments, being added to "the Steventon Edition."[7] As with so many of Austen's familiar references, it's not clear exactly what she meant by this, but the phrase and its context suggest an album in which the family verses were collected. James Austen's own poems and verse prologues have survived largely because his three children made copies of them in similar quarto volumes.[8]

Almost every item in Jane Austen's juvenilia has an elaborate, mock-serious dedication to one or another member of the family circle: her brothers, both parents, her cousins Eliza de Feuillide and Jane Cooper, and friends Martha and Mary Lloyd. Cassandra, who had provided Jane with thirteen charming watercolor vignettes as illustrations to "The History of England," received this dedication to "Catharine, or The Bower," Jane's unfinished but ambitious early novel:

> Madam
> Encouraged by your warm patronage of The beautiful Cassandra, and The History of England, which through your generous support, have obtained a place in every library in the Kingdom, and run through threescore Editions, I take the liberty of begging the same Exertions in favour of the following Novel, which I humbly flatter myself, possesses Merit beyond any already published, or any that will ever in future appear, except as may proceed from the pen of Your Most Grateful Humble Servt.
> The Author[9]

Behind the humor is a familiarity with book production and distribution as well as patronage, and a tacit acknowledgment of her own ambitions, which "Catharine, or The Bower" (the only substantial non-burlesque story by Jane to have survived from these early years) was clearly meant to advance.

Jane's writing was encouraged in particular by her father, with whom she was something of a favorite (Mrs. Austen favored her first-born, James). The portable writing desk that Jane bequeathed to her niece Caroline, which is now on display in the British Library, is thought to have been a gift from him.[10] He certainly gave her the white vellum notebook that became "Volume the Second" (she inscribed it "*Ex Dono Mei Patris*"), and probably also provided "Volume the Third," as he wrote a mock commendation inside the front cover: "Effusions of Fancy / by a very Young Lady / Consisting of Tales / in a Style entirely new," sportingly joining in the spirit of her enterprise. In Austen's surviving letters, the earliest of which dates from 1796, it is her father who is depicted as most close to her own interest in books, literary periodicals, and the circulating library, and with whom she shares and discusses the latest novels.

James Austen later characterized the family bookishness in this way:

> *We love, & much enjoy with ivory knife*
> *To sever the yet damp & clinging leaves*
> *Of some new volume; & can pleased discuss*
> *With critical acumen & due skill,*
> *An Author's merit: Authors too ourselves*
> *Not seldom, & recite without much fear*
> *To hearers kindly partial, verse or prose,*
> *Song, parody or tale, whose themes of high*
> *But local import, well record the fate*
> *Of cat or pony: or, from satire free*
> *Raise against other's follies or our own*
> *Perchance, the fair & inoffensive laugh.*[11]

Writing and reading—and sharing both with like minds in the family—was not a mere pastime for the Austens but an essential part of their lives. They were a very verbal tribe, and Jane's contributions to the family's entertainment, however original, would have appeared to them to corroborate a shared trait, not necessarily to display an individual one. The family was full of people who prided themselves on their own writing talent and wit, "Authors too ourselves," not least Jane's mother, a keen, sometimes unstoppable versifier.[12] More pertinently, for the development of Jane Austen's sense of herself as a writer, the family had plenty of committed, quasi-professional authors in their circle, too. Two of her brothers, two first cousins, an aunt, two second cousins, and a neighbor were all published authors,[13] and others in her circle strove to be.

James Edward Austen-Leigh later emphasized his aunt's "entire seclusion" from the literary world, "neither by correspondence, nor by personal intercourse was she known to any contemporary authors,"[14] giving a very misleading impression of her isolation and ignorance. Though it is true that Austen declined the few opportunities that she got in adult life to meet celebrity authors, she grew up in an atmosphere of informed interest in all aspects of print culture and had before her a surprising number of writers and would-be writers to learn from.

The first published writer Jane Austen had the chance to observe at close quarters was a poet called Samuel Egerton Brydges, the younger brother of Jane's friend and mentor, Anne Lefroy. Mrs. Lefroy, who was married to the rector of the nearby village of Ashe, was a highly cultivated and intelligent woman, herself a poet who had been published in *The Poetical Register*.[15] According to her brother's later tribute, she had "a warm and rapid poetical genius; she read voraciously; her apprehension was like lightning, and her memory was miraculous."[16] Brydges was only twenty-three when he came with his new bride, Elizabeth, and younger sister, Charlotte, to live in the vicinity of Mrs. Lefroy and her husband in 1786, but he was already suffering from thwarted poetical ambition due to the disappointing reception of his first book, *Sonnets and Other Poems; with a Versification of The Six Bards of Ossian*, which includes the quatrain,

> *Yet, o beloved Muse, if in me glow*
> *Ambition for false fame, the thirst abate!*
> *Teach me, fair fields and flocks, mankind to know,*
> *And ope my eyes to all, that's truly great.*[17]

If this was his agenda on arrival in Deane, the poet didn't keep to it but sank into a melancholy quite as powerful as any he'd been able to imagine. Looking back on the years 1785–91, he thought them "amongst the most wearisome and low-spirited of my life ... in which my pride was most mortified and my self-complacence most disturbed."[18]

Brydges found fame in the 1790s as a novelist, but he never got over his early failure as a poet; his 1834 autobiography is full of complaints about the unjust neglect of his genius and how it had exacerbated his "morbid sensitiveness."[19] He must have harped on the theme a great deal during his time at Deane, when he wasn't enacting it in gloomy reverie.

Jane was only ten when the melancholic poet became their neighbor. She was virtually beneath his notice—until, many years later, her fame prompted him to recall that she had been "very intimate" with his brilliant older sister, "and much encouraged by her. . . . When I knew Jane Austen I never suspected that she was an authoress," he wrote in 1834. "The last time I think that I saw her was at Ramsgate in 1803: perhaps she was then about twenty-seven years old. Even then I did not know that she was addicted to literary composition."[20] The phrase is an excellent one for Jane, who was indeed gripped by a sort of mania for writing in her early teens and who later told her niece Caroline she wished she had "read more, and written less" in those years, when she had been "much taken up with" her own compositions.[21]

The fellow addict whom Brydges did recognize at Deane was James Austen, undoubtedly the most ambitious, talented, and promising writer in the young Jane Austen's immediate circle. His seniority, his sex, and his choice of the art of poetry over prose meant that even after his sister had become a highly praised novelist, he was in all important respects still regarded as the writer of the family. A distant figure to the younger children, Cassandra and Jane (who were only five and three when he went up to St. John's College, Oxford, at the age of fourteen), James was also precociously talented; his earliest surviving poem, addressed to his boyhood friend Fulwar Craven Fowle, imagines them in later life, Fowle a successful statesman and James a secluded poet, whose fate is "to woo in lowly strain / The nymphs of fountain, wood or plain / To bless my peaceful lays." Imminent retreat from "tumultuous strife" was a theme the world-weary sixteen-year-old kept returning to:

> Nor er'e shall I with envy view their fate
> Whilst solid bliss that ne'er can cloy
> Thro' life's retired vale my steps await.[22]

His plan was to take his degree and Holy Orders and lead a life given over mainly to poetry and his other great enthusiasm, the hunt. "Place me in farthest Scythia's trackless waste" could be taken to mean a nice Hampshire living where he could keep a pack of harriers and court his muse, for James was not an urban creature like his younger brother Henry and valued solitude and rural quiet rather more than is natural in a youth, even a poetical youth. Gray and Cowper, the most popular poets of the age gone by, were his models in language and form, but his melancholic sensibility was more in tune with the coming romantics.

All through Jane's childhood, the visits home of this sophisticated, ambitious, and scholarly brother must have impressed her deeply. He was the moving force behind the home theatricals that were put on at Steventon, in the parlor and in the barn across the road, for seven consecutive years in the 1780s. As with the amateur theatricals that Jane later described so vividly in *Mansfield Park*, these productions must have galvanized the whole household, with all the demands of scenery and costume making, learning lines, and rehearsing. Jane was too young to take part until the later productions but would have been a keen observer of all the preparations for *Matilda* and *The Rivals* in 1782 and 1784, with James in charge of an excited group of young people drawn from the family, the Reverend Austen's pupils, neighbors, and friends. The productions were also showcases for James's own writing talents, as he composed prologues and epilogues for most of the plays they performed. Some were lengthy and elaborate, such as the prologue to Fielding's *Tragedy of Tom Thumb*, in which James surveyed a number of favorite sports and pastimes, wittily pointing out how arduous leisure can be, and ending with an evocation of his own preferred occupation, being a writer:

*To please no numerous crowd he e'er pretends—*
*He writes & lives but for his private friends.*
*Their vacant hours to amuse, his favourite toil,*
*And his best thanks are their approving smile—*[23]

When they put on *The Wonder*, the Austens' glamorous and flirtatious cousin, Comtesse Eliza de Feuillide, was visiting Steventon and took the part of Violante. James, who was under his cousin's spell for many years (as was Henry, whom she later married), must have enjoyed putting these words into her mouth:

*Such was poor woman's lot—whilst tyrant men*
*At once possessors of the sword & pen*
*All female claim, with stern pedantic pride*
*To prudence, truth & secrecy denied,*
*Covered their tyranny with specious words,*
*That called themselves creation's mighty Lords—*
*But thank our happier stars, those days are o'er,*
*And woman holds a second place no more.*
*Now forced to quit their long held usurpation,*
*These men all wise, these Lords of the Creation!*
*To our superior rule themselves submit,*
*Slaves to our charms, & vassals to our wit.*[24]

Of course, such sentiments, coming from a young man who thinks of himself as "possessor of the pen," are as much an expression of his own anxieties as a welcome to the changing status of women. Jane, aged twelve, had fully absorbed the ambiguous messages of the day about women's rights in general and female "scribblers" in particular, and in her juvenilia (contemporary with these pieces by James) was already showing her complete awareness that the cardinal sin for a woman writer was a lack of humor about her own position. Even if one was not prepared to be self-deprecating, the subject had to be treated lightly.

Six years after earning his BA, James Austen returned to Oxford with an ambitious plan to start up his own literary periodical. Henry had gone up to St. John's in 1788, ten years after James's own promising start there, and the younger brother's high spirits and literary talent may have been behind the scheme to venture into print. In the years following his graduation, James had been traveling on the Continent, had taken Holy Orders, and had received his MA and first curacy. But as it approached, the retirement he had imagined for himself must have begun to look a little less attractive, for this was exactly the moment when he decided to take the only big risk of his life and "go public" as a man of letters.

James's son, James Edward, said later that his father "used to speak very slightingly" of the *Loiterer*,[25] but this says more about James's disappointments in later life than the lively publication he produced every Saturday, without a hitch, from January 1789 to March 1790. For all the *Loiterer*'s provincial origins, the Austen brothers clearly did not intend to limit its potential audience to that of Oxford university or town. The title, a witty rejoinder to the *Idler*, the *Rambler*, the *Tatler*, and the *Spectator*, ought, they reckoned, to appeal to "four-fifths of the English nation."[26] Within five issues, they had found distributors in Birmingham and London (the publisher Thomas Egerton) and a month later had spread out to Bath and Reading. At threepence a copy, the price was low. The issues were short, often consisting of a single essay or article, but the necessity of writing and printing them with such frequency, and the business of dealing with printers and distributors, must have taken up most of James's time and energy that year, when, one presumes, he was more often in Oxford than Hampshire.

Back at Steventon, the thirteen-year-old Jane Austen would have been among the magazine's keenest readers, having been privy to excited planning among James, Henry, and their cousin Edward Cooper (also an Oxford undergraduate at the time) when everyone was together at Steventon for Christmas 1789. The first issue of the *Loiterer* was published just a month later by this "small Society of Friends, who have long been accustomed to devote our winter evenings to something like learned pursuits."[27] The optimism with which it was launched suggests that the project had the full backing of the Austen parents (it is hard to see how it could have happened without some financial support as well), and the editorial stance of the *Loiterer* was completely in tune with the Austen family manner of gentle mockery and disingenuous self-deprecation. The editors justified their enterprise by claiming that "to keep our talent any longer wrapt in the napkin would be equal injustice to our writings, the world, and ourselves,"[28] and the content, which started off mostly in the vein of short, slightly pompous musings on life and literature, evolved gradually into displays of individual taste, with James, the most frequent contributor, showing an increasing interest in writing fiction. His tale of "Cecilia" takes up two issues of the magazine—a risky editorial decision—and deals with just the themes that were to become central in Jane's novels, the moral choices that young women face in courtship and matrimony. "Though an union of *love may* have some misery," the author concludes, "a marriage of interest *can* give *no* happiness."[29]

The temptation for the young Jane Austen to join in this exciting publishing venture in her own family must have been overpowering, and one contribution in particular, a letter published in number nine of the *Loiterer*, has attracted the attention of critics as possibly having been written by her, constituting her first appearance in print. The letter, signed "Sophia Sentiment," is a comically overstated (but sincere-sounding) complaint that the *Loiterer* is not only too reliant on Oxford in-jokes but ignores female tastes and female readers (it predates James's "Cecilia" story by several months): "You have never yet dedicated one number to the amusement of our sex, and have taken no more notice of us, than if you thought, like the Turks, we had no souls." The writer has many suggestions of the kind of thing that would do instead: "Let us see some nice affecting stories, relating the misfortunes of two lovers, who died suddenly, just as they were going to church. Let the lover be killed in a duel, or lost at sea, or you may make him shoot himself, just as you please; and as for his mistress, she will of course go mad . . . only remember, whatever you do, that your hero and heroine must possess a good deal of feeling, and have very pretty names."[30] Though this could, at a pinch, have been written by Henry, the absurd tone and bravado are exactly those of Jane's own pastiches of sentimental literature, "Love and Freindship," "Lesley Castle," and "The Three Sisters," which she was writing at the same time, and which everyone at home knew about. Writing to the *Loiterer* would have been just the sort of pert joke Jane specialized in.[31]

The fact that James worked so hard on the *Loiterer* for over a year and then gave up so abruptly suggests that he was cutting his losses. He was also, possibly, sorely disappointed. There is a plangent tone to his farewell essay, in which he thanks the friends who had contributed to the magazine and cites several of "many sufficient causes" for the periodical closing, "the short list of my subscribers, and the long bill of my publisher" being perhaps the most pressing.[32] But he also admits to a certain degree of editorial miscalculation, having changed tack from his initial objective of making his main matter "the circles of Oxford ... some portraits and some scenes," to a broadening out of subjects in the hope of appealing to a wider audience (in exactly the way suggested by Sophia Sentiment's letter). The *Loiterer* actually achieved as much as, if not more than, the editor in chief could have expected, but perhaps his expectations had not been reasonable. George Holbert Tucker, one of the few biographers to pay much attention to James Austen, has described his personality as "an unequal blending of sociability and brooding melancholy, the latter predominating as he grew older."[33] James retired to his country living and in 1792 married a well-to-do young woman, Anne Mathew. He published nothing after the *Loiterer*—perhaps he disdained to, preferring to remain an unrecognized genius—but he certainly continued to write. As he had said in the first issue of his magazine, "of all chymical mixtures, ink is the most dangerous, and he who has once dipped his fingers in it—."[34]

The skits and stories of Jane's earliest surviving manuscript, "Volume the First" (all completed well before her fifteenth birthday), show that she was every bit as ambitious as her brother had been at the same age but would never open herself up to the charge of self-importance by appearing to take herself too seriously. She sought to amuse and amaze her family circle with knockabout comedies full of abductions, abandonments, exotic accidents, adultery, and death (all the sort of spicy drama that is absent or carefully backgrounded in her adult fiction). From the dedication of her absurd sketch "The Visit," which mentions two earlier works that have not survived, it is clear that she had written short comedies as early as 1788 or 1789. The title of one of these lost plays, "The School for Jealousy," immediately recalls that of Sheridan's *School for Scandal* (and perhaps lampooned Henry and James's joint infatuation with their cousin Eliza?); the other, "The Travelled Man," might well have taken James's Continental tour of 1786–87 as its subject.[35] "The Visit" itself is dedicated to James and is fondly and jokingly recommended "to your Protection and Patronage." Although she was ten years his junior, Jane was already aligning herself with "the writer of the family" and seeking to be the cadet comic counterpart of this much-admired older brother.

One wonders what James made of his little sister's skits, which she must have hoped would be taken up in some way by the older siblings at their theatricals. "The Visit," which ends with three proposals and engagements effected in four lines, involves an absurd scene where eight guests are provided with only six chairs and two of the ladies have to have men sitting on their laps: "I beg you will make no apologies," Sophy says. "Your Brother is very light."[36] But could any of the amateur actors at Steventon have done justice to the brilliance of "The Mystery," in which all the characteristics of drama are deliberately absent? In one scene, a lone character, Corydon, enters and says, "But Hush! I am interrupted"; in another, the action is already over, and the characters, having nothing to tell one another, decide to leave. The second scene is entirely made up of this brief dialogue between a father and son:

> Enter Old Humbug and his Son, talking.
> OLD HUM:) It is for that reason I wish you to follow my advice.
>     Are you convinced of its propriety?
> YOUNG HUM:) I am Sir, and will certainly act in the manner you
>     have pointed out to me.
> OLD HUM:) Then let us return to the House. (Exeunt)[37]

At thirteen or fourteen, Jane Austen was like a jolly Samuel Beckett! The juvenilia are full of sophisticated absurdity like this, as in "Jack and Alice": "A lovely young Woman lying apparently in great pain beneath a Citron tree was an object too interesting not to attract their notice"; or this deadpan description from "Lesley Castle": "She is remarkably good-tempered when she has her own way, and very lively when she is not out of humour."[38] The young author lights on one style after another with remarkable virtuosity, impatient of longer, extended writing. Perhaps that was a sign of her eagerness to get things out before an audience and enjoy their response. Their response had almost always been very carefully anticipated and engineered.

SEVERAL OF JANE'S RELATIONS on the distaff side also had thoroughly inky fingers. James Henry Leigh, the heir to Stoneleigh Abbey in Warwickshire, had published his book of verse, *The New Rosciad*, in 1785, and Cassandra, Lady Hawke's novel *Julia de Gramont* appeared in 1788. Among the unpublished writers was Mrs. Austen's first cousin, Mary Leigh, elder of the two daughters of Dr. Theophilus Leigh of Balliol (who was still master when the Austen brothers went up to the university). Mary Leigh was a scholarly, childless woman who was the family historian and made "copious extracts and abridgements" of historical and theological works, according to a biographical note written by her husband, the Reverend Thomas Leigh. Rev. Leigh also, fleetingly, mentions that his wife "spent more time than agreed with her health" writing "some Novels highly moral and entertaining."[39] Nothing about these novels—not even a title—has survived, but it is highly likely that they were known and read by the Austen family, in whom Mary Leigh took a great interest.

Mary's younger sister, Cassandra Cooke, was to play an important role in Jane Austen's early contact with the literary world, not so much because of her own writing (though the progress of Mrs. Cooke's novel *Battleridge* through the press in 1798–99 and its indifferent reception must have fascinated Jane), but due to an accident of location. In 1793, Fanny Burney, the literary celebrity whom Jane Austen considered "the very best of English novelists,"[40] came to live in a house almost opposite the Cookes in Great Bookham, Surrey. Madame d'Arblay (as Burney was known after her marriage) liked her new neighbors at once. Rev. Cooke officiated at the baptism of her only child,

Alexander, in December 1794, and she and his wife were soon sharing newspapers and periodicals (including the *Critical Review*) and speculating primly together over the morals of their neighbors.[41]

Cassandra Cooke became particularly animated and active around the publication of Burney's long-awaited third novel, *Camilla*, in 1795–96. Burney was one of the bestselling authors of the day, but it was publishers, not she, who had made money from the books: *Evelina* had been sold outright for a mere £30 and *Cecilia* for £250. Mrs. Cooke must have been discussing the novelist's losses with her contacts in Oxford, one of whom passed on the warning to Madame d'Arblay "not to be again, as he hears I have been, the dupe of Booksellers."[42] Further in her capacity as agent/adviser, Mrs. Cooke passed on to the novelist the information that "a Relation of hers" involved in the publishing business with Robson of Bond Street had heard that Payne and Cadell, the publishers of *Cecilia*, "*cleared* 1500 pounds *the first Year!*"[43] The new novel, Mrs. Cooke believed, should be published by subscription, giving the author a large, guaranteed profit. Burney followed her advice, and it paid off handsomely: She raised about £1,000 from the subscription to *Camilla* and went on to sell the copyright for another £1,000 soon after publication—a record sum at the time.

Burney's thirty-five-page list of subscribers to *Camilla* included a dazzling array of the nation's great and good (she had been at court for five years, and was extremely well connected) and a number of people from the Leigh and Austen circles, including "Miss J. Austen, Steventon." It must have been thrilling to the nineteen-year-old to have a stake, however small, in her favorite author's new work and to see her name printed in the first volume (the only time she would have ever seen her name in print; her own novels were all published anonymously). The book itself influenced her deeply and is, along with Samuel Richardson's *Sir Charles Grandison*, the most frequently mentioned in her letters. It was singled out in Austen's famous defense of the novel in *Northanger Abbey* as a work in which "the most thorough knowledge of human nature, the happiest delineation of its varieties, the liveliest effusions of wit and humour are conveyed to the world in the best chosen language."

By this date, Austen had probably already written the first version of "Elinor and Marianne" (which became *Sense and Sensibility*), and possibly the undated epistolary novel "Lady Susan"; later in the same year she began writing "First Impressions." Her own story (whose final title, *Pride and Prejudice*, may derive from the repetition of those words in the final paragraph of Burney's *Cecilia*) has so many resonances with *Camilla* as to constitute a form of elaborate homage; Darcy being haughty at the Meryton ball, the Bennet sisters being held back at Netherfield by the rain, Mary Bennet's piano playing, Mr. Bennet's regret over his wife's silliness: All have equivalents in characters and situations in Burney's novel. Even Austen's famous first sentence has an echo in one of Burney's: "[It is] received wisdom among matchmakers, that a young lady without fortune has a less and less chance of getting off upon every public appearance."[44]

Austen was an ardent, but not doting, fan. Her enjoyment of *Camilla* didn't prevent her from penciling in a droll joke at the end of her copy (now in the Bodleian Library), acknowledging how artificially Burney had prolonged the novel's central crisis: "Since this work went to the press a circumstance of some assistance to the happiness of Camilla has taken place, namely that Dr Marchmont has at last died." Similarly, Austen was far from starstruck by Burney's recent accessibility in Bookham and friendship with her aunt Cooke. There are no recorded instances of their meeting, but given the Austens' regular visits to Bookham and the frequent commerce between Madame d'Arblay and the rector's wife (not least at church services) it is highly likely that Austen had sightings of the novelist and may well have been introduced to her. Madame d'Arblay, her gentle émigré husband, and their adored toddler son were, for the three years they lived opposite the Cookes, the most exciting residents Bookham had ever known. But to a thoughtful observer such as Jane Austen, it would have been clear that contact with the celebrities was much more likely to disillusion than gratify.

Mrs. Cooke's own novel, privately printed in 1799, *Battleridge: An Historical Tale, Founded on Facts*, "by a Lady of Quality," is not mentioned either in her surviving letters to Fanny Burney, nor in Burney's voluminous journals and letters, so it seems likely that she kept her authorship a secret from her famous acquaintance. The Austens, however, were fully aware of the book's progress; Jane remarked in a letter of October 1798 that Mrs. Cooke was disappointed by a series of delays with the printer, Cawthorn, and "never means to employ him again." The Steventon family almost certainly enjoyed the novel in the way they enjoyed all such nonsense—noblemen going feral, ladies having fits, evil-minded men indulging their lusts—and Mrs. Cooke's pedantry would have afforded the author of "The History of England" some wry smiles (Mrs. Cooke disdains to describe the Restoration because "the majesty of history would be disgraced by the flow of fiction"). But the one review that *Battleridge* received, in the very periodical Mrs. Cooke was sharing with the d'Arblays, was devastatingly bad: "The work is not very amusing; and in point of composition, it is despicable," wrote the *Critical Review*.[45]

By the end of the 1790s, the examples of Mrs. Cooke and Egerton Brydges interested Jane Austen for professional as well as literary reasons. Brydges had become surprisingly successful after leaving Deane, founding a periodical called the *Topographer* with an old friend from Cambridge and then taking to fiction writing. Of all his publications, the *Topographer* probably appealed most to young Jane Austen, who loved William Gilpin's books on the picturesque and would very likely have read and discussed the magazine and its interesting illustrations with Anne Lefroy. One commentator has gone as far as to suggest that Austen's description of Pemberley in *Pride and Prejudice* owes something to Brydges's series of articles about a journey through the Midlands that included Chatsworth in Derbyshire and "the most perfect house in England," Kedleston.[46]

Brydges indulged some absurd pretensions about his novels, claiming that they were pure gifts of inspiration; all he did was write down "as carelessly as they rose, some of the thoughts that were playing about my fancy."[47] He said that he composed his first novel in a trancelike state of "fervid rapidity,"[48] sending the sheets to the printer as fast as they were finished. Unlike Mrs. Cooke, Brydges didn't publish at his own cost but sold the copyright to a firm in Dublin, glad to avoid liability for the expenses. But when the novel subsequently did quite well, he probably came to regret the loss of the rights.

The author of *Mary de Clifford* showed frequent lapses of ingenuity. At the end of a duel scene, where the hero half-utters the name of the heroine before his mighty soul departs for a better place, Brydges concludes, "I cannot attempt to describe the remainder of this affecting scene. To those who feel as I do, the recital would be too terrible to give pleasure."[49] This begged to be lampooned, and no doubt the Austens read passages aloud to one another with relish. As Mr. Bennet says in *Pride and Prejudice*, "For what do we live, but to make sport for our neighbours, and laugh at them in our turn?"[50] By the time Brydges's next novel, *Arthur Fitz-Albini*, was published in 1798, Jane was twenty-two and the author of several unpublished novels herself. George Austen ordered a copy of the new book, against Jane's "private wishes," as she wrote to Cassandra, "for it does not quite satisfy my feelings that we should purchase the only one of Egerton's works of which his family are ashamed."[51] By "family," she almost certainly meant Mrs. Lefroy, who might well have been distressed at her brother's thinly veiled picture of life at Deane, Ashe, and Steventon. Years later, Brydges professed himself puzzled that the book "gave great offence to some of my country neighbours, who supposed their characters alluded to,"[52] but as he describes all the country folk as uncongenial boobies, provoking in the hero "disgust . . . driving him to the society of his books, his own thoughts, and a few sensible friends," their reaction was not surprising. And, as Jane wrote to her sister: "My father is disappointed—I am not, for I expected nothing better. Never did any book carry more internal evidence of its author. Every sentiment is completely Egerton's. There is very little story, and what there is is told in a strange, unconnected way. There are many characters introduced, apparently merely to be delineated."[53]

Here we get a unique glimpse of Austen, in her midtwenties, scrutinizing the work of someone known to her. Her tone of impatience is surely not just due to the shortcomings of Egerton's novel but to the fact that productions of its kind were preferred over her own. Jane had moved on, in her late teens, from burlesques and stories for family consumption to a different sort of writing altogether, the full-length novel. "Catharine, or The Bower" was the beginning of one (that she kept, and tinkered with, all her life); another was "Elinor and Marianne," the early version of *Sense and Sensibility*, which she is thought to have written, or conceived, as an epistolary novel. Cassandra, the only source of information about the dates of Jane's compositions, was a bit vague about "Elinor and Marianne," saying that as far as she could remember "it had something of the same story & characters" as the published book.[54] Jane's revisions, then, must have amounted to an almost complete rewrite or series of transformations, lasting years.

The novel that Jane had begun in October 1796, "First Impressions," might also have been epistolary—there are still forty-three letters in the book it became, *Pride and Prejudice*, and letter writing is integral to the plot. "First Impressions" was finished in ten months and immediately passed around and read aloud to members of the family, who were, not surprisingly, charmed and delighted by it. Jane's father was so completely sure that it could and should be published that he took the bold step of writing to the well-known London publisher Thomas Cadell, the firm that the year before had published Fanny Burney's *Camilla*:

1 November 1797

Sirs,

I have in my possession a Manuscript Novel, comprised in three Vols. About the length of Miss Burney's Evelina. As I am well aware of what consequence it is that a work of this sort should make it's first Appearance under a respectable name I apply to you. Shall be much obliged therefore if you will inform me whether you chuse to be concerned in it; What will be the expence of publishing at the Author's risk; & what you will venture to advance for the Property of it, if on perusal, it is approved of?

Should your answer give me encouragement I will send you the Work.[55]

This letter came to light only seventy years later, among Cadell's papers, and is the only evidence that there was any attempt before 1803 to solicit publication for one of Jane's works. (It should be noted that the letter doesn't specify *which* novel or, indeed, which author is involved, but the assumption has always been that the author was Jane and the novel her most recently completed one, "First Impressions.")

George Austen's comparison of the novel's length with Burney's *Evelina* is clearly meant to suggest other similarities with the charming 1778 best seller, not least that that debut novel made a fortune for its publisher, Thomas Lowndes. But Cadell's answer was far from "giving encouragement": By return post he declined Rev. Austen's offer and so "the Work" never left Steventon.

Lucky Jane, though, to have a parent who was so active on her behalf and whose pride in his daughter's achievement shines through this slightly misaimed business letter. There's no reason to assume this was an isolated experiment or that Jane was seriously put off by the disappointing outcome, for the next year she had started on a remarkably funny satire of the Gothic novel, called "Susan," which was to be her first success.

JANE AUSTEN BECAME A great writer partly because she was a great reader and had a highly developed consumer's understanding of her favorite form. Her novels are full of books and readers: Catharine Perceval and Camilla Stanley in "Catharine, or The Bower" read novels together, as do Catherine Morland and Isabella Thorpe in *Northanger Abbey*; Darcy is a bibliophile and "always buying books"; Anne Elliot and Fanny Price, from *Persuasion* and *Mansfield Park*, respectively, are passionately engaged readers of Cowper; Marianne Dashwood is devoted to recent poetry as well as to the classics; and Henry Tilney, one of the most discerning characters in any Austen novel, has read all and admires "most of" Ann Radcliffe's work.[56]

Austen's taste in reading was eclectic and guided purely by the pleasure principle. When Mrs. Martin of the Maidenhead Inn was planning to open a new circulating library in the Steventon area, Jane was one of the people she wrote to as a likely subscriber, mentioning, as an inducement, that "her Collection is not to consist only of Novels, but of every kind of Literature &c &c." "She might have spared this pretension to our family," Jane reflected, "but it was necessary I suppose to the self-consequence of half her Subscribers."[57] Mrs. Martin should perhaps have attended more closely to the tastes of her clientele, for she went out of business within a couple of years, presumably from not stocking *enough* novels in her library.

There was a circulating library in Alton, and another in Basingstoke, but provincial establishments of the kind were not very large, with stock ranging on average between three hundred to a thousand books only. Austen increased her access to new publications through her membership in reading societies in Steventon and later in Chawton—the original "Jane Austen Book Clubs." The societies worked by subscription: members chose the books to be purchased, and titles were rotated around the group, with everyone expected to read (or at least house for a fortnight) one another's "picks." The rules were strict: there were penalties for keeping a book beyond the agreed date, and the stock was monitored jealously, "every smudge, burn and candlewax blot carefully recorded and charged for," according to the historian William St. Clair.[58] Later in her life, Austen was proud of the book club she helped run in Chawton, and on hearing that the Miss Sibleys of West Meon wanted to establish one "like ours" wrote to her sister, "What can be a stronger proof of that superiority in ours over the Steventon & Manydown Society, which I have always foreseen & felt?—No emulation of the kind was ever inspired by their proceedings."[59]

Austen knew that her own works were as good as, if not a great deal better than, most of the titles in the circulating library, and everything suggests that she both hoped and expected to see one of her novels in print some day. Quite how she would square her ambitions and talent with the conventional requirements of middle-class female life was not so clear. The situation at Steventon rectory in the late 1790s was very different from a decade earlier. The brothers had all left, there were no more pupil boarders, Rev. Austen was in his late sixties, and he and his wife were thinking about retirement. Three of their sons had married: James for the second time, in 1795, after the sudden death of his first wife (he had one child from each marriage at this date, Anna and James Edward); Henry to his widowed cousin Eliza; and Edward, now a landed gentleman in Kent, to Elizabeth Bridges, with whom he already had five children. Cassandra and Jane, good-looking, clever, and lively young women, were naturally expected to marry as well. Cassandra had been engaged since 1795 to one of her father's former pupils and a family friend, Tom Fowle, who was waiting for an appointment to a suitably lucrative clerical living, in the gift of a patron with property in Shropshire.

Mrs. Austen wrote to her prospective daughter-in-law Mary, James's second wife, in 1796, "I look forwards to you as a real comfort to me in my old age, when Cassandra is gone into Shropshire, & Jane—the Lord knows where."[60] Mrs. Austen's somewhat impatient bemusement over her younger daughter's future prospects suggests Jane's difference from the norm, but being a professional writer was certainly not one of the options being canvased for her; marriage was the expected course for any dependent woman, and Jane's suitors had not yet been very promising. Charming Tom Lefroy, Mrs. Lefroy's nephew, came and flirted and went away again; the young cleric Samuel Blackall hovered around, suggesting he might be about to fall in love; Jane dallied and danced with her brothers' friends and her cousins and worked up crushes to entertain herself and her girlfriends, but none of it seemed serious. Their former neighbor Mrs. Mitford recalled Jane at this period in her life as "the prettiest, silliest, most affected, husband-hunting butterfly she ever remembered,"[61] enforcing the idea that an act was being put on. Jane had always emulated her elder sister, prompting their mother's remark that "if Cassandra's head had been going to be cut off, Jane would have her's cut off too."[62] Cassandra was engaged to be married and would soon leave home. Jane probably thought she had better make steps, or at least gestures, in the same direction.

Cassandra's engagement came to a tragic end in the spring of 1797 when her fiancé died of yellow fever while serving as chaplain on a voyage to the West Indies. Though Cassandra was still very young, she entered what Carol Shields has described as a "symbolic widowhood" at Fowle's death and seems to have resolved to live in retirement and spinsterhood. Although the possibility of marriage was not over for Jane (and she was to come very near it in 1802), the pull to do as Cassandra did now worked in the opposite direction.

Although many commentators claim that Jane Austen was so traumatized by moving house in 1801 that she was unable to settle to writing for eight years, no one has pointed out that during the far more testing year of 1797, with the household in turmoil over Cassandra's bereavement, Jane completed in a matter of months the first version of one of the most cheerful and cheering books in the English language. Though Cadell hadn't wanted to read "First Impressions," it was enough of a hit among those who did read it to gratify the author deeply. Cassandra requested the manuscript so often that Jane could tease her, "I do not wonder at your wanting to read first impressions again, so seldom as you have gone through it, & that so long ago,"[63] and their friend Martha Lloyd was almost as ardent. In the summer of 1799 Jane joked about not relending it to her; "I would not let Martha read First Impressions again upon any account, & am very glad that I did not leave it in your power.—She is very cunning, but I see through her design;—she means to publish it from Memory, & one more perusal must enable her to do it."[64] It's a confident joke, displaying satisfaction with the quality of her own work and its chances of appearing in public soon. Jane was in Bath at the time and had the manuscript with her; she seems to have been intending to work on it during her stay—and perhaps on other stories too.

But, devastatingly, the next year someone else *did* publish a novel called *First Impressions*, a poet and dramatist, Margaret Holford.[65] The appearance of this rival didn't simply mean that Jane would need to change the title of her own novel—a relatively easy procedure—but that she was being beaten in a race that she hadn't yet been able to join. The manuscripts were beginning to pile up in the sisters' shared sitting room at Steventon: In 1799 she finished "Susan," her brilliant story satirizing the books and reading habits of the 1790s. But the 1790s were closing, and the novel, for all its amazing originality, ran the risk in topical satire of built-in obsolescence.

At the turn of the century, Austen was twenty-five years old, unmarried, unpublished, and unsure if there was any future in her highly individual style of writing. She had the manuscripts of the early versions of *Sense and Sensibility*, *Pride and Prejudice*, and *Northanger Abbey* sitting on a shelf in her room, where, for all she knew, they would remain till doomsday, taken down every now and then and laughed over by Cassandra or Martha or one of the sisters-in-law, but that would be all.

Frustrating though this must have been for the author, the benefit to posterity could hardly have been greater. If Thomas Cadell had asked to read "First Impressions," he would very likely have published it; it would have been followed to the press by "Elinor and Marianne," and then—goodness knows what, but certainly not the novels for which Austen is now so famous and loved. The longer Austen remained unpublished, the more experimental she became, and the more license she assumed with bold, brilliant moves. These are particularly characteristic of the novel written deepest in her obscurity, as it were, "Susan" (later *Northanger Abbey*), with its authorial interjection about how we must be near the denouement of the love story, as the number of pages remaining are so few, and the passage where the heroine and her friend take a break from the ardors of the plot in order to read novels:

Yes, novels;—for I will not adopt that ungenerous and impolitic custom so common with novel writers, of degrading by their contemptuous censure the very performances, to the number of which they are themselves adding—joining with their greatest enemies in bestowing the harshest epithets on such works, and scarcely ever permitting them to be read by their own heroine, who, if she accidentally take up a novel, is sure to turn over its insipid pages with disgust. Alas! if the heroine of one novel be not patronised by the heroine of another, from whom can she expect protection and regard? Let us leave it to the Reviewers to abuse such effusions of fancy at their leisure and over every new novel to talk in threadbare strains of the trash with which the press now groans. Let us not desert one another; we are an injured body. Although our productions have afforded more extensive and unaffected pleasure than those of any other literary corporation in the world, no species of composition has been so much decried. . . . "And what are you reading, Miss—?" "Oh! It is only a novel!" replies the young lady; while she lays down her book with affected indifference, or momentary shame.—"It is only Cecilia, or Camilla, or Belinda;" or, in short, only some work in which the greatest powers of the mind are displayed, in which the most thorough knowledge of human nature, the happiest delineation of its varieties, the liveliest effusions of wit and humour are conveyed to the world in the best chosen language.[66]

It would take another hundred and seventy years or so before this could be described as "postmodern"; even today, amour propre about the limits of realism keeps characters in soap operas away from their television sets and the residents of Ambridge mysteriously incapable of tuning in to Radio 4. Such touches weren't Austen's only innovations: No one had reproduced dialogue so naturalistically before, no one had reined in so skillfully from caricature to character, no one had been as honest about female motivations or so efficient in telling a story. As W. D. Howells remarked a century later, "The wonder of Jane Austen is that at a time when even the best fiction was overloaded with incident, and its types went staggering about under the attributes heaped upon them, she imagined getting on with only so much incident as would suffice to let her characters express their natures movingly or amusingly."[67] Almost single-handedly, Austen moved the novel into the modern era—and did much of it before she got a single word in print.

# Praise and Pewter

 IN HIS MEMOIR OF JANE AUSTEN, JAMES EDWARD AUSTEN-
Leigh said of his aunt,

> I do not think that she was herself much mortified by the want of
> early success. She wrote for her own amusement. Money, though ac-
> ceptable, was not necessary for the moderate expenses of her quiet
> home. Above all, she was blessed with a cheerful contented disposi-
> tion, and an humble mind; and so lowly did she esteem her own
> claims, that when she received 150*l.* from the sale of "Sense and Sen-
> sibility," she considered it a prodigious recompense for that which
> had cost her nothing.[1]

Even given the conventions of Victorian biography and the fact
that the writer was the subject's nephew, this is a remarkably inaccurate view of Jane Austen's attitude to her profession. Austen *was* mortified by the humiliating rejections and delays she faced in the first
half of her career, *did* want to make money, and had no intention of
"writing for her own amusement" alone. While she never needed or
desired to adopt the difficult life of a full-time female "hack," like

Mary Wollstonecraft or Elizabeth Inchbald or Ann Radcliffe, neither was she ever the bland dabbler of James Edward's imagining (or of Henry Austen's earlier portrait, on which it is based). She may not have craved the society of other writers, but she did want readers—lots of readers—and money, which, like fame, was very "acceptable" to her indeed. "Tho' I like praise as well as anybody," she wrote in 1814, with bracing directness, "I like what Edward calls *Pewter* too."

Perseverance was the quality Jane Austen recommended to her niece Anna, a fledgling writer, in 1815[2] and which she possessed herself almost to the point of bloody-mindedness. She needed a powerful work ethic to see her through years of writing, revising, and adapting a growing collection of unpublished and—as far as she knew—possibly unpublishable works. Hardly any of Austen's original manuscripts have survived; only the fragmentary "Sanditon" and "The Watsons," the finished but unpublished "Lady Susan," a short and unpolished dramatization of scenes from Richardson's *Sir Charles Grandison*, and two canceled chapters of *Persuasion*, so it is difficult to reconstruct Austen's working methods and Austen's *work*. The six major novels exist for us only as finished items, as if they really had been produced effortlessly by that "cheerful contented" person whose writing "cost her nothing." But a memorandum compiled by Cassandra gives some idea of the timescale involved in their composition, and the doggedness of this genteel lady writer:

First Impressions begun in Oct 1796
Finished in Augt 1797—Published afterwards, with alterations & contractions under the Title of Pride & Prejudice.
Sense & Sensibility begun Nov. 1797
·  I am sure that something of the same story & characters had been written earlier & called Elinor & Marianne.
Mansfield Park, begun somewhere about Feby 1811—Finished soon after June 1813
Emma begun Jany 21st 1814, finished March 29th 1815
Persuasion begun Augt 8th 1815
Finished Augt 6th 1816
North-hanger Abby was written about the years 98 & 99 C.E.A.[3]

The most persistent theory about Austen's creative life, put forward by James Edward Austen-Leigh and repeated endlessly ever since, is that she had two "phases" of composition, in the 1790s and after 1809, which were divided by eight years of dearth; that the family's move to Bath in 1801 silenced her and that her muse returned only when she settled back in Hampshire. Austen left no diaries or pocketbooks, very few letters from the period before 1800, and no letters at all from May 1801 to September 1804, so these are, indeed, difficult years to reconstruct. But while it is impossible to quantify the extent of Austen's writing activity and business with publishers during this time, there is no reason to suppose she didn't have any. We know that she had three full-length novels finished or in progress in 1801, that her father solicited publication for one of them in 1797, and that she was successful in selling "Susan" in 1803, so she may have sent manuscripts to other publishers too and had other rejections. In fact, it's hard to imagine how the author of "First Impressions" and "Elinor and Marianne" could have borne to leave them festering in a drawer year after year.

The Austens' move to Bath gave them excellent access to booksellers, literary societies, circulating libraries, and the general gossip about books and authors that the family—and especially Jane and her father—loved. In Bath, they would have felt far better connected with the world of books and print than in rural Hampshire; there were plenty of bookshops and one of the country's largest circulating libraries on Milsom Street. Since there is nothing to suggest that George Austen withdrew his approval of his daughter's writing after the snub from Cadell, it seems entirely possible that he renewed his efforts on her behalf. It was through a bookseller in Bath, according to her nephew, that Jane Austen had her first contact with the London publisher Benjamin Crosby, known for his list of Gothic romances and trade in remainders. Crosby had been joint publisher with a Bath bookseller called Cruttwell in 1800 of an account of the trial for shoplifting of Jane Austen's aunt Jane Leigh Perrot. Perhaps there was pressure on Jane to maintain the connection; Mrs. Austen had been particularly keen to show solidarity with her wealthy, childless sister-in-law over many smaller matters.[4] In the spring of 1803, Jane Austen sold Crosby the manuscript of her Gothic satire, "Susan," for £10 out-right.[5] The business, conducted anonymously through Henry and his lawyer friend William Seymour, seemed to please the publisher as much as the author: He promised "an early publication" and adver-tised "Susan; a Novel, in 2 vols" as one of the new and useful books that he had "in the press."[6]

For twenty-seven-year-old Jane Austen and her family, this must have been an intensely exciting time. Crosby's acceptance of the man-uscript crowned a decade of effort on the part of the author and re-warded her family for their support. It came at a very significant moment in Austen's life. A few months earlier, on a visit to her Hamp-shire friends Catherine and Alethea Bigg, Jane had received a proposal of marriage from her friends' younger brother, Harris Bigg-Wither, heir to a splendid and substantial family home, Manydown House, near Basingstoke. It is usually assumed that Harris's offer came out of the blue, but without any letters from this year or the previous one, it is impossible to tell how intimately acquainted the couple were. The fact that Jane accepted his proposal—even though she withdrew her accep-tance within hours and fled from Manydown—indicates that she had anticipated his move and considered in advance the possibility of mar-rying him. The visit itself may have been structured around a courtship that had been going on for months; it's hard to imagine that Bigg-Wither would have dared risk speaking to her otherwise.

Whatever the circumstances, Jane's reversed decision was a turn-ing point in her life. In December 1802, Austen teetered on the edge of becoming the mistress of a beautiful estate near to her native Steven-ton and, almost inevitably, becoming the mother of lots of little Bigg-Withers; in the spring of 1803, she was a free woman and about to be a published writer. The acceptance of "Susan" must have helped her to justify to her family her refusal of Bigg-Wither. The £10 she re-ceived from Crosby would not, of course, have gone far toward her upkeep (apart from her disabled brother George, Jane was the only one of her siblings who was wholly dependent and incomeless) but helped to show that her preoccupation with writing wasn't entirely solipsistic.

Austen was buoyed up enough by the prospect of having her first novel in print to set to work on an entirely new one, "The Watsons," the story of a young woman, Emma Watson, who reenters her own family after twelve years of living with richer and more refined relations. If her later experience is anything to go by, Austen would have been focusing intensely on the forthcoming publication of "Susan," for when in 1811 she was in a similar position, waiting for the appearance of *Sense and Sensibility*, she said to Cassandra that she was "never too busy" to think of it; "I can no more forget it, than a mother can forget her sucking child."[7] Months passed, however, and "Susan" never appeared, nor was there any communication from Crosby in explanation. Austen must have gotten tired of having to account for it to those of her intimates who inquired when the novel would be out; like any form of abandonment, it could only have caused her deep mortification and embarrassment.

When the Reverend George Austen died suddenly at home in Bath in January 1805, aged seventy-three, Jane lost both a beloved, like-minded parent and the best supporter of her literary endeavors. George Austen had been anticipating his younger daughter's debut as a novelist for several years but never lived to see one of her books in print. His death left the Austen women heavily dependent on the charity of the remaining Austen men, and Jane's new situation, as an unmarried, unprotected, and now virtually penniless twenty-nine-year-old, was borne in on her forcefully as she and her sister and widowed mother moved to and from a series of rented houses in Bath and Southampton during the next four years, ending up sharing the home of her sister-in-law Mary and brother Frank (who, as a captain in the navy, was often on active service in the war with France at this time).

While it was clearly a time of retrenchment and change, Austen is unlikely to have given up her habit of writing in these years: it's as unlikely as her not having written any letters in the same period. We just don't have the documentation anymore. The novel begun in Bath, "The Watsons," had started promisingly but was put aside after about seventeen thousand words. However, the watermark of another manuscript, the completed epistolary novel "Lady Susan," shows that it was written—or rewritten or copied—in 1805. Scholars are divided on dating its origins; though there is no rule saying that authors all have to "progress" from one mode to another, in form and tone "Lady Susan" seems to belong to the juvenilia rather than the mature novels, and the surviving 1805 manuscript is very clean (unlike "The Watsons," which is full of evidence of working). The inference is that "Lady Susan" is older than its paper. Perhaps Austen meant to submit it for publication at this date or change it more; it would, after all, have been odd to have two novels in circulation with such similar titles as this and "Susan."

Austen clearly still had manuscripts going around the family for their private enjoyment. Cassandra, who made a particular pet of their eldest niece, Fanny Knight, after the death of Fanny's mother in 1808, must have shown the teenager one of Jane's manuscript novels as a mark of favor and intimacy when she was visiting their brother Edward's house at Godmersham in Kent. Responding to this news in a letter of January 1809, Jane makes some interesting remarks to Cassandra about this very small expansion of her readership. She feels her prose is already affected by the consciousness of an audience and fears further "hurt":

> I am gratified by [Fanny] having pleasure in what I write—but I wish the knowledge of my being exposed to her discerning Criticism, may not hurt my stile, by inducing too great a solicitude. I begin already to weigh my words & sentences more than I did, & am looking about for a sentiment, an illustration or a metaphor in every corner of the room. Could my Ideas flow as fast as the rain in the Storecloset, it would be charming.[8]

Austen was perhaps feeling nostalgic for the helter-skelter brilliance of her youth and the reassuring degree of control she used to have over her well-disposed home audience. There is a lot of freedom in being unpublished, and she had been unpublished a long time. Her letter also shows a deep self-consciousness about being entertaining and making it look effortless. The metaphor of the rain in the storecloset is brilliant, not only enacting her self-critique of "looking about for an illustration in every corner of the room," but suggesting what trouble such luck might be. Even more striking is the sense of watchfulness over her own development, a concern with the danger of falling off or stiffening. This evidence of writerly anxiety and self-monitoring, from an unpublished author, is surely very unusual. It shows how seriously Austen took her own vocation, published or not.

In the first years of the nineteenth century, she was, of course, expecting that Crosby's edition of "Susan," however long delayed, would eventually appear. But having sold the copyright outright and anonymously, she had no rights over her own book, no dealings with the publisher, and had to resign herself to waiting. In 1809 an anonymous novel called *Susan* was advertised in the press, which Austen and her family must have thought at first was her book, negligently brought out at last, without notification, by Crosby; further investigation would have shown that, as with "First Impressions," she had been preempted again, and her title used by someone else. On April 5, 1809, she was moved to write to Crosby, under an assumed name, to complain about the nonappearance of her own "Susan." Six years of frustration and bottled-up disappointment came to the surface in this, her angriest letter, written in the person of "Mrs. Ashton Dennis" (perhaps in an attempt to sound older and more significant than a mere Miss). The incognito helped her to be especially forthright, telling Crosby that she could only account for his negligence "by supposing the MS by some carelessness to have been lost; & if that was the case, am willing to supply You with another Copy if you are disposed to avail yourselves of it, & will engage for no farther delay when it comes into your hands."[9] The offer of another copy was possibly just to call his bluff, as Austen does not seem to have been in the habit of keeping copies of manuscripts (though she did copy this letter; it is our only record of it). But she was clearly furious at the treatment she had received and Crosby's likely decision not to publish "Susan" at all. She insisted on no more delays, not even to her letter, which should be answered "as soon as possible, as my stay in this place will not exceed a few days. Should no notice be taken of this Address, I shall feel myself at liberty to secure the publication of my work, by applying elsewhere." The assumed name allowed her to sign off dramatically, "I am Gentlemen &c &c MAD.—"

Mrs. Dennis's ultimatum, coming so vehemently out of the blue, seemed to irritate rather than shame the publisher. In his curt, prompt reply, Crosby's son Richard denied that there had ever been any agreed timetable for publication and pointed out that the firm owned, but was in no way bound to publish, the manuscript. He even slipped in a threat—"Should you or anyone else [publish it] we shall take proceedings to stop the sale"—before admitting that he was nevertheless prepared to sell the goods back to her "for the same as we paid for it."[10]

It was a very unsatisfactory conclusion: Crosby sitting on the rights and obviously unwilling to publish; Austen forced to find £10 if she wanted to retrieve the work and submit it elsewhere. The £10 was a large sum for her but not an impossible one. Judging from her later careful marshaling of her earnings from writing, she might have saved some or all of the money she got for the book in 1803 or have put some by over the years from her modest allowance of £10 a year. Henry spent as much as this every time he and his wife threw a party—and to Edward, who had inherited the Knight fortune and name by this date, and whose income from the Hampshire estates alone averaged £5,000 a year, it would have been a very small sum indeed. But Jane never would have dreamed of borrowing from her brothers, even to ransom back her book; her professional and personal pride would not have allowed it. One only has to look at how carefully she budgeted for possible losses later to see how much store she set by remaining independent in these matters.

The year 1809 was difficult for the family's finances generally. The death of the Reverend Austen had left his widow and daughters with only Mrs. Austen's sinking stock in the South Seas and Cassandra's annuity from the money left her by Tom Fowle. Edward covered the expense of settling his mother and sisters in a new home, a cottage belonging to his estate in Chawton, Hampshire (getting the cottage plumbed properly cost over £35 alone), and all the brothers were paying cash to maintain the household, an arrangement that was a struggle for the youngest, Charles, in particular. The transition from being a not-yet-married daughter to being a spinster sister and long-term burden must have been extremely distasteful to Jane, and the last thing she would have spent £10 of anyone's money on in 1809 was the repurchase of a manuscript. She might have been cutting her losses in another sense too, for "Susan" was getting old and would have needed time and work to bring up to date. In fact, "Susan" may have seemed to her a lot more out of date in 1809 than it did in 1816, when she did finally regain possession of the novel after the bankruptcy of Crosby & Co.

The stalemate over "Susan" didn't stop Austen's continuation with writing during these years, reflected in the production-line efficiency of her output from the year she did first get published, 1811, to her death in 1817. Though in 1809 she didn't get the opportunity to review her Gothic satire, she had the other 1790s novels, "First Impressions" and "Elinor and Marianne," still on hand, and must have been working on both of them in the years between 1805 and 1810. "Elinor and Marianne" emerged as *Sense and Sensibility*, presumably to chime with *Pride and Prejudice*, the new name for "First Impressions." In the first year at Chawton, she was still making adjustments to "Catharine, or The Bower," the fragmentary novel begun in 1791; in the manuscript she has replaced an illegible detail (probably "parasol") with "Regency walking dress" and inserted a reference to Hannah More's 1809 novel *Coelebs in Search of a Wife*. Many other changes, including the heroine's name to Catharine from Kitty, may date from the same set of revisions. It seems rather extraordinary that Austen was keeping this story from her teens in play at all, but she displayed a strong reluctance to abandon any of her work entirely, however old or incomplete.

The manuscript of "The Watsons" intriguingly reveals Austen's method of revising by pinning slips of paper over sections of text to be amended where there isn't room simply to cross through and write above the line—a nineteenth-century version of cut and paste. The sheets of paper are small and her writing economically tiny, indicating that Austen was probably in the habit of making a draft or drafts like this and fair copying at least once (to produce the evenly spaced and beautifully clear script of "Susan" and her letters, for example). Her use of dressmaking pins to attach corrections to "The Watsons" and as staples in "Sir Charles Grandison" (written on paper watermarked 1796 and 1799), is a nice connection between her writing life and her domestic life, displaying "a particular feminine frugality," as Kathryn Sutherland has remarked.[11] The two manuscripts show another habit of composition, which they share with "Sanditon" too: Austen liked to write these early drafts on large sheets of paper cut and folded to make small booklets of around eight pages, which were easily portable and became a series of quires. She certainly had time to expend on the labor. Some critics think that "The Watsons" was subsumed into *Pride and Prejudice* or *Emma*, but the similarities are tentative, and though Austen was unwilling to throw anything useful away, she doesn't seem to have kept drafts for which she had no further use.

By 1810, *Sense and Sensibility*, rewritten at least twice, was completely revised and ready to be sent out as Austen's latest bid for publication. This is unlikely to have excited her family much; they were possibly getting a bit tired of Jane's lack of success. Henry was her agent again and knew the man they sold to, Thomas Egerton, from Egerton's printing of the *Loiterer* in 1789–90. The deal was to publish on commission, with Egerton paying all the costs and getting a 10 percent commission on sales, and the author liable for all losses. It was quite a gamble for Austen, who, as Henry later recalled, "actually made a reserve from her moderate income to meet the expected loss."[12] Did she really expect a loss, or was this the spendthrift Henry's inability to understand financial caution? He also claimed that his sister published *Sense and Sensibility* only against her own inclinations, but all the evidence in Austen's own letters is quite to the contrary.

The relief and joy to the author of selling the book can be gauged by the fact that, as after the acceptance of "Susan," she began immediately on an entirely new novel. This one, known later as *Mansfield Park*, was carried on and finished within two years and four months, the first of Austen's books not to be composed in fits and starts over a much longer period. She must also have been working on the revision of "First Impressions" into *Pride and Prejudice*, since it was lined up ready to be offered to the publisher after the publication of *Sense and Sensibility*, and from what she said in 1813 of having "lopt & cropt" it extensively,[13] the work of revision took time.

Jane spent several weeks in London in April 1811, at Henry and Eliza's house on Sloane Street, a busy visit full of social events, coinciding—deliberately, one imagines—with the arrival of the first proof pages from Egerton. The proofs needed little adjustment, though Austen attempted to bring the book right up to date by adding a reference to the twopenny post—introduced in 1809—and *Marmion*, the best-selling poem published anonymously by newcomer Walter Scott in 1808. Austen had initially expected her novel to be published in May, but hope of that was fading; even June sounded unlikely. "Henry does not neglect it," Jane told Cassandra, who was staying at Godmersham and had been discussing the forthcoming event with Edward's adoptive mother, Mrs. Knight. "He has hurried the Printer, & says he will see him again today."[14] But there was a long delay before the book finally appeared in October, leaving Jane plenty of time to fear a repeat of the Crosby debacle. Meanwhile, other writers were making impressive debuts, and she was getting left behind. This was worse than bad novelists stealing her titles. Hearing the anonymous 1810 novel *Self-Control* (by Mary Brunton) talked up among her friends, Austen tried to get hold of a copy but was feeling anxious about it, as she told Cassandra: "I . . . am always half afraid of finding a clever novel too clever—& of finding my own story & my own people all forestalled."[15]

The circle of people who knew about Jane's authorship was small up to this point, and among the many nieces and nephews, only the eldest, Fanny Knight, was in on the secret. She had more than one letter that autumn from her aunt Cassandra "to beg we would not mention that Aunt Jane Austen wrote 'Sense & Sensibility.' "[16] In truth, there wasn't much need to worry about secrecy; the author must sometimes have hankered for less of it and probably didn't even know the momentous date on which the novel, in three volumes, "By A Lady," was eventually published. She had the congratulations, or otherwise, of her closest family and friends, and James composed a poem for her on the occasion, but news of the book's reception in the wider world filtered through to Chawton Cottage only slowly. Thomas Egerton had advertised the "Interesting Novel" at the end of the year, but it took three more months for the first of only two notices of the book to appear, a long article in *Critical Review*, in which the author praised *Sense and Sensibility* as "one amongst the few"[17] good examples of the genre. Austen must have been pleased with this (if she saw it) and the enthusiastic review in *British Critic* three months later: "We think so favourably of this performance that it is with some reluctance we decline inserting it among our principal articles."

Unknown to her, the novel was generating plenty of interest among the reading public, especially in the fashionable world. Countess Bessborough recommended it warmly to Lord Granville Gower, as "a clever Novel. They were full of it at Althorp," and the prince regent's only legitimate child, the teenage Princess Charlotte, wrote to a girlfriend that she had "*just finished*" reading it and was in the grip of a strong identification with the more romantic of the Dashwood sisters; "it certainly is interesting, & you feel quite one of the company. I think Maryanne & me are very like in *disposition*, that certainly I am not so good, the same imprudence, &c, however remain very like. I must say it interested me very much."[18] There was gossip about who the author of this charming book might be: Egerton had transposed "By A Lady" in one advertisement as "By Lady A"—typo or sales stratagem is hard to say—and some, like the regent's brother, the Duke of York, imagined that the author was Lady Augusta Paget (a rather outré suggestion, as Lady Augusta was a divorcée). This sort of literary guessing game was a popular pastime in an age where anonymity was standard practice for most authors, especially women authors. Other candidates for authorship of *Sense and Sensibility* over the next months included Elizabeth Hamilton and Mrs. Dorset, now almost completely forgotten except in this context. As Austen's friend Mrs. Pole said of Austen's novels a year or two later, "Everybody was desirous to attribute them to some of their own friends, or to some person of whom they thought highly."[19]

For Austen, anonymous and uninformed in her Hampshire village, the sense of being a published author remained rather abstract. There was one amusing incident, during a visit to the circulating library in Alton with James's daughter Anna, when the teenager came across a copy of *Sense and Sensibility*, "which she threw aside with careless contempt, little imagining who had written it, exclaiming to the great amusement of her Aunts who stood by 'Oh that must be rubbish I am sure from the title.' "[20] Austen was best able to measure her success through the book's sales. By July 1813 the first edition of around 750 copies (cheaply produced for the circulating library trade at a price of 15 shillings a set) had sold out, earning Austen a profit of £140. Having published on commission, she, of course, still possessed the copyright, "if that shd ever be of any value," as she remarked to her brother Frank.[21] The £140 was a very respectable sum, though nothing compared to the record-breaking deal Fanny Burney was about to sign with Longmans for *The Wanderer*, an advance of £3,000 that made even Lord Byron's eyes water (and on which the publisher lost a fortune: the second impression was pulped in 1817). To Austen, £140 was, of course, a huge increase in her personal wealth, but more important, it was a solid justification of her faith in herself. At last, she had reason to hope that the manuscripts she had piled up at home could be put before the public and that she could go ahead with new novels with some certainty of their reaching an audience.

In his verse "To Miss Jane Austen the reputed Author of Sense and Sensibility," James Austen had praised his sister's personification of those qualities and given her his best wishes, perhaps a little wistfully, "Oh then, gentle Lady! continue to write / And the Sense of your Readers t'muse & delight."[22] James's life had contracted very much since the days when he was the impresario of the Steventon theatricals and energetic editor of the *Loiterer*. He had taken over the curacy of Steventon (and the rectory that went with it) on his father's retirement in 1801, and had been rector since his father's death, but there was no return of the old gaiety in the former family home, and though James continued to write poems, there is no evidence that he sought publication for them. James's middle age was characterized by increasing melancholy and stasis. His poems became more introspective, his cadences interestingly halting, as in this description of himself:

> *By the long habits of retired life*
> *Unfitted to give pleasure, or be pleased*
> *In large & noisy parties; and at times*

> But scarcely able to maintain my share
> Of conversation[23]

The poem's subject was James's reticence, bordering on inability, to accept a different post in the church, but neither his deliberations nor his language were exactly what one would expect of a man of God: "Here . . . I am known, & borne with; but who there / Would care for me?" Of all the brothers, he seemed the one who had the most early promise and who had achieved least. Edward was master of Godmersham; Henry was a successful banker, cutting a stylish figure with Eliza in London; Captain Francis Austen was earning a high reputation for rectitude and leadership in the navy; and Charles Austen was also leading an active and successful life at sea. Perhaps James had been immobilized by waiting for the substantial inheritance he was promised by the Leigh Perrots, whose great wealth got even greater in 1806 after part of the Leigh family's Stoneleigh estate came to them. Mrs. Austen's deep agitation about the Leigh Perrot money was almost entirely on behalf of her eldest son, endlessly promised and never receiving a fortune almost equal to that of his younger brother Edward. No wonder James was brooding and embittered and spent most of one visit in 1807 "walking about the House & banging the Doors," as Jane was distressed to notice.[24]

Samuel Egerton Brydges had been far more successful in literary life, first with his two novels and in the new century as a connoisseur and collector of antiquarian books. At his son's grand home, Lee Priory, he ran his own small press devoted to the republication of Tudor works and eventually became a member of Parliament who helped change copyright law for authors. The Austens' cousin and *Loiterer* collaborator Edward Cooper had also become a man of letters. Cooper was a rather stringently principled young cleric, very much of the coming manner in the church, who insisted on residing in his Staffordshire benefice rather than subcontracting his parish duties to a curate, as many ministers did. Jane had found her cousin very attractive and congenial in his youth and admired his stance on clerical residence (the defining characteristic of Edmund Bertram in *Mansfield Park*), and they corresponded regularly enough for Jane to mention his "chearful

& amusing letters" in 1801, though she guessed that religious zeal was already getting the better of him, and that he would feel "obliged to purge himself from the guilt of writing Nonsense by filling his shoes with whole pease for a week afterwards."[25]

Cooper did get more and more evangelical, and his sermons, the first volume of which was published in 1805, was notably hard-line: "God sees through every disguise. He distinguishes the true character of men with infallible certainty. He now notices the specious pretender to religion. He will ere long bring to light his hypocrisy, and will at last load him with merited infamy and punishment."[26] The Hampshire Austens found all this too full of "Regeneration & Conversion" for their taste,[27] but Cooper's books sold extremely well. The 1809 collection went into four editions within a year, and he published many more, with numerous selections and reprints appearing all through the 1820s and '30s. James Edward Austen-Leigh remembered them "much preached in many pulpits in my youth."[28] Jane Austen may have had good reason to envy her cousin's success as an author: His first publisher, gallingly, was that very Thomas Cadell who had passed over the opportunity to read "First Impressions" in 1797, and even after Jane was published, Edward Cooper sold consistently better than she ever did.

Though the publication of *Sense and Sensibility* didn't measure up to the success of Edward Cooper's sermons, Jane scarcely needed her brother James's encouragement to keep on writing, and Thomas Egerton was interested in publishing more. She had *Mansfield Park* under way and *Pride and Prejudice* ready for the press. "The 2nd vol. is shorter than I cd wish," she told Cassandra when all the revisions were done, "—but the difference is not so much in reality as in look, there being a larger proportion of Narrative in that part. I have lopt & cropt so successfully however that I imagine it must be rather shorter than S.&S. altogether."[29]

The experience of publishing on commission had been successful, but put the onus on the author, or her agent, to oversee a great deal of business, which perhaps busy Henry wasn't able to attend to as promptly as he might have wished in 1811, when Eliza became ill. Austen clearly wanted to hand the matter over this time so agreed to

sell Egerton the copyright of her next book for the bargain price of
£110. She wrote to Martha Lloyd, "I would rather have had £150,
but we could not both be pleased, & I am not at all surprised that he
should not chuse to hazard so much—Its being sold will I hope be a
great saving of Trouble to Henry, & therefore must be welcome to
me."[30] It's strange that she valued *Pride and Prejudice* at so much less
than *Sense and Sensibility*, but perhaps—it's an odd thought—she was
simply glad to get it off her hands after so many years. She certainly
derived nothing but pleasure from the contemplation of her earnings so far, writing to her brother Frank, "I have now therefore written myself into £250.—which only makes me long for more."[31]

"I want to tell you that I have got my own darling Child from
London," Jane wrote triumphantly to her sister on January 29, 1813,
when the first set of *Pride and Prejudice* arrived at Chawton. "On
Wednesday I received one Copy, sent down by Falknor. . . . The Advertisement is in our paper to day for the first time;—18s." Austen's
surprise at what the publisher was charging (and making in profits
for himself) is reflected in her next remark, "He shall ask £1-1- for
my two next, & £1-8- for my stupidest of all."[32] Her observations
were shrewd, as Egerton had not only upped the price of her book
but shaved production costs by cramming more lines on a page and
using cheaper paper, since he was paying this time as well as getting
the profits. The print run of the first edition isn't known but is likely
to have been around seven hundred copies. It sold fast enough for a
second edition to appear later the same year, which was still available
in 1815; a third edition came out in 1817. A conservative estimate of
these sales (based on the print runs of other Austen novels) would be
1,500 copies—and of the gross profit to Egerton about £575: £465 more
than he had paid for the rights.[33]

The same day that the book arrived at Chawton, Austen and her
mother tested it out on their unsuspecting neighbor, Mary Benn:

> We set fairly at it & read half the 1st vol. to her—prefacing that hav-
> ing intelligence from Henry that such a work wd soon appear we
> had desired him to send it whenever it came out—& I beleive it
> passed with her unsuspected.—She was amused, poor soul! *that* she

c^d not help you know, with two such people to lead the way; but she really does seem to admire Elizabeth. I must confess that *I* think her as delightful a creature as ever appeared in print, & how I shall be able to tolerate those who do not like *her* at least, I do not know.[34]

The copy sent to Godmersham was read immediately by Fanny Knight and her friend Mary Oxenden, who scribbled in Fanny's diary, "This morning we finished 'Pride & Prejudice' . . . perfection!!!"[35] Cassandra sent on their praise from Kent, which for Jane came at an opportune moment: In Chawton with only Miss Benn as audience and Mrs. Austen gabbling her part of the reading, Jane had "had some fits of disgust" about the book. "Upon the whole however I am quite vain enough & well satisfied enough," she wrote, facetiously suggesting some of the ways in which the book might be improved and have its sparkle tamped down a bit. Thanks to the local Reading Society, Chawton was awash with books and readers, and word was already circulating about the new novel "By the Author of 'Sense and Sensibility.'" Mrs. Digweed called at the cottage with Miss Benn one morning and mentioned the book, though of course neither of them had any idea who they were talking to.

It was an "agreable surprise" to Jane that her secret was being guarded cautiously in Steventon by James and his wife, but no surprise at all that several of Henry's London friends had got to hear of it. On a visit to him that spring, she was told that one of them, a Miss Burdett, wished particularly to be introduced. "I am rather frightened by hearing that she wishes to be introduced to *me*," she wrote at this first evidence of lionization. "If I *am* a wild Beast, I cannot help it. It is not my own fault."[36] Austen had little idea how much impression *Pride and Prejudice* was making on its first readers. At a dinner party at the brewer Samuel Whitbread's house in the year of publication, the playwright Richard Brinsley Sheridan turned to his neighbor and asked if she had seen the novel, urging her to "buy it immediately, for it was one of the cleverest things he ever read."[37] The young lady was a Miss Shirreff, who took the great man's advice and subsequently became such an admirer of Austen's work that she used to hope for a carriage breakdown every time she passed through Chawton in order to contrive acquaintance with the author, whose cottage (as she must have discovered) was right on the corner of the busy Alton to Winchester road. Miss Shirreff was Austen's first obsessive fan.

Another early reader, Annabella Milbanke, wrote to her mother that she considered *Pride and Prejudice* "a very superior work": "It depends not on any of the common resources of novel writers, no drownings, no conflagrations, nor runaway horses, nor lap-dogs and parrots, nor chambermaids and milliners, nor rencontres and disguises."[38] She thought it the *"most probable"* fiction she had ever read and felt that "the interest is very strong, especially for Mr Darcy." Miss Milbanke had identified Austen's most unusual quality in a market suffused with sensational literature: that she could arouse the reader's "strong interest" without gimmickry. Miss Milbanke's remark about the novel's hero is also, I believe, the first recorded instance of a condition that has gripped millions of other "fair readers" since: Darcy-philia. Austen's astonishingly powerful creation of the supreme bourgeois fantasy man, aristocratic, handsome, heterosexual, and possessed of Pemberley, rather gave the lie to the novel's ostensible antiromanticism, as Miss Milbanke (who the very next year was courted by and accepted England's most wanted bachelor, Lord Byron) must have appreciated at many levels. *Pride and Prejudice* strove to be "probable," but in the service of erotic and materialist dreaming.

The novel attracted two reviews, from the same sources as before. The *British Critic* thought the book "far superior to almost all the publications of the same kind which have lately come before us" and praised the simplicity of the plot and complexity of the characters. The *Critical Review*, at much greater length, told the whole plot and quoted copiously, chuckled over the characterization of Mr. Bennet and Mr. Collins ("indeed a notable object"), and flatteringly likened Elizabeth Bennet to Shakespeare's Beatrice. This reviewer had guessed or heard the sex of the author and seemed surprised—not to say amazed—at the intelligence she displayed and "the lively manner" in which the heroine "supports an argument." Altogether he felt "this performance . . . rises very superior to any novel we have lately met with in the delineation of domestic scenes" and that the sentiments of the book "do great credit to the sense and sensibility of the authoress.

... It is unnecessary to add, that we have perused these volumes with much satisfaction and amusement, and entertain very little doubt that their successful circulation will induce the author to similar exertions."[39]

The fact that she had sold the manuscript cheap did not in the least affect Austen's happiness that spring and summer at the long-awaited appearance of her "darling child." She was still thinking about the characters as her own private property and was as fond of them as real people. At a watercolor exhibition in London in May, she picked out the portrait she imagined was of Jane Bennet, "now" Mrs. Bingley. She looked for a corresponding portrait of "Mrs. Darcy," but wrote to Cassandra that she was not surprised at its absence: 'I can only imagine that Mr D. prizes any Picture of her too much to like it should be exposed to the public eye.—I can imagine he w^d have that sort [of] feeling—that mixture of Love, Pride & Delicacy."[40] Still kept comfortably from "the public eye" herself, Jane savored the novel: when her brother Edward and his family were in Chawton that summer she read it aloud to Fanny Knight, apparently doing all the parts herself, with theatrical relish.[41]

The publication of the book brought surprises for everyone: Charles Austen (along with half the nation) was busy praising Walter Scott's first novel, *Waverley*, at a dinner in 1814 when a young man, who turned out to be a nephew of Charles James Fox, countered with the opinion that "nothing had come out for years to be compared with Pride & Prejudice, Sense & Sensibility etc."[42] This must have been quite stunning for the anonymous novelist's younger brother but was also an obvious signal to him, and other members of the family, that there was little point and no pleasure in withholding the identity of the author any longer. Henry certainly had no qualms about it. On a visit to Scotland, he heard Lady Robert Kerr warmly praising *Pride and Prejudice* with a friend and immediately blurted out that it was, in fact, the work of his own sister! Jane excused him, understanding that he was acting "in the warmth of his Brotherly vanity & Love," but also knew that this wasn't an isolated incident: "He, dear Creature, has set it going so much more than once." Reporting this to Frank, who was safely away at sea, she said: "The truth is that the Secret has spread so far as to be scarcely the Shadow of a secret now—& that I beleive whenever the 3ᵈ [novel] appears, I shall not even attempt to tell Lies about it.—I shall rather try to make all the Money than all the Mystery I can of it. People shall pay for their Knowledge if I can make them."[43] This is a remarkably hard-nosed remark, a world away from the portrait later painted by Henry Austen and James Edward Austen-Leigh of the woman who wrote only "for her own amusement." Critical success was gratifying, but Austen also coveted sales dearly. She also enjoyed the idea of fame enough to joke that her own picture might yet appear at the Royal Academy annual exhibition, along with the other beauties and celebrities of the year, "all white & red, with my Head on one Side," as she wrote to Cassandra; "or perhaps I may marry young Mr D'arblay,"[44] Fanny Burney's nineteen-year-old son, then a student at Cambridge.

Five months after the appearance of *Pride and Prejudice*, she had *Mansfield Park* ready to publish, "which I hope on the credit of P.&P. will sell well, tho' not half so entertaining."[45] As Austen's first contemporary book, not using material generated in her teens and early twenties, *Mansfield Park* was also something of a leap in the dark for the thirty-seven-year-old author. The themes—of neglectful parenting, bad ministering, sexual transgression, and the dubious origins of many a good man's gains—were much more somber than before, and the stifled central character, Fanny Price, quite a challenge to readers just getting used to the charms of the Dashwood sisters and Elizabeth Bennet. Fanny Price, with her blushes and scruples, has always been the least popular of Austen's heroines, though she suited the more stringent moralism of the 1810s and the reaction against upperclass vice (personified by the lax new prince regent). Thomas Egerton thought the book had "no weak parts"[46] but didn't offer to buy the copyright this time, publishing on commission again in May 1814. The further economies evident in the production of *Mansfield Park*— even thinner paper than *Pride and Prejudice*, and even more lines to the page—reflected the steeply increasing price of book production during the long war years but may have been ordered by the author in emulation of Egerton's own practices, to maximize profits. In business terms, *Mansfield Park* was Austen's most successful venture, and the invested profits from it gave her an income of about £30 a year.[47]

Austen had engaged the help of Cassandra, Henry, Martha, and Frank with minor queries during the writing of *Mansfield Park* and seemed to enjoy a collaborative or conspiratorial element in its composition; she also enjoyed having made an impression on her older nieces in Godmersham, and, as one of the excluded younger nieces recalled later, used to shut herself up in a bedroom with them and read the current work in progress aloud. Austen kept a record of "Opinions" of the novel—many of which had been solicited from, rather than volunteered by, her family and friends—which shows just how large a group the "insiders" now made. The compilation of this record is itself a mark of the author's pride in her achievement and deep interest in its reception, as she wrote to Fanny Knight: "The pleasures of Vanity are . . . within your comprehension & you will enter into mine, at receiving the *praise* which every now & then comes to me, through some channel or other." To her niece Anna she wrote, "Make everybody at Hendon admire Mansfield Park."[48]

While the "Opinions" contain many expressions of delight from family and friends, some seem to have been preserved as examples of the crass things nearest and dearest feel licensed, or even obliged, to say to one of their own who has attracted praise elsewhere. Mrs. Austen thought the heroine insipid; Anna "could not bear" her; Mrs. Cooke liked the treatment of clergy, but "wished for a good Matronly Character"; Mrs. Sophia Lefroy "liked it, but thought it a mere novel." There were rather unaccountable identifications (one lady chose to see herself in Lady Bertram) and appalling rudeness too, such as Mrs. Augusta Bramstone taking the opportunity to say that she thought Jane's first two novels had been "downright nonsense," but "expected to like Mansfield Park better, & having finished the Ist vol.—flattered herself she had got through the worst." The book was constantly held up for comparison with *Pride and Prejudice* and found wanting in liveliness but superior in morality.

So there was not much danger of Jane Austen getting above herself at home. Her family seemed full of experts on fiction, and a new generation of writers was springing up at her feet; in 1814 Anna Austen admitted that she too was writing a novel and sent it in batches to be read and commented on by her aunts. Anna's young half-sister Caroline was also writing and sending stories for commentary, and James Edward, about to go up to Oxford, was busy writing poems and sketches. James Edward was a much more frequent correspondent after he discovered, three novels into Jane's career, that he "had the honour to have a relation / Whose works were dispersed through the whole of the nation." The witty verses he sent her on the occasion marveled at the fact:

> *That you made the Middletons, Dashwoods & all,*
> *And that you, (not young Ferrars,) found out that a ball*
> *May be given in cottages never so small*
> *And though Mr Collins so grateful for all*
> *Will Lady de Burgh his dear patroness call,*
> *Tis to your ingenuity really he ow'd*
> *His living, his wife, & his humble abode.*[49]

Sales of *Mansfield Park* were enough to raise the prospect of a second edition, of which Austen told her niece, "I am very greedy & want to make the most of it."[50] But perhaps Henry asked too much from Egerton, as the idea seems to have died on the vine. Moving as he did in far more wealthy and worldly circles than his sister, Henry was keen for her to maximize her celebrity and take whatever opportunities arose to mingle with wits and the literati. Madame de Staël was in London that year and had borrowed a copy of *Pride and Prejudice* from Henry Colburn, and although privately she pronounced Austen's novels "vulgaire,"[51] she was interested in meeting the author. Austen firmly quashed the suggestion. Nothing was less likely than she would enjoy the company of the great French novelist, with her famously big personality, thick skin, and loud voice, from whose eloquence Byron said "the sovereign himself . . . was not exempt."[52] Austen was far too satirical to insert herself into such a scene.

A very interesting view of how fame affected Jane Austen in the few years she was granted it comes from the novelist and playwright Mary Russell Mitford, another local parson's daughter, twelve years Austen's junior and brought up in nearby Alresford.[53] Miss Mitford was delighted to discover, in 1815, that the author of "*Pride and Prejudice* etc" was someone her mother had known as a girl. She also heard this gossip about Austen from an unnamed mutual acquaintance, suggesting that Austen's behavior in front of strangers had modified dramatically now that she was a figure of interest:

> A friend of mine, who visits her now, says that she has stiffened into the most perpendicular, precise, taciturn piece of "single blessedness" that ever existed, and that, till "Pride and Prejudice" showed what a precious gem was hidden in that unbending case, she was no more regarded in society than a poker or a fire-screen, or any other thin upright piece of wood or iron that fills its corner in peace and quietness. The case is very different now; she is still a poker—but a poker of whom every one is afraid. It must be confessed that this silent observation from such an observer is rather formidable. Most writers are good-humoured chatterers—neither very wise nor very witty:—but nine times out of ten (at least in the very few that I have known) unaffected and pleasant, and quite removing by their conversation any awe that may have been excited by their works. But a wit, a delineator of character, who does not talk, is terrific indeed![54]

The specific linking of this terrific new social power to Austen's debut as a published writer says a lot about how she decided to conduct her fame. "A poker of whom every one is afraid" could have been a useful mode to adopt when faced with impertinent gawpers, though the impression here is of Austen being actively unpleasant to her admirers rather than simply trying to protect her own privacy. "Nine times out of ten" a writer in such a position would make an effort to put people at their ease. But not Jane Austen.[55]

DESPITE SOME DOUBTS ABOUT how long her inspiration could go on, Austen now thought of herself as a full-time novelist, and the five years from 1811 to 1816 were an almost constant round of writing, revising, correcting proofs, and getting published. She finished *Mansfield Park* in June 1813 and was perhaps planning an early version of

"Sanditon" that autumn.[56] Egerton brought out second editions of *Sense and Sensibility* and *Pride and Prejudice* late in 1813, and in January 1814 Jane began *Emma*, finishing the book within fourteen months. In May 1814, *Mansfield Park* was published; *Emma* was published the next year; *Persuasion* was started; and the long-neglected "Susan" was retrieved from Crosby and revised.

Austen got the chance to show her hand as a businesswoman toward the end of 1815 when Henry was taken ill during the negotiations over the sale of her new novel, *Emma*. They had made the decision to leave Egerton and offer the book to John Murray, the most prestigious and fashionable literary publisher of the day. Murray's desk on Albemarle Street was groaning with submissions from novelists and poets who sought "the honour of the name of Lord Byron's publisher on the title-page," as Samuel Smiles wrote at the end of the century,[57] so his prompt interest in Austen was very much a mark of distinction. Murray wanted to buy the copyrights to all three available titles, *Sense and Sensibility*, *Mansfield Park*, and *Emma*, but the £450 he was offering was dismissed by Henry rather haughtily:

> The Terms you offer are so very inferior to what we had expected, that I am apprehensive of having made some great Error in my Arithmetical Calculation.—On the subject of the expence & profit of publishing, you must be much better informed than I am;—but Documents in my possession appear to prove that the Sum offered . . . is not equal to the Money which my Sister has actually cleared by one very moderate Edition of Mansfield Park . . . & a still smaller one of Sense & Sensibility.[58]

Jane must have approved the letter and possibly composed much of it, as it was dictated to her from Henry's sickbed, but when his illness worsened sharply, and the family rushed to London to help, Jane had to continue the negotiations on her own. She had no trouble with this, writing under her own name to arrange a meeting with Murray at Henry's house in Hans Place. Nor was she intimidated by the great man, whom she judged "a Rogue of course but a civil one."[59] She was right to think "it will end in my publishing for myself, I dare say"; Austen hung on to the copyrights and Murray published *Emma* on commission, in an edition of two thousand (much larger than Egerton had ever ventured), and reissued *Mansfield Park*. The printing progressed with a speed almost unimaginable in the industry now, and within three weeks, Austen felt justified in sending an irritable letter complaining about delays with the proofs: "Instead of the Work being ready by the end of the present month [November 1815], it will hardly, at the rate we now proceed, be finished by the end of the next."[60] Again, the tone is that of an assertive businesswoman, not a meek amateur.

In the meantime, one of the doctors treating Henry revealed that, as physician to the prince regent, he knew that His Royal Highness was "a great admirer" of Miss Austen's novels and kept a set in each of his residences. Few people could have been less flattered by this information: Jane thoroughly disapproved of the regent and had sided strongly with his wife during their scandalous public wrangling at the time of the divorce proceedings. But when the doctor informed the prince that the author was presently in London, Jane received an invitation to visit his library at Carlton House and be received by the librarian, the Reverend James Stanier Clarke. This questionable treat took place on November 13, 1815. Jane was given a tour of the ornate and garishly colored palace, stuffed with gilt and ormolu and velvet hangings, and in the Gothic library Rev. Clarke repeated the prince's praises and passed on his permission—which she had never sought, of course—to dedicate her next book to him.

Such an offer was tantamount to a command and caused Austen some anxiety about protocol, though Murray was pleased with the honor and found the correct, fulsome form of words for the dedication. In the meantime, Rev. Clarke had begun to pester the author with suggestions for future subjects, something about a clergyman perhaps, who passes his time between the town and the country, who is fond of literature and is "no man's Enemy but his own"—someone, indeed, rather like himself. Austen's attempts to rebuff him and Clarke's increasing insistence on the value of his advice make one of the most amusing exchanges in Austen's surviving correspondence but also give us a glimpse of what she had to put up with as a woman of extraordinary talent and originality being patronized by nincompoops. When she answered politely that such a character as Clarke suggested would be beyond her range and would require "A Classical Education, or at any rate, a very extensive acquaintance with English Literature,"[61] he countered helpfully with a much fuller outline of the proposed novel, complete with just such little touches of sophistication as she had confessed lacking:

> Make all your friends send Sketches to help you—and Memoires pour servir—as the French term it. Do let us have an English Clergyman after *your* fancy—much novelty may be introduced—shew dear Madam what good would be done if Tythes were taken away entirely, and describe him burying his own mother—as I did— because the High Priest of the Parish in which she died—did not pay her remains the respect he ought to do. I have never recovered the Shock. Carry your Clergyman to Sea as the Friend of some distinguished Naval Character about a Court—you can then bring forward like Le Sage many interesting Scenes of Character & Interest.[62]

Clarke insisted that his rooms in Golden Square, "my Cell . . . where I often hide myself," were ever at her disposal, with a small library and maidservant in constant attendance. Perhaps the Reverend Clarke, who has gone down in literary history as one of the great fools, was a little in love with the creator of Emma Woodhouse and Elizabeth Bennet and Elinor Dashwood and Fanny Price, and who can blame him?

The satirical "Plan of a Novel, according to hints from various quarters" that Austen wrote as a private response to Clarke's advice is a very funny pastiche of his suggestions (and incidentally bears some resemblance to the story lines of Madame d'Arblay's 1814 flop, *The Wanderer*). It takes malicious revenge on Clarke and those like him who had pointed out ways in which Austen could improve her writing. Two friends are in the joke with her, Mary Cooke and Fanny

Knight; the other names that appear neatly in the margin, next to their attributed suggestions, are themselves victims of the satire: Murray's reader, William Gifford; a clergyman called Mr. Sherer who had not liked *Emma*; Martha Lloyd's aunt Craven; and, of course, James Stanier Clarke. The beautiful and virtuous heroine of Austen's "Plan" is "often reduced to support herself and her Father by her Talents, and work for her Bread;—continually cheated and defrauded of her hire, worn down to a Skeleton, and now and then starved to death":

> —At last, hunted out of civilized Society, denied the poor Shelter of the humblest Cottage, they are compelled to retreat into Kamschatka where the poor Father, quite worn down, finding his end approaching, throws himself on the Ground, and after 4 or 5 hours of tender advice and parental Admonition to his miserable Child, expires in a fine burst of Literary Enthusiasm, intermingled with invectives against Holder's of Tythes.[63]

The "Plan" is thought to have been circulated among Austen's friends and family, but, like her recording of "Opinions" about *Mansfield Park* and *Emma*, the joke could be even more private than that, a symptom of profound (not necessarily unhappy) isolation. Why seek an audience, after all, for an attack on how one is received? The phenomenon had rapidly gone beyond satire: In the "Opinions of Emma" that Austen was gathering at about the same time as writing "Plan of a Novel," most of the contributors felt free to point out Austen's shortcomings in no uncertain terms: Mrs. Guiton thought the novel "too natural to be interesting," while Mrs. Digweed, perhaps stung by the emergence of such vast literary talent among the ranks of the Chawton Reading Society, said that "if she had not known the Author, [she] could hardly have got through it."[64]

What the prince regent made of *Emma*, if *he* ever "got through it," is not recorded, but the dedication of the book to him, and Murray's elegant imprint, ensured a certain amount of notice in the literary press. Most of it was extremely conventional. The *British Critic* described the book as "inoffensive and well principled"; the *Gentleman's Magazine* thought it had "no tendency to deteriorate the heart." For the first time, the author had some connection with the book's reception in fashionable society and was required to send a copy to the Countess Morley, a lady with literary interests whose husband Henry Austen was trying to secure as a patron for himself. Jane's careful drafting of a note to her, which still exists in two versions—one in pencil, gone over in ink, the other in ink (but presumably a copy, as there is no seal, postmark, or address)—betrays a painful degree of consciousness. It's a lot of practice for a thank-you note, and the differences between the two drafts are few and trivial. Was Jane Austen intimidated by writing to a member of the aristocracy, annoyed at having to toady to Henry's patrons, or did she often (always?) take this much trouble composing?

Austen was understandably annoyed that Murray's dispersal of copies of *Emma* "among my near Connections—beginning with the P.R. and ending with Countess Morley"[65] meant there wasn't one available for her younger brother Charles. Among the other "near Connections" of the author to whom the publisher had sent prepublication copies were the celebrated novelist Maria Edgeworth (who was puzzled that the book had "no story") and Augusta Leigh, Lord Byron's half sister. Augusta took it with her, in December 1815, when she moved into her brother and sister-in-law's home to assist at the birth of their first child, Allegra. Augusta was not perhaps the expectant mother's first choice of companion, as Lady Byron already had her suspicions about the relationship between her mercurial husband and his half sister (which was to cause such scandal later), but we can be fairly sure that the book went down well, at least. Lady Byron, already thoroughly miserable in her marriage, was the former Annabella Milbanke who had been such an enthusiastic reader of *Pride and Prejudice* in 1813. As Christine Penney has remarked in a bibliographic note about this copy (which sold in 1995 for £16,000), "one must hope that Emma gave both women some relief from their domestic hell."[66]

Three months after the publication of *Emma*, an unsigned article by Walter Scott, about four thousand words long, appeared in the *Quarterly*, acknowledging publicly for the first time that "the author of Pride & Prejudice etc etc" was a force to be reckoned with. Scott's thoughtful, deeply appreciative overview of *Sense and Sensibility*, *Pride and Prejudice*, and *Emma* was all the more interesting given his very different mode of novel writing from Austen's, the "big Bow-wow strain," as he was to characterize it later. He recognized her kind of novel as something new in the past fifteen or twenty years, replacing the improbable excitements of sensational literature with "the art of copying from nature as she really exists in the common walks of life, and presenting to the reader, instead of the splendid scenes of an imaginary world, a correct and striking representation of that which is daily taking place around him."[67] Readers, he said, were made to feel they really knew the characters and could spot their counterparts in everyday society. The risk of this "naturalness," Scott realized, was that everyone felt free to criticize "that which is presented as the portrait of a friend, or a neighbour."

Austen was not overcome by praise from the best seller. Though grateful for the distinction of such a long notice, she expressed displeasure to Murray at Scott's complete neglect or ignorance of *Mansfield Park*: "I cannot but be sorry that so clever a Man as the Reviewer of Emma, should consider it as unworthy of being noticed."[68] *Mansfield Park* was still, for her, something of a special case, a contemporary book touching on serious themes, not likely to get its due. It didn't receive a single review during the author's lifetime and ranked low in the "Opinions," except among a minority of high-minded people who tended to disapprove of the frivolity of the other books. In the emerging pecking order of the novels, *Pride and Prejudice* was constantly referred to as the very best of Jane's efforts so far; Mr. Collins was often praised (except by clergymen), and characters in *Emma* such as Miss Bates and the Eltons proved popular, though not Emma herself, interestingly. Austen had said when she was writing the book that Emma was a heroine "nobody but myself will much like," anticipating the responses of the home audience almost exactly.

Austen's letter to Murray also contains an acid little aside about how the only comment on *Emma* that had reached her from the prince regent was on the book's appearance. She was becoming sensitive to such slights—to any sort of criticism. Murray's friend and reader William Gifford, for example, hardly deserved being held up to ridicule in "Plan of a Novel" for his suggestion that she should write about a clergyman's daughter; he was an intelligent and keen supporter of her. But an air of anxious disillusionment hangs around her letters of this time, as if Austen was losing faith—not in her own work, but in the ability of others to appreciate it in the "right" way. Perhaps her experience of being unpublished so long, and being her own principal reader, had left her hard to please when it came to outside judgment of her "darling children." In her reply of April 1, 1816, to some of James Stanier Clarke's renewed suggestions for her future plots, she seems to be addressing herself more than him: "I must keep to my own style & go on in my own Way; And though I may never succeed again in that, I am convinced I should totally fail in any other."[69]

Jane's letter of thanks to Countess Morley contains a similarly lonely, self-reflective sentiment:

> Accept my Thanks for the honour of your note & for your kind Disposition in favour of Emma. In my present State of Doubt as to her reception in the World, it is particularly gratifying to me to receive so early an assurance of your Ladyship's approbation. It encourages me to depend on the same share of general good opinion which Emma's Predecessors have experienced, & to beleive that I have not yet—as almost every Writer of Fancy does sooner or later—overwritten myself.[70]

The idea of having "overwritten herself" was not the only thing preying on Austen's mind early in 1816. Henry Austen's banking business, which prospered during the war years, suffered a corresponding slump in 1815 when farmers began to default on their debts. The country branches Henry had set up in Alton, Petersfield, and Hythe came under severe strain, and over the winter of 1815–16, the Alton bank crashed. Henry's partnerships dissolved in a flurry of asset stripping and last-ditch mortgaging, and in March the London branch failed and Henry was officially declared bankrupt. The catastrophe brought financial losses all through the family (Jane herself lost £13.7s, though this was nothing compared to Edward's £20,000 loss, or the Leigh Perrots' £10,000). It also brought social and professional shame, which Jane felt much more acutely than her brother, who was soon negotiating for a career in the church. She had to make alternative money arrangements with Murray and let him in on the "late sad event in Henrietta St."[71] Henrietta Street itself, Henry's spacious house in Hans Place and the access it had afforded to London, plays, parties, literary gossip, books, and publishers, all had to be given up, of course.

According to Cassandra's memorandum, Jane had begun writing her next novel (called "The Elliots" at this stage, later *Persuasion*) in August 1815, that is, while *Emma* was in production. She finished it—or finished *with* it for the time being—a year later. When her niece Fanny inquired about her work, she said, "I have a something ready for Publication, which may perhaps appear about a twelvemonth hence. It is short, about the length of Catherine."[72] It is notable that Austen was anticipating such an interval between the book being "ready for publication" and being published. In her 1920 biography, *Personal Aspects of Jane Austen*, Mary Augusta Austen-Leigh claimed (on family authority) it was Austen's practice to let works "rest" like this, to dissipate "the charm of recent composition" and give herself time to make final changes in the light of second or third thoughts. This seems entirely consistent with a lifetime of keeping control over her manuscripts (albeit unwillingly), to the extent that Austen may have really felt comfortable only about her unpublished, still-improvable books.

Two manuscript chapters of *Persuasion*, the only such drafts of any part of any Austen novel to have survived, have given scholars fascinating insight into Austen's working methods. The wholescale changes that she made to the story and style show that, even at this late stage in her career, "conception and execution were neither instinctive nor unerring," as Brian Southam has remarked.[73] In the canceled draft, the resolution of the love story is made to turn on a very artificially engineered meeting between Anne Elliot and Captain Wentworth at the Crofts' lodgings; it has none of the drama or emotional weight of the later version, in which Anne's heartfelt conversation with Harville about the differences between men's and women's constancy is overheard by Wentworth at the White Hart and prompts his renewed declaration to her by letter. The thoroughness of the revision shows the effort that Austen was prepared to put in to improve her work; "a triumph of rethinking," in Southam's words again, "won through trial and error." Austen clearly had little respect for those who, like Egerton Brydges, dashed off work and sent it straight to the printer; she drily suggested that an 1809 novel called *Ida of Athens* "must be very clever, because it was written as the Authoress says, in three months."[74]

The same year that she was writing "The Elliots" (*Persuasion*), Austen was making extensive changes to the manuscript of "Susan," which had just come back from its long sojourn in Benjamin Crosby's slush pile. She was strongly motivated to update and resell the book, money being more of an issue than ever in 1816 (when the tenancy of Chawton Cottage also came into doubt, owing to litigation against her brother Edward), but she found the work difficult and after a year felt it still wasn't ready. She reported to her niece Fanny Knight that "Catherine," as the story was now called, was "put upon the Shelve for the present, and I do not know that she will ever come out."[75]

As part of its revision, Austen had written a short preface to explain the novel's datedness. It is the only autobiographical writing of its kind by her and shows just how much Crosby's dog-in-the-manger behavior still rankled:

This little work was finished in the year 1803, and intended for immediate publication. It was disposed of to a bookseller, it was even advertised, and why the business proceeded no farther, the author has never been able to learn. That any bookseller should think it worth while to purchase what he did not think it worth while to publish seems extraordinary. But with this, neither the author nor the public have any other concern than as some observation is necessary upon those parts of the work which thirteen years have made comparatively obsolete. The public are entreated to bear in mind that thirteen years have passed since it was finished, many more since it was begun, and that during that period, places, manners, books and opinions have undergone considerable change.

Even with this rider, Austen hesitated to send the book out into the world. By the middle of 1816, she was suffering from pains in the back and chronic fatigue. On a summer visit to the Fowles at Kintbury, her hosts noticed how ill she looked and were struck by her "peculiar manner—as if she did not expect to see them again."[76] By the time Jane made up the booklets in which she began her next novel, "The Brothers" (later given the title "Sanditon"), she had been ill for some months, though hopeful of a recovery. She wrote about twenty-four thousand words before putting the story aside in March 1817. It went "on the Shelve" along with "The Watsons," "Lady Susan," "Catharine, or The Bower," and the two short novels that she had, technically speaking, finished, but which were somehow not yet deemed ready to be submitted for publication, "Susan"/"Catherine" and "The Elliots." In June, Austen was moved to lodgings in Winchester to be nearer the professional skills of the surgeon Dr. Lyford. It is not certain what was wrong with her; Bright's disease, Addison's disease, or cancer are the more recent suggestions. Her symptoms included severe debilitation, discolored skin, and pains.

Usually, when she was going away from home, Austen would have taken work to do, but not this time. Lyford's prognosis was bad, and whether Jane had been told it or not, James Austen believed she was "well aware of her situation."[77] The family hung on every sign of a rally, and the patient herself, showing remarkable courage and fortitude, remained "composed and cheerful." She became so weak that she was able only to totter around the rented rooms in College Street; for excursions she was taken out in a sedan chair. When she had the strength, she wrote letters or dictated them, and on July 15, 1817, composed some verses on the subject of Winchester races. The speaker is St. Swithun:

*Oh! subjects rebellious! Oh Venta depraved*
*When once we are buried you think we are gone*
*But behold me immortal! By vice you're enslaved*
*You have sinned and must suffer, then farther he said . . .*[78]

Margaret Anne Doody has pointed out that the second and fourth lines of this stanza break the rhyme scheme of the whole poem, which instead of "gone" demands "dead." Perhaps Jane Austen couldn't say the word—or, more likely, Cassandra couldn't write it.[79] "Behold me immortal!" presumably underlined by Cassandra at a later date, seemed prophetic, for these unexceptional comic verses were the last thing Jane Austen ever wrote. Two days after composing them, she was dead.

# Mouldering in the Grave

"WHAT A TERRIBLE LOSS!" MARY RUSSELL MITFORD WROTE to her friend Sir William Elford on September 13, 1817. "Are you quite sure that it is our Miss Austen?"[1]

Jane was the first of George and Cassandra Austen's eight children to die. She was only forty-one. The funeral took place on July 24, 1817, in Winchester, the family having been granted permission by the bishop to have her buried in the north aisle of the cathedral. Her only mourners were Henry, Edward, Frank, and young James Edward Austen, who rode over from Steventon to represent his father. James felt too ill to attend.

The death notice that appeared in the *Courier* on July 22, 1817, made the first public acknowledgment of Jane Austen's authorship, naming all four novels.[2] No reference to her writing appeared, however, on the memorial inscription that was later added to her black marble gravestone, which lauded "the benevolence of her heart, the sweetness of her temper" with a rather generalized tribute to "the extraordinary endowments of her mind." It would have been surprising if the family had used any more specific wording in this most permanent and formal context, but the omission seems glaring now. By the 1860s, when the first tourists sought out the writer's grave in Winchester Cathedral, the verger had no idea what she was famous for.

At home in Steventon, James was composing a poem to his sister's memory, which was later copied and circulated around the family "as a fitting tribute by the acknowledged family poet."[3] "Venta! within thy sacred fane" begins with a grandiloquent evocation of the cathedral, now the final resting place of the "Beauty, Sense & Worth" of the poet's late sister. Then he pays tribute to Jane's quick fancy, warm heart, and even temper, praises her rectitude as a writer, and concludes with the aspect of his sister's character he judged the most important, her fulfillment of duties to home and family:

> *But to her family alone*
> *Her real & genuine worth was known:*
> *Yes! They whose lot it was to prove*
> *Her Sisterly, her Filial love,*
> *They saw her ready still to share*
> *The labours of domestic care*
> *As if their prejudice to shame;*
> *Who, jealous of fair female fame*
> *Maintain, that literary taste*
> *In woman's mind is much displaced;*
> *Inflames their vanity and pride,*
> *And draws from useful works aside.*[4]

Useful works around the house were not neglected by Jane Austen, for all her indulgence of "literary taste." She paid her dues to the status quo. But James's wording is interesting. "As if their prejudice to shame" implies that Jane's dutifulness was strategic. And who were "they" whose latent prejudice and jealousy of "fair female fame" Austen strove to head off, if not members of her own family?

There is an interesting flash of candor in the middle of this otherwise conventional poem, when James is speaking of his sister's self-regulation as a writer:

*. . . not a word she ever pen'd*
*Which hurt the feelings of a friend*
*And not a line she ever wrote*
*"Which dying she would wish to blot"* . . .

The poet suggests that this was all the more remarkable given the subject's natural inclinations:

*Though quick and keen her mental eye*
*Poor nature's foibles to descry*
*And seemed for ever on the watch*
*Some traits of ridicule to catch.*

The evocation of Jane's vigilance over other people's "traits of ridicule" is very much in keeping with what Miss Mitford had said privately about Austen turning into "a poker of whom everyone is afraid" in the years after her books began to be published. James makes his sister sound like a cat watching over a mouse hole, recreationally malign. Subsequent family reminiscences steered well clear of anything as unflattering as this, but its appearance here, in the first of all of them, is revealing. Coming from a brother, it could seem almost too coldly objective and "watchful" itself.

James Edward, James's son, had also been moved to write a memorial verse and also took ancient Winchester Cathedral as his starting point (he was a former Wykehamist, so the site was significant to him personally). James Edward was only eighteen at the time and had just completed his first year at Exeter College, Oxford. His poem contrasted the deep private grief the family was experiencing at Jane's loss and the happy ignorance of ordinary readers of her works:

*The purple Floweret of the Vale,*
*Around its perfume throws,*
*But, though it scent the evening Gale,*
*We know not when it grows.*

*E'en so, thy Volumes to the world*
*Have half thy merit spread,*
*Yet were those graces yet unfurl'd*
*The Eye alone could read.*

*And who of all the Tribe, to whom*
*Thy works amusement gave,*
*Have felt one sorrow for thy doom,*
*Or know thy early grave?*
. . . . . . . . . .
*But we, to whom, unbidden Guests*
*That feast was always spread;*
*In private who enjoy'd thy Jests,*
*And in thy presence fed;*

*We, who the closest kindred claimed*
*With one so doubly dear,—*
*From us may fall, perchance unblamed,*
*One half-repining Tear.*[5]

James Edward is much more direct about his aunt's career than his father had been, specifying "thy Volumes" and acknowledging their readership ("the world" allows for future readers as well). It makes James's poem look more concerned with putting a lid on Jane's fame than considering its continuation. However much James admired his sister's talents, the sibling relationship, with all its undercurrents, had set her up as a sort of rival. James Edward had none of that to deal with, and his poem seems subsequently more generous and thoughtful. His distinction between what the public could ever know of his aunt (beyond what the "Eye" could find in her texts) and what she meant to those who habitually enjoyed the "feast" of her presence makes his praise, effectively, unquantifiable. It also implies that the subject put her family first, not just in terms of doing her duty by them domestically (the aspect that James Austen managed to make sound more like the honoring of a contract than a free choice) but as the focus of her artistic efforts, the spur to her highest flights of inventiveness. Her true audience was "closest kindred," and the books were only half of what she offered *them*. No wonder James Edward had some trouble being persuaded, almost fifty years later, to become his aunt's first biographer.

In 1817, the idea of such a biography, like the idea of Jane leaving any artistic legacy, was unimaginable. Compared with the global fame of Scott and Byron, Austen's little group of admirers and sales of a few thousand copies were negligible, and although plenty of her readers had declared themselves delighted, no one yet seemed moved to consider her novels as more than light entertainment for the current day, and as unlikely as any to survive (with one notable exception in 1818, as we shall see). Her fame seemed temporary and localized, most of all among members of her own family, who had been much more used to Jane being an unpublished writer than a published one. Her early death made her years of success seem like a short episode in a much patchier story of effort and rejection, and, in her mother's eyes at least, she never displaced James as the child blessed with literary gifts. After James died in 1819, without having published a single poem in his lifetime, his mother wrote to her sister-in-law, Mrs. Leigh Perrot, of the "Classical Knowledge, Literary Taste and the power of Elegant Composition" that "my dear James . . . possessed to the highest degree."[6] This was something of a diversion from the subject of her letter, which was the earning potential of Mrs. Austen's remaining sons, but she was never diverted enough to mention her late daughter's "power of Elegant Composition," even in passing.

As a single woman in possession of no fortune to speak of, Jane Austen's material estate was easily dispersed. She had drawn up a will three months before her death, leaving everything she owned to "my dearest Sister Cassandra Eliz[th],"[7] with a £50 bequest to Henry's former housekeeper, Madame Bigeon (who had lost savings in the collapse of Henry's bank), and £50 to Henry, probably on the understanding that he would help Cassandra to manage and pay for any outstanding publishing business. In the months before she died, Jane had also been making a list of her profits from writing, which amounted to almost £700 (£600 of which was prudently invested in the Navy Fives—bonds with a guaranteed 5 percent interest). At her death, she was owed another £90 or so by John Murray.

Among the papers that Cassandra inherited (about which she knew so much more than anyone else) were the two manuscript novels, "Susan" (which Jane had renamed "Catherine") and "The Elliots." Though there is no indication that Austen was negotiating the publication of either book in the last year of her life, or that she even considered them completely finished, they were both immediately sent to Murray, who paid £500 to publish on commission. "Susan"/"Catherine," now retitled *Northanger Abbey*, and "The Elliots," now *Persuasion*, were shorter novels than the four Austen had seen through the press in her lifetime, and would appear together as a four-volume work, with a biographical preface announcing the author's identity and death and giving an outline of her life all in one package. It was a "wrapping-up" operation, a closing of the account, done at a speed that indicates that Cassandra and Henry were as keen to finish with the business of their sister's authorship as any other executorial matter.

Murray mentioned the books to Lord Byron as forthcoming titles on his list less than two months after the author's death: "Two new novels left by Miss Austen—the ingenious Author of Pride & Prejudice—who I am sorry to say died about 6 weeks ago."[8] When the joint edition appeared at the very end of the year, these two extremely different books, yoked together for years through the accident of posthumous publication, were reviewed as if in competition with each other, and as a result neither was really given its due. And not surprisingly, the novels themselves got less attention than the "Biographical Notice," revealing the melancholy fact that the author had died and that she had not been Lady Boringdon or Elizabeth Hamilton or Mrs. Dorset or Lady Augusta Paget but an unmarried parson's daughter from Hampshire.

Henry's note is full of the "warmth of his Brotherly vanity & love"[9] that made him such a poor custodian of his sister's secrets during her lifetime, now tempered with his deep sadness at her loss. His provision of some personal details about the author was not, he made clear, to satisfy the vulgar curiosity of the reading public, but to draw a line under her life and work, to put an end to curiosity. He is able to reveal her identity at last—no longer "the author of Sense and Sensibility, Pride and Prejudice, etc" but "Jane Austen"—only because the story is over, or, as he puts it, only because the hand that guided her pen "is now mouldering in the grave."

"Short and easy will be the task of the mere biographer," Henry continued briskly. "A life of usefulness, literature and religion, was not by any means a life of event." Indeed, it was a bit of a problem, describing that eventless life, and Henry, like James in his memorial poem, had to fall back on his sister's qualifications as a conventional, domesticated female, full of "cheerfulness, sensibility and benevolence," modestly competent at music, dancing, and drawing, satisfied with her lot, happy in her family life, and who never had a bad word to say about anyone. Henry edged rather uneasily around the issue (a glaring one for female writers of the time, and the main inhibition behind the convention of anonymity) of how this refined and pious female could have understood worldly matters well enough to represent them so acutely in her fiction. "Though the frailities, foibles and follies of others could not escape her immediate detection, yet even on their vices did she never trust herself to comment with unkindness," he said, nervously rushing on into hyperbole. "Faultless herself, as nearly as human nature can be, she always sought, in the faults of others, something to excuse, to forgive or forget. . . . Where extenuation was impossible, she had a sure refuge in silence." What kind of silence that might have been, Henry naturally didn't specify.

In attempting to give a physical description of his sister, Henry relied almost entirely on vague evocations of her "quiet, yet graceful" deportment, elegant but not excessive height, sweet voice, and happy "assemblage" of features that were "separately good." No chance of summoning up a mental image of Jane from that, and why would one need to? Henry was more revealing about his sister's experience of authorship, while continuing to extol her sweet temper, intellectual modesty, and unworldliness. "Neither the hope of fame nor profit mixed with her early motives," he claimed. "She became an authoress entirely from taste and inclination." He went on to say that Jane had hoarded her manuscripts for years with no thought of publication and could only be prevailed upon "with extreme difficulty" by her friends to offer them to the world. Henry depicts these strenuously encouraging friends as having superior judgment of the situation to that of the naïve author, whose anxiety about covering possible losses on her first book (such an un-Henry-like trait) and childish delight at turning a profit of £150 earn his fond admiration.

The message of the "Biographical Notice" is, again and again, that the author of the four well-received novels was herself well loved, quiet, unambitious—a kindly wit and an acute but never unkind observer. Henry stresses that she was a very private person and as such would always be unknown to the public: "No accumulation of fame would have induced her, had she lived, to affix her name to any productions of her pen. In the bosom of her own family she talked of them freely, thankful for praise, open to remark, and submissive to criticism. But in public she turned away from any allusion to the character of an authoress."

But his sister's defining attribute, in Henry's opinion, was her religious devotion. He ended his memoir—which as far as anyone in the family expected was literally going to be the last word on the subject of Jane Austen—with a tribute to her piety and an assurance that her opinions "accorded strictly with those of our Established Church." Then he signed and dated his work and sent it off to Murray. Amen.

As a publishing "event," *Northanger Abbey and Persuasion, with a Biographical Notice of the Author*, had far more interest to reviewers than any of the books that Austen had published in her lifetime and prompted several thoughtful overviews of her achievement. Richard Whately, archbishop of Dublin, wrote a long piece on Austen in the *Quarterly Review* of January 1821 that placed her at the head of writers of the new realistic novel. A great deal of his essay was about this new style of novel and how much it had raised the status of the genre, "neither alarming our credulity nor amusing our imagination by wild variety of incident, or by those pictures of romantic affection and sensibility, which were formerly as certain attributes of fictitious characters as they are of rare occurrence among those who actually live and die."[10] He continued, "The delights of fiction, if not more keenly or more generally relished, are at least more readily acknowledged by men of sense and taste; and we have lived to hear the merits of the best of this class of writings earnestly discussed by some of the ablest scholars and soundest reasoners of the present day."[11]

Given that Whately is crediting Austen with a significant part in this radical improvement, it is strange that he thought no better of *Northanger Abbey*—a satire on the "old style" novel in the manner of the new—than to give it only one paragraph out of his many thousands of words. *Persuasion* was the book he preferred, judging it "one of the most elegant fictions of common life we ever remember to have met with."[12] "Miss Austin" (as he refers to her throughout) "has the merit of being evidently a Christian writer"; her works were morally useful without recourse to preaching (interesting praise from a professional moralizer). Whately also considered her to be virtually unique in being candid about her own sex:

> Authoresses can scarcely ever forget the esprit de corps—can scarcely ever forget that they *are authoresses*. They seem to feel a sympathetic shudder at exposing naked a female mind. Elles se peignent en buste, and leave the mysteries of womanhood to be described by some interloping male, like Richardson or Marivaux, who is turned out before he has seen half the rites, and is forced to spin from his own conjectures the rest. Now from this fault Miss Austin is free. Her heroines are what one knows women must be, though one can never get them to acknowledge it.[13]

No one took up this point again for years, that Austen gave away more about how women think and behave than any previous writer had cared or thought right to do. Elizabeth Bennet's reply to her sister's question of how long she has loved Darcy—"It has been coming on so gradually, that I hardly know when it began. But I believe I must date it from my first seeing his beautiful grounds at Pemberley"[14]—could be called a watershed in this context: a great joke about female materialism and painfully shrewd about its causes. The range of follies that Austen's women display might well have left the archbishop reeling:

Mrs. Bennet, Lady Bertram, Mrs. Norris, Mrs. Elton, the Steele sisters, Fanny Dashwood, Elizabeth Elliot, Mrs. Clay, Lady Catherine de Bourgh . . . all differentiated, all unique in their unpleasantness. Her heroines too are, like Emma Woodhouse, "faultless in spite of their faults." The books exposed female fallibility so brilliantly and with such sporting candor that, as men picked up on the fact that these might not simply be "ladies' novels," Austen's male readership grew enormously. Not just among the kinds of men who were relieved to find some genuinely attractive heroines in a novel but among the misogynists too, of course.

An anonymous writer in the *Retrospective Review* was clearly among the former and seems to have fallen madly in love with the dead author, whose works "stole into the world without noise,—they circulated in quiet,—they were far from being much extolled,—and very seldom noticed in the journals of the day." He imagined her "strong in innocence as a tower, with a face of serenity, and a collectedness of demeanour, from which danger and misery—the very tawny lion in his rage—might flee discomfited,—a fragile, delicate, feeble and most feminine woman! . . . O lost too soon to us!"[15] Few readers worked themselves up to such a pitch, and some forgot the convention of *de mortuis nil nisi bonum* enough to be forthrightly critical, like the reviewer in the *British Critic* who wrote, "in imagination, of all kinds, she appears to have been extremely deficient; not only her stories are utterly and entirely devoid of invention, but her characters, her incidents, her sentiments, are obviously all drawn from experience." The same reviewer also accused Austen of "a want of delicacy" in *Northanger Abbey* "in all the circumstances of Catherine's visit"[16]—the very last fault that anyone would think applicable to Austen today, when she is held up as the personification of rectitude and refinement.

Only the reviewer in *Blackwood's*, in May 1818, seemed to be addressing the future millions who now revere Austen and hold her genius to be self-evident. He praised her truth to life, "seemingly exhaustless invention," and her "good sense, happiness and purity," but what made Austen really remarkable, in his eyes, was the extent to which she went against the grain of the time, "the prevailing love of historical, and at the same time romantic incident" that Scott and Byron, Edgeworth and Godwin, specialized in, and which the public seemed to love and crave. Her simple representations of common life, expressed "in pure English," are thus presented as the truly bold and revolutionary works in an age of strenuous high romanticism. "Yet the time, probably, will return, when we shall take a more permanent delight in those familiar cabinet pictures, than even in the great historical pieces of our more eminent modern masters."

"When this period arrives," the anonymous reviewer concluded, with remarkable prescience, "we have no hesitation in saying, that the delightful writer of the works now before us, will be one of the most popular of English novelists."[17]

THE ACTUAL NUMBER OF Austen's books in circulation was extremely small in the years immediately following her death—just a few thousand in total—but her readership grew slowly (not least through the circulating libraries), and she began to have a certain impact on literary fashions. In 1821, Byron's spurned mistress, Lady Caroline Lamb, was trying to reprise the scandalous success of her 1816 roman à clef, *Glenarvon*, and in a letter to her friend Thomas Malthus said that though she was having trouble thinking of what to put in the new story, she had at least hit on a title, "Principle & passion," "since the fashion is to call every thing in the manner of Pride & prejudice, sense & sensibility."[18] It was hardly the sort of influence Austen could have anticipated or desired but shows how "fashion" had picked up on certain reverberations around the books.

Such connections are likely to be tangential and predatory, as was the almost immediate appropriation of "Austen-like" qualities by a long-forgotten set of 1820s novelists, characterized as the "silver-fork" or "Dandy" school. The name came from an acerbic article by William Hazlitt in 1827, condemning the vogue for escapist novels that idealized high society life in the age just gone and concentrated on fashions and accessories rather than plot or characterization: "A writer of this accomplished stamp," Hazlitt wrote, "comes forward to tell you, not how his hero feels on any occasion, for he is above that, but how he was dressed . . . and also informs you that the quality eat fish with silver forks."[19]

Henry Colburn was publisher of many of these utterly forgettable novels and advertised them as written "by aristocrats, and for aristocrats." Some were genuinely "By A Lady," or even "By Lady A—": Lady Charlotte Bury, Lady Morgan, Countess Blessington; but on the whole, the genre was sustained by and for the aspirant middle classes, who felt that they were gaining some sort of entrée into elite manners and mores through tales of aristocratic life such as Edward Bulwer-Lytton's *Pelham, or The Adventures of a Gentleman* (1828) or Thomas Lister's *Granby* (1826). These, and the many inferior examples of the genre that rolled off Colburn's presses in the 1820s and '30s, were fantasy literature for the Age of Reform, inventing a version of Regency England, its lost elegance and comforting social inequalities, around which readers could manufacture a little nostalgia.

Thomas Lister seems to have read Austen's works with care and reproduced a great many scenes, characters, and even names from them in his own novels. The bibliographer and critic David Gilson has spotted dozens of parallels with Austen in *Granby* (1826), *Herbert Lacy* (1828), and *Arlington* (1832), from a flirtation scene like that between Henry Tilney and Catherine Morland, to home theatricals involving a Crawford.[20] Lister's borrowings from Austen were clearly conscious: In *Granby*, a character called Lady Harriet says, "I hope you like nothing of Miss Edgeworth's or Miss Austen's. They are full of commonplace people, that one recognises at once."[21] But was Lister aiming these jokes at his readers generally, or just at his own circle, which included the very Countess Morley with whom Austen had corresponded briefly in 1815? The in-group was small and rather incestuous. In 1830, Lister married Countess Morley's niece, one of whose friends, Emily Eden, was a would-be novelist also engaged in writing a story suspiciously close in plot, setting, and tone to one of Austen's: "Mrs Douglas had been an heiress which perhaps accounts for Mr Douglas having married her. . . . He let her have a reasonable share of her own way . . . but kept his own opinion."[22] *The Semi-Attached Couple* was not published until the 1850s but had been written in the 1830s, when Austen still seemed like a fairly untraceable source.

Lister, reviewing Catherine Gore's *Women as They Are* in 1830, digressed on to the subject of Miss Austen's novels, lamenting the fact that her art had not "in this age of literary quackery" received its reward. Strikingly, he refers to her audience in the past tense: "It was even so with many of the readers of Miss Austen. She was too natural for them. . . . They did not consider that the highest triumph of art consists in its concealment; and here the art was so little perceptible, that they believed there was none."

Lister possibly felt free to expound this past author's virtues because it was, by 1830, very hard to get hold of a copy of any of her books; unlike his own novels, which sold well—better than Austen's ever had (*Granby* went into three editions in the first year). It makes one wonder if his appropriation of bits of *Northanger Abbey* might have been casual attempts at plagiarism rather than wry acts of homage.

But it is likely that many of her early imitators hadn't even read Austen's novels; what they were attempting to do was not imitate her but replicate some of her effects, the generally conservative air of her stories and strong materialist undertow. Austen had introduced a "feel-good" factor into the popular novel that no one had yet thought to analyze, but that people recognized as instantly gratifying and desirable. The fact that Austen was in any way a model for the "silver-fork" novelists says more for her power to represent social anxiety than for their power to interpret it. One of the most consistent criticisms made by early reviewers was that Austen's novels were too concerned with "the middling sort": It was a pity, for example, the *Gentleman's Magazine* had said in 1816, that Austen had not thought to introduce in *Emma* "highly-drawn characters in superior life" like those "which are so interesting in Pride and Prejudice." For Lady Catherine de Bourgh to be thought of as raising the tone of *Pride and Prejudice* must be one of the more bizarre comments the book has ever prompted. One is meant to admire Darcy, of course, but only after he has gone through the rigorous de-classification (or perhaps middle-classification) demanded by the heroine. Her great coup is to gain a share in hereditary wealth without changing her own social attitudes one iota, and part of the reader's satisfaction with the imagined outcome of the novel is that the marriage of Darcy and Elizabeth will combine his "aristocratic" good breeding with her social inclusiveness; it rewards a fine-minded woman with the worldly goods that only aristocrats habitually received and tames the pride of old families who may not have recognized that their heritage is under threat of revolution if they don't change.

During Jane's lifetime, there had been a pirated edition of *Emma* in America and French translations of *Emma, Sense and Sensibility,* and *Mansfield Park*, none of which she is likely to have heard about. French translations proliferated in the following years, though their relationship to Austen's originals was more exploitative than respectful. One translator, Isabelle de Montolieu, was already a popular novelist in her own right in Switzerland, and it was her name, rather than Austen's (which appeared in much smaller type on the title page), that was meant to attract readers. The titles of some of these translations indicate how freely the core material was used: *Raison et Sensibilité, ou Les Deux Manières d'Aimer* (Reason and Sensibility, or Two Ways of Loving); *La Nouvelle Emma* (The New Emma); and *La Famille Elliot, ou L'Ancienne Inclination* (The Elliot Family, or The Old Inclination) (the latter interestingly nearer to Austen's own working title, "The Elliots," than *Persuasion*). Madame de Montolieu took other liberties too, cutting scenes from the originals and adding new ones, with plenty of coloring. When the text of her *La Famille Elliot* was used instead of the original *Persuasion* by a Swedish translator in the 1830s, the resulting hybrid was predictably weird.[23]

Even farther away, in Russia, Austen's novels were becoming known without any translation. The author would have been amazed to hear that as early as June 1816, an article in a Russian journal praising contemporary English women novelists singled out the anonymous author of *Emma* for her successful "pictures of quiet family life." And though there is no direct evidence that Alexander Pushkin ever read *Pride and Prejudice*, the similarities between the novel and his masterpiece, *Eugene Onegin* (published in serial form between 1825 and 1832), have convinced several critics that he knew the book very well, perhaps in one of its early French versions.[24]

A more traceable Austen influence can be found in a strange novel called *Precaution*, published in America only two years after *Persuasion* by a first-time author called James Fenimore Cooper. In later years, the story of Cooper's debut was told over and over again by his daughter Susan, with decreasing amounts of clarity and consistency. Her father, a well-to-do and somewhat under-occupied retired navy officer, was living the life of a country gent in Scarsdale, New York, and devoting his time mostly to landscape gardening. One of his projects was to build a ha-ha on his property, then and always "a novelty in this country."[25] Cooper hadn't thought of turning his hand to writing until an occasion when, reading aloud from one of the many recent English novels to which his wife was addicted, he found it so vapid that he threw it down and declared he could write a better novel himself. His wife challenged him to do so, and the result was *Precaution*, a story of English life and manners set in the last decades of the previous century.

As an exercise in marital defiance and sheer chutzpah, *Precaution* has its merits, but it is not an easy or enjoyable read (George E. Hastings, who made a detailed study of the book in 1940, reckoned he was one of the very few people who had finished it), and in terms of Cooper's later oeuvre it must represent one of the most bizarrely uncharacteristic books of any author. Cooper had not visited England in 1820, though the ha-ha suggests that he had read plenty about it (in *Mansfield Park*, perhaps). In his daughter's secondhand account, he was of two minds whether or not to seek publication but did so after testing the novel out on his friend John Jay. The verdict of the Jay family was favorable, and Cooper went ahead with publication, though one of the ladies who had been at the reading "said that she had heard the tale before and that the author was a woman."[26]

Susan Cooper thought that the book that had disgusted her father, and the one he was supposed to have emulated, were both "Mrs Opie's or one of that school," but in a study of 1938, Maurice Clavel pointed out the unlikelihood of Cooper seeking to make "an elaborate imitation in plot and character" of a novel he thought too trashy to finish reading. More likely, Clavel argued, he was setting out to better the trashy novel by imitating authors of what, in a review of

John Gibson Lockhart's *Life of Scott*, Cooper had categorized as "the healthful class of novels," among whom he counted Edgeworth, Burney, Mrs. Opie, and Austen.

George Hastings went further than this and made a detailed comparison of *Precaution* and the Austen novel nearest in date (and title) to Cooper's, *Persuasion*, which makes a convincing case for Austen being the copied novelist but not the loathed one. Both books begin with a baronet renting out one property and retiring to another; both baronets have three daughters and a favorite among them. Both books have heroines who are not the father's favorite; the heroines both have an older female mentor and an admiring brother-in-law, and both are courted unsuccessfully by a cousin. And so on . . . the similarities are "so numerous that one has difficulty in believing them all to be accidental," and Cooper's book, though twice as long as *Persuasion* and much more elaborate, "repeats almost every detail of situation, setting, character and plot used by Jane Austen."[27]

Cooper thought he had put *Precaution* behind him when he found fame with his later novels of American frontier life, *The Pioneers* and *The Last of the Mohicans*, but his British publisher and ardent advocate, Richard Bentley, wanted to include it in his Standard Novels series, necessitating a large-scale revision of the book. In an embarrassed preface, Cooper explained that he had never intended *Precaution* for publication, and once it had been accepted never expected to write another like it. It had "many defects in plot, style and arrangement, that were entirely owing to precipitation and inexperience"; "its English plot, and, in a measure, the medley of characters . . . no doubt will appear a mistake in the conception." The book disappeared from his acknowledged oeuvre but remains the unlikely springboard from which his later novels—and so much of American national literature— were launched.

IF AUSTEN CAN EVER be said to have had a period of obscurity, it was during the 1820s, when her books were out of print, out of demand, and almost out of mind. During her lifetime, Austen's most successful book (in terms of sales) had been Murray's first edition of *Emma*, which sold 1,250 copies in its first year. He had printed around 2,000 in 1815, and still had 565 copies unsold in 1818. Two years later, hardly any of these had shifted, and he remaindered the last 535 copies for two shillings a set. The initial price had been 21 shillings. A single copy of this edition sold in 1999 for £8,500.

*Emma* was not the only title to be wasted. In 1820, Murray also sold off his stock of *Mansfield Park* (almost two-thirds of the original 750 copies of the 1816 second edition—a bad failure) and after one more year remaindered *Northanger Abbey* and *Persuasion*, which had sold 1,400 copies in the first year, then sank to almost no sales at all. Egerton had kept *Sense and Sensibility* in print for several years, but the small 1813 edition does not seem to have sold out, and he probably remaindered the stock at the same time that he remaindered the third edition of *Pride and Prejudice*, in 1817. He held the copyright on the latter, so throwing in his hand indicates that he really didn't think there was any more money to be made out of the title.

Cassandra and Henry Austen may well have been relieved to hear of these developments, as they had to bear the cost of the losses for four of the five publications. At least, in 1821, they knew where they stood. Cassandra, now aged forty-eight and still living at Chawton with her elderly mother and Martha Lloyd, was modestly well-off, but Henry's fortunes were declining all the time. He had not recovered from bankruptcy as little scathed as he had anticipated, and his career in the church was proving both demanding and ill-paid. His first appointment after taking Holy Orders in 1816 had been as curate of Chawton, and in 1819, after the death of his elder brother James, he succeeded to the old family living of Steventon. Quite why he didn't maintain this position in his old home isn't clear, but perhaps there was a financial advantage to resigning Steventon and taking up the curacy of Farnham, about twenty miles away, in 1822. Henry's juggling of appointments within the church seems to have had more to do with his taste for speculation than with parish needs or even private convenience.

In 1820, seven years after his wife Eliza's death, Henry got married again, to Eleanor Jackson, the niece of the previous Chawton vicar. Eleanor was a very different character from the late comtesse, a pious and studious woman (author herself of *An Epitome of the Old Testament* in 1831) who encouraged Henry to live much more modestly than before. Retrenchment was absolutely necessary, as the financial repercussions of Henry's bankruptcy continued to affect all corners of the family. Edward Knight and Uncle James Leigh Perrot had been the largest losers, but the poorer creditors rightly elicited most of Henry's remorse. "I only mourn to see so little chance of my being able to heal those wounds by me inflicted on the property of others—and on you in particular," he wrote to his younger brother Charles in 1822. Henry was trying to make some extra money by tutoring boys and was disappointed not to attract more pupils (the following year, he took on the superintendence of Farnham's ancient Free Grammar School). Meanwhile, he had been forced to lower the Steventon tithes and couldn't yet calculate the value of his Farnham curacy but hoped it would bring in no less than £140 a year, of which they would lose £40 in rent. He was cutting down on all luxuries, he told Charles, had given up shooting (for the duration), dining out (unless with the bishop), and socializing. But there was still too much work for one person to do "without a dangerous degree of exertion," so Henry had incurred another expense—£40 a year—to employ an even poorer clergyman to take one of his Sunday services.

This plan clearly wasn't about saving exertion so much as maximizing earning capacity, for Henry was only paying a delegate so that he could set up "what is called a Clergyman's book" and start an additional, subscribers-only service on Sunday evenings. He must have hoped that his parishioners were snobbish and competitive enough to make this a successful venture, but Farnham was possibly not the best place to try the maneuver. At the time he moved there, the town's best-known son was the radical pamphleteer and soon-to-be parliamentarian William Cobbett, and I wonder if there is not some reflection of Cobbett's influence in what Henry says to his brother, a little nervously, of his overall performance in the first year at Farnham: "I believe that I give on the whole a predominating satisfaction in the Church. There must always be some faultfinders. My predecessor had a strong party among *tag rag* & radicals—But his influence seems nearly decayed."[28]

Henry didn't ever flourish as a clergyman, despite everyone's hopes to the contrary. The cheerful spirits with which he had weathered so many previous difficulties seemed to have abandoned him, and Jane would hardly have recognized the brother who wrote in 1822 of past "days of Sunshine—of sunshine never to return as far as regards my worldly circumstances."[29] In a letter to Cassandra from his vicarage in Bentley he described how hard he found it to concentrate on the job at hand: "I have been writing a sermon till my brains are dry. Not a drop of divinity left. But there may be a stream of other matters."[30] By 1828, he was appealing to his nephew James Edward to defer until after his own death (and that of Eleanor) the £400 debt he still owed his dead brother James's estate and ended this difficult and embarrassing letter with the lament, "my dreams of affluence, nay of competence are closed."[31]

The family was divided more than ever between the haves and have-nots; despite the expense of maintaining two grand estates and eleven children, Edward couldn't help but make large amounts of money, and James Edward Austen became a similarly fortunate heir in 1836 when Jane Leigh Perrot finally died and made him the master of her handsome Berkshire estate, Scarlets, and recipient of the long-discussed Leigh Perrot thousands. Captain Charles Austen's salary was lowish at best and very variable, and his "little all" in the 5 percents (the Navy Fives) had been liquidated.[32] Francis had fared better and was by 1825 living comfortably in Portsdown with a £10,000 settlement from the Leigh Perrot estate. Mrs. Austen's long-nurtured South Sea stock (which she had bought in the early years of her marriage partly with the proceeds of selling property left to her by her father) had fallen in value over the years from £3,350 in 1769 to a mere £2,185 in 1827—a disastrously bad investment from which her children benefited to the tune of only £437 each after her death in 1827. Edward generously made over his share "for the use of my brother George," the son Mrs. Austen had overlooked altogether in her will, who lived on for a further eleven years in whatever cottage or asylum he had been sent to. Perhaps Edward had taken over the support of that all-but-invisible brother many years before.

Cassandra had a small income from her Fowle annuity still, £1,000 from the eventual settling of the Leigh Perrot estate, her legacy from her mother, and whatever remained of Jane's bequest to her. This was a comfortable amount for an unmarried woman, trained to expect and require as little as possible for personal maintenance. By 1828, she was living alone at Chawton Cottage, following Martha Lloyd's late marriage to the widowed Frank Austen and removal to Portsdown. As in his mother's day, Edward charged Cassandra no rent on the house and provided plenty of wood from the estate for fuel, so her basic overheads were covered. She managed her affairs far better than Henry, it hardly needs saying.

In May 1831, Cassandra received a letter from John Murray, inquiring if he could buy the rights to her sister's novels. Cassandra replied that she was "not disposed to part with the Copy-right" but was interested in seeing new editions after so many years out of print. Even in this first letter to the publisher, Cassandra asked very pertinent questions: Had Murray approached Egerton's heirs about the rights to *Pride and Prejudice*? How big an edition was he thinking of? How many volumes would there be, and of what size and price? What proportion of the profits would he pay to "me or my Agent"?[33] But her businesslike approach was wasted, for Murray must have stuck to his request for the copyrights or nothing, and the offer died. Perhaps Cassandra regretted having so quickly discouraged an outright sale. It is quite possible that she didn't consult Henry in the six days between getting and answering Murray's letter (thinking that negotiations would go on), for the following year, when the family was approached by the publisher Richard Bentley with a similar offer, Henry accepted quickly on behalf of them both. Murray would have been the better imprint and would have charged and paid more, so this was clearly something of a collapse. But the siblings must have decided that they had less negotiating power than they had imagined, and that if they wanted to see their sister's works in print again (and make any money whatsoever) they had better smile on the next comer.

That was Richard Bentley, and his purchase of the five remaining copyrights went through quickly in 1832, for the bargain price of £210. Bentley was in the process of dissolving a soured partnership with Henry Colburn (the publisher of so many "silver-fork" books) and setting up a sole imprint from offices on New Burlington Street. He was keen to establish a coterie as well as a list and furnished a comfortable "Red Room" for entertaining his authors, who included Charles Dickens (editor of Bentley's *Wits' Miscellany*) and the poet Thomas Campbell. Bentley's ambitious business plans (and the lavish *Miscellany* dinners where "all the very *haut ton* of the literature of the day" gathered)[34] were paid for mostly by his Standard Novels series, a pioneering imprint of low-cost, compact productions of which *Sense and Sensibility* appeared early in 1833 as number twenty-three, followed by *Emma*, *Mansfield Park*, *Northanger Abbey* and *Persuasion*, and *Pride and Prejudice*. It was a sign of Bentley's business acumen as well as his literary taste that he persuaded the Austens to sell to him and then whittled down his initial offer of £250 by the £40 it was going to cost to buy *Pride and Prejudice* from Egerton. Henry's disinclination to haggle shows that, on the family's side, they were glad of whatever they could get. Fifteen years earlier, limited rights to just two of the four titles had fetched £500. Although she was back in print again, Jane Austen's market worth had dropped very dramatically.

But Henry enjoyed business of this sort and did all he could to oblige Bentley. When they met in London before agreeing to the contract, Henry had assured the publisher (who had expressed an interest in "any biographical relics of the Authoress") that there was a sketch of his sister somewhere. He had to retract this later, writing, "On further enquiry and inspection, I find that [the sketch] was merely the figure and attitude—The countenance was concealed by a veil—nor was there any resemblance of features intended—It was a 'Study.'"[35] The image he is referring to is generally agreed to be the only authenticated one of Jane Austen, not the full-face sketch now in the National Portrait Gallery (which is almost certainly by Cassandra and of Jane, but which has no signature, date, or identification), but the pencil and watercolor drawing, still in the Austen family, showing a back view of Jane seated outdoors on a warm day. It has Cassandra's initials and the date, 1804, and was fondly remembered many years later by Anna Lefroy as a picture of her aunt,[36] but as it shows none of the subject's face, it would, of course, have been useless to Bentley as an illustration, and he went about getting some steel engravings made of scenes from the novels instead. Each of his Austen volumes appeared with a specially commissioned frontispiece and second-title-page vignette illustrating pivotal episodes from the stories, with hair and clothes all in the styles of the 1830s.

The "veil" Henry mentions in his letter as concealing Jane's features is either his way of describing the bonnet in Cassandra's drawing, or Cassandra's way of describing the picture to him; in other words, when Henry asked about the available images of Jane, Cassandra may have dismissed them as unusable without producing anything for her brother to view. She doesn't seem to have reminded him about the full-face drawing, which he might have wanted to use or at least show to Bentley. What is odd is that in all those years of living with Jane, Cassandra had made or kept so few likenesses of her sister. Drawing was meant to be her particular interest, after all, and Jane was her most available model. If she had winnowed down a number of attempts to the two that we know today, it says little for the likely quality of any of the rejected ones; those two are so rough and amateurish.

It is also rather odd that no images of Jane by other members of the family exist. Like verse writing and amateur musicianship, drawing was an accomplishment every young person was meant to try their hand at, and the Austen circle was full of competent artists. James had studied painting while he was at Oxford, and Henry had been so adept with the pencil that his first employment had been as a drawing master to a family in Kent. Perhaps his expertise inhibited Cassandra in some way. James Edward was also an excellent draftsman (as Jane herself remarked), and made some extraordinarily good cut-paper pictures of domestic scenes for his children. But no one apart from Cassandra seems to have taken Jane's likeness.

Henry provided a new version of his "Biographical Notice of the Author" for Bentley's edition, which shows some interesting changes from the one he composed in 1817. Some of them reflected the passage of time and changing tastes—he omitted, for instance, the comparison of his sister's work with that of "a D'Arblay and an Edgeworth"; others validated his sister's literary credentials with lengthy quotes from the best reviews, as well as the anecdote about Sheridan (who, like the others, is not actually named) and the story of Jane electing not to meet Madame de Staël. The whole of the opening of the original note was scrapped, with its emotional evocation of the author's hand "mouldering in the grave," and Henry removed the small details of Jane's drawing skills, musical talent, love of dancing, and temper "of the happiest kind." He was asking that the author—now openly referred to as Miss Austen—should be judged more on her literary merits than her personal virtues. This was a significant change of emphasis.

Bentley, or one of his employees, added an editorial note after Henry's that pressed the claims of the author further, pointing out that Miss Austen had founded a school of novelists that included men as well as women, some (he was perhaps thinking of Thomas Lister) "of considerable merit."[37] He also paid tribute to Austen's originality and special genius "in the power by which, without in the slightest degree violating the truth of portraiture, she is able to make the veriest everyday person a character of great interest. This is, indeed, turning lead into gold; but it would be difficult to detect the secret of the process." It was a remarkably perceptive and warm appraisal, which when Virginia Woolf echoed it a century later in her famous dictum about Austen being of all great writers the hardest to catch in the act of greatness, struck people afresh.

Bentley didn't coin a very substantial amount of "gold" from his republication of Austen in 1833–34, nor from the four or five reprintings the firm made up till 1854; they sold quietly but steadily in first runs of 2,500 to 3,000 copies, with small reprints every few years. *Emma* sold the most copies (by a small margin); *Mansfield Park* the fewest. But publication in Bentley's Standard Novels, a pioneering imprint that set out "to register the permanent fame of certain novels . . . not hitherto fittingly reprinted in handy and cheap form," was significant for Austen.[38] Having all her six novels in print for the first time, in an accessible and inexpensive uniform edition, kept Austen's readership steadily growing throughout a period when she received next to no critical attention at all.

One of Bentley's pet authors (and the first in his Standard Novels series) was the very same Mr. Cooper who had started out as an Austen imitator but had now moved on to *The Pilot*, *The Spy*, and

*Lionel Lincoln*, all of which were included in the series. Bentley mentioned his name, and Austen's, in a letter he wrote in October 1835 to another "neglected" author whose early works he had his eye on, Madame d'Arblay. The venerable author was by then eighty-three years old and living alone in Mayfair, a strange relic from the age of Johnson and Thrale. The only work she had published since *The Wanderer* (not on Bentley's wants list) was her 1832 *Memoirs of Dr. Burney*, which had been widely derided for its convoluted language and hagiographical approach to a figure who was of little public interest or relevance in the 1830s. Bentley undoubtedly thought he was doing the author a favor by offering to include *Evelina*, *Cecilia*, and *Camilla* on his thriving reprint list, pointing out as an inducement that "your fictions will appear with those of Mr Bulwer, Mr Morier, Mr Cooper, Mr Theodore Hook, Miss Austen, etc."[39] It was a strange fate for Burney to survive so long past the next generation and see her own eclipse. She did not reply to Bentley's letter but kept it.

Austen's rout of Burney continued after the older woman's death in 1840, for when Thomas Babington Macaulay was reviewing Madame d'Arblay's posthumous six-volume *Diary and Letters* in 1843, he was diverted (with some relief, one senses) from the difficult task of summing up her achievement to consider instead the merits of "a woman of whom England is justly proud," Jane Austen. "Shakespeare has neither equal nor second. But among the writers who, in the point which we have noticed, have approached nearest to the manner of the great master, we have no hesitation in placing Jane Austen."[40] How crushing to the memory of Madame d'Arblay to have her encomium interrupted by this extraordinary praise of another writer—a female writer, and a novelist, compared with Shakespeare! But worst of all, one of those nieces of Mrs. Cooke!

THE FIRST PUBLISHED REMINISCENCE of Jane Austen, apart from Henry's "Biographical Notice," came from an unlikely source, Samuel Egerton Brydges, who was by 1832 living in Geneva, in exile from creditors. His mention of Austen in his *Autobiography* seems to acknowledge other people's admiration of her more than his own, for he can't conceal a note of surprise that the pleasant but unimpressive young girl "with cheeks a little too full," whom his sister, Anne Lefroy, had befriended back in the 1780s and '90s, had turned out to be an acclaimed novelist. Austen had a great many true admirers among her contemporaries whose opinions were far more flattering than Brydges's but were recorded in diaries and correspondence that remained unpublished for years, delaying the spread of her renown. Robert Southey, Maria Edgeworth, Samuel Taylor Coleridge, Edward Bulwer-Lytton, Sidney Smith, and Henry Crabbe Robinson all privately expressed their high view of her work, and Benjamin Disraeli—the man who once said that if he needed to read a good novel, he would write one—claimed to have read *Pride and Prejudice* seventeen times.

Sir Walter Scott's own set of Austen's novels became worn with rereading, and in a famous journal entry of 1826 he reflected on what she had achieved and how far beyond his own range it was:

> Read again and for the third time at least Miss Austen's very finely written novel of Pride and Prejudice. That young lady had a talent for describing the involvement and feelings and characters of ordinary life which is to me the most wonderful I ever met with. The Big Bow-wow strain I can do myself like any now going, but the exquisite touch which renders commonplace things and characters interesting from the truth of the description and the sentiment is denied to me. What a pity such a gifted creature died so early![41]

When this was quoted in John Gibson Lockhart's biography of Scott, Sarah Harriet Burney, Fanny Burney's half sister, was delighted to find that Sir Walter "thought so highly of my prime favourite Miss Austen." She had imagined herself to be alone in her fandom, having "quite raved" about the books since 1813. Sir Walter boasted of having read *Pride and Prejudice* three times, but as Sarah Harriet noted, "*I* have read it as bumper toasts are given—*three times three*!"[42]

Austen's popularity with her romantic contemporaries perhaps suggests they saw more of the "modern" in her than other people, more of a break with the past than had been supposed. Austen's attacks on the cult of sensibility, her matter-of-fact anti-Wertherism, her rational—but not unfeeling—demolition of the clichés surrounding true love: All were as revolutionary in their way as anything in *The Prelude* or *Don Juan*. What love story had ever contained such sentiments as this, for instance, from *Sense and Sensibility*: "After all that is bewitching in the idea of a single and constant attachment, and all that can be said of one's happiness depending entirely on any particular person, it is not meant—it is not fit—it is not possible that it should be so."[43]

Just how modern Austen was wasn't remarked upon until much later; the adjective employed in the early nineteenth century was "pure" or "natural." Not everyone shared the same idea of "natural," of course, and William Wordsworth, unlike Coleridge and Southey, was not an admirer of Austen. Sara Coleridge remembered that her father's friend "used to say that though he admitted her novels were an admirable copy of life, he could not be interested in productions of that kind; unless the truth of nature were presented to him clarified, as it were, by the pervading light of imagination, it had scarce any attractions in his eyes."[44] But as a proviso, Sara Coleridge added that Wordsworth "never in his life appreciated any genius in which [humor] is a large element."

"Truth to nature" was enough for the poet laureate Robert Southey, who told Samuel Egerton Brydges in a letter of April 1830, "You mention Miss Austen; her novels are more true to nature, and have (for my sympathies) passages of finer feeling than any others of this age. She was a person of whom I have heard so well, and think so highly, that I regret not having seen her, nor ever having had an opportunity of testifying to her the respect which I felt for her."[45] Southey realized how narrowly he had missed that opportunity, for his uncle, the Reverend Herbert Hill, was married to Jane's great friend Catherine Bigg, and the novelist's name was frequently mentioned at the Hills' house in Streatham. Perhaps Southey had heard the story of Mrs. Hill's brother and his proposal back in 1802; it's odd to think that if Jane had married Harris Bigg-Wither, she and Southey would have been related.

There was another story about Southey's strong admiration for Austen that was passed on to Henry Austen by his friend Henry Sandford. The poet laureate had, apparently, picked up on an oblique quotation from one of Austen's novels that Sandford had let slip and taken this as his cue to hold forth, all the way up a very long hill in Montreal, on his favorite novelist. The anecdote, dating from about 1823, survives because Henry Austen sent it on to Cassandra for what was clearly a collection of such snippets that his sister gathered slowly over the years. The cut-out paragraph is now in the collection of the British Library.

Cassandra was the person who exercised ultimate control over Jane's posterity and who, a few years before her own death in 1845, destroyed a large quantity of her papers, leaving the life record famously scanty and unrevealing. Her motives have often been brought into question and are usually thought to have been either mean-spirited or self-protective, but the evidence points a different way. Far from thwarting the passing on of information about her sister, Cassandra Austen kept the archive intact for twenty-five years and *added* to it assiduously during those years, preserving every scrap of praise for her sister that she encountered.

Cassandra's involvement in Jane's writing career is very clear from the letters that have survived (and that may have been selected by her, consciously or unconsciously, to illustrate just that point). In one of November 6–7, 1813, having mentioned the latest news on the second edition of *Sense and Sensibility* and gossip about its authorship, Jane says, "I cannot tire you I am sure on this subject, or I would apologise."[46] The sense is that Cassandra could often be as eager (if not more so) for news like this as Jane herself.

Jane's frequently deferential tone toward her older sister and mysterious tribute in 1796 to Cassandra's superior talents as "the finest comic writer of the present age"[47] are difficult to square with the humorless nature of Cassandra's few remaining letters (as opposed, say, to letters by Mrs. Austen, who was a notably lively writer and proud of her "sprack wit"). If anyone deserved comparison with a poker, it would seem to be the young woman who bore up with such rigid self-control under the loss of her fiancé in 1797; as Eliza de Feuillide reported, "Jane says that her Sister behaves with a degree of resolution & Propriety which no common mind could evince in so trying a situation."[48] Cassandra's fortitude is surely a model for that of Elinor

Dashwood in *Sense and Sensibility*, whose lone outburst against her more expressive younger sister is to protest that her composure of mind is the result of "constant and painful exertion," not lack of feeling.[49] Cassandra's own capacity for both was dramatically demonstrated in the letter she wrote to Fanny Knight from Winchester between Jane's death and burial, very likely in the presence of the corpse: "I *have* lost such a treasure, such a Sister, such a friend as never can have been surpassed,—She was the sun of my life, the gilder of every pleasure, the soother of every sorrow, I had not a thought concealed from her, & it is as if I had lost a part of myself."[50] But this outpouring of feeling is instantly checked by the following consideration: "I loved her only too well, not better than she deserved, but I am conscious that my affection for her made me sometimes unjust to & negligent of others, & I can acknowledge, more than as a general principle, the justice of the hand which has struck this blow." The absolute Christian correctness of this seems too violent for sympathy.

Cassandra, who had spent much of her youth mourning for Tom Fowle, spent her later years keeping the memory of her sister sacred. "Aunt Cassandra's loss in her sister was great indeed and most truly a loss never to be repaired," Fanny Caroline Lefroy wrote later, repeating the impressions of her mother, Anna. "They were everything to each other. They seemed to lead a life to themselves, within the general family life, which was shared only by each other. I will not say their true but their full feelings and opinions were known only to themselves. They alone fully understood what each had suffered and felt and thought."[51] Little chinks of these strong feelings can still be glimpsed. In Cassandra's own copy of *Persuasion*, next to the passage in which Anne Elliot reflects, "She had been forced into prudence in her youth, she learned romance as she grew older—the natural sequel of an unnatural beginning," she wrote feelingly, "Dear dear Jane! This deserves to be written in letters of gold."[52]

The scraps of praise for Jane that were kept by Cassandra and left to their brother Charles include her writing-out of the quote from Lockhart's *Life of Scott* (published in 1830), Henry's letter relating Southey's praise, an extract from one of Charles Austen's letters, copied out by his daughter, and a piece cut from a letter recording

Miss Shirreff's dinner-party conversation with Sheridan back in 1813. The fragment, addressed to Cassandra in an unknown hand, ends "I know you like to hear any thing of this kind," indicating that friends and family were on the lookout for such items.[53] They didn't necessarily reach Chawton very quickly. After the sale of the copyrights to Bentley in 1832, the family had no more control over Jane's works, no income from them, and no connection with the publishing world. It was almost two years after its publication that Henry sent on a poetic tribute in the *Keepsake for MDCCCXXXV*. Next to an illustration of a woman reading was this verse titled "The Lady and the Novel," by the Earl of Carlisle:

> *Beats thy quick pulse o'er Inchbald's thrilling leaf,*
> *Brunton's high moral, Opie's deep-wrought grief?*
> *Has the mild chaperon claimed thy yielding heart,*
> *Carroll's dark page, Trevelyan's gentle art?*
> *Or is it thou, all perfect Austen? Here*
> *Let one poor wreath adorn thy early bier,*
> *That scarce allowed thy modest youth to claim*
> *Its living portion of thy certain fame!*[54]

When her mother died at the age of eighty-seven in 1827, Cassandra adopted the title "Mrs. Austen," as was conventional for mature unmarried women as well as married ones. Not that there was much family left at Chawton among whom distinctions of rank could be made. Chawton House had long been let by Edward, and the year after old Mrs. Austen's death Martha left to marry Frank (who was knighted in the early 1840s). Cassandra made long visits to them and to her other brothers. The favored nieces and nephews were all grown up by this time, some with children of their own.

Martha, who had been so close to both Austen sisters, had been Cassandra's intended executrix, but when she died first, in 1843, a new will and instructions had to be drawn up. Cassandra turned to her youngest brother Charles to take on the task, with his daughter Cassy Esten Austen to help "examine and apportion" Cassandra's jewelry and mementos, bequeathed to nine of her nieces; to Henry; to

James Edward's wife, Emma; and to Fulwar Craven Fowle's daughter Elizabeth Caroline. The occasion made her reconsider what was and was not appropriate to pass on, as she wrote to Charles in May of that year: "As I have leisure, I am looking over & destroying some of my Papers—others I have marked 'to be burned', whilst some will still remain. These are chiefly a few letters & a few Manuscripts of our dear Jane, which I have set apart for those parties to whom I think they will be mostly valuable."[55]

In other words, Cassandra's main purpose in retaining some manuscripts at this date was to make appropriate keepsakes within the family. Charles was to have "Volume the First" (Cassandra pasted a note in the back, "For my Brother Charles. I think I recollect that a few of the trifles in this Vol. were written expressly for his amusement"[56]); "Volume the Second" was for Frank, and "Volume the Third" for James Edward Austen-Leigh. Caroline Austen was to receive "The Watsons," Anna Lefroy "Sanditon" (neither of these fragmentary works had a title at this date) and the rejected chapters of *Persuasion*, but the greater part of the remaining manuscripts went to Fanny Knight, now Lady Knatchbull. She was to get almost ninety letters and "Lady Susan," the only complete unpublished story.

Caroline Austen corroborated the fact that Aunt Cassandra had "looked over . . . and burnt the greater part" of her letters from Jane "2 or 3 years before her own death" and that, of the ones given as legacies, "several had portions cut out."[57] Catherine Anne Hubback gave some idea of the material that was destroyed, remembering how Aunt Cassandra used to relish rereading letters of Jane's "triumphing over the married women of her acquaintance, and rejoicing in her own freedom"[58]—not the traditional image of the good-natured spinster sisters! But the fact that Cassandra waited so late in her life before effecting a final purge seems very significant. Cassandra acted in an unusual way in not destroying *all* the letters, regardless of their contents, as proven by their niece Anna's assumption, twenty years later, that she had done so. "The occasional correspondence between the Sisters when apart from each other would as a matter of course be destroyed by the Survivor," Anna wrote to her half brother James Edward when he was compiling material for his biography. "I can fancy what the indignation of Aunt Cass[a]. would have been at the mere idea of its being read and commented upon by any of us, nephews and nieces, little or great."[59] This is undoubtedly true. The sisters considered letters as private, unless they signaled otherwise; when Mrs. Austen "had the perusal" of one of Cassandra's to a Miss Irvine in 1804, Jane alerted her of the fact, adding that it was something which "in your place I should not like."[60] Yet this is one of the letters saved from the bonfire, bequeathed to Charles Austen, and now available in print in dozens of languages the world over, perused by hundreds of thousands, possibly millions, of people. Cassandra's feelings of propriety about the content being private must have been overridden by other, even stronger, feelings.

Of the few letters from Cassandra herself that have survived, one to Anna Lefroy of February 1, 1844, shows her still gratefully collecting scraps of praise for her sister's works in her seventy-second year. Anna had sent a cutting from a review of four novels, which digressed on to Jane Austen, calling her "the greatest of all female novelists . . . great in her absence of affectation, in her wonderful knowledge of the secrets of the heart, in her power of investing common-place with interest." Cassandra's response shows her pleasure at this but also a residual surprise that the wider world might agree with her own opinion:

> The first subject which calls for my gratitude is the Extract from the Foreign & Colonial Review respecting your Aunt's works which you were so good as to send. The Article was quite new to me & could not fail of being highly gratifying to my feelings. It was evidently written by a person of taste & discrimination. Is it not remarkable that those Books should have risen so much in celebrity after so many years? I think it may be considered as a proof that they possess intrinsic merit.[61]

The idea that the intrinsic merit of Jane's novels was debatable comes as almost as much of a surprise as Cassandra's perception of them as having had their day long ago. Her interest in the books' wider fame has a detachment and objectivity about it that underlines her own much more powerful and unfluctuating sense of proprietorship. She had been

Jane's confidante, the first reader of all the works (both the ones that are known to us and perhaps some unknown), the person whose tastes and opinions most heavily influenced Jane's writing, and whose approval was pivotal. But there must have been a terrible loneliness to such a position, when everyone who had understood it properly was dead. "Prayers composed by my ever dear sister Jane," Cassandra wrote on a copy of some precious remnants, but to whom was such an explanatory note addressed?

Cassandra's later life on her own in Chawton was remembered by John White, a villager who died in 1921, aged one hundred. He recalled that she lived "at the corner house by the Pond" and that the front door opened straight into a room, either the dining room or the drawing room. She "took a great interest in young girls" of the village and taught them reading, the catechism, and sewing, and had a nice dog called Link who used to go up to Chawton House for the milk with Cassandra's manservant, William Littleworth, and bring it home in a pail held in his mouth.[62]

In 1840, the railway came through the area, with the nearest station, at Alton, telescoping the time it took to get from Chawton to London to an almost incredible two hours. "People could not at first believe that coaches could be made to run without horses," John White recalled. Cassandra lived to see the quiet of the area disturbed in other ways too. At the height of the troubles arising from the high food prices and low wages for laborers in the 1830s, there was rioting and a wave of vandalism that included the total destruction of the Selborne workhouse. The soldiery was called out to contain the violence, but it took time and some tentative promises from local farmers to increase pay. Nevertheless, Chawton was not a particularly happy or thriving community during these years, and in 1841 several of the village's young men decided to emigrate en masse to New Zealand. The move had a sad outcome, as nearly all their children died on the five-month sea voyage, perhaps among them some of the girls in whom old "Mrs. Austen" had taken an interest at home.[63]

Cassandra in her old age was remembered as "a pale, dark-eyed old lady, with a high arched nose and a kind smile, dressed in a long cloak and a large drawn bonnet, both made of black satin."[64] She died at age seventy-two on a visit to her brother Frank in 1845, and was taken back to Chawton for burial at St. Nicholas's Church on a blustery day in March. Her nephew Charles Knight, who conducted the service, could hardly be heard in the churchyard above the wind, and the pall almost blew away. "It struck me as remarkably emblematic of her age & condition," James Edward Austen-Leigh wrote afterward to his sister, "that the wind whisked about us so many withered beech leaves, that the coffin was strewn with them before the service closed."[65]

# CHAPTER 4

# A Vexed Question

JANE AUSTEN'S NOVELS WERE NOT ESSENTIAL READING FOR the high Victorians and certainly were not "beloved." She had become a half-forgotten niche writer, with a readership that looked insignificant compared with that of Dickens, Collins, and Thackeray, all selling in their hundreds of thousands to the new mass market. When the copyrights expired on *Sense and Sensibility*, *Pride and Prejudice*, and *Mansfield Park* in 1839, 1841, and 1842 respectively, and on *Emma*, *Northanger Abbey*, and *Persuasion* in 1857 and 1860, there was no rush by publishers to pick up the free texts. Bentley, unchallenged as her main publisher, kept up with demand for Austen's novels by ordering another five hundred to one thousand copies of each title every eight or ten years. The books were available but hardly flooding the market, and the author remained "a critic's novelist—highly spoken of and little read."[1] In the 1850s, G. H. Lewes complained about the number of people he met who remembered having read Austen's novels but who had forgotten by whom they were written: " 'Miss Austen? Oh yes; she translates from the German, doesn't she?' "[2] And as late as 1866, *Notes & Queries* published a request for the name of the author of a book mentioned by Macaulay, *Mansfield Park*.[3]

In the fifty-two years between her death and the publication of the first biography in 1870, only six essays were published on the subject of Jane Austen, and she was hardly mentioned in the public sphere. James Austen's granddaughter Mary Augusta Austen-Leigh had a rather literal explanation for the slow growth of Austen's fame in the 1830s, '40s, and '50s, blaming the smallness of the print used in the Standard Novels series, "ill-suited to any but young and strong eyes."[4] But Austen was being "overlooked" in all sorts of ways. Though Queen Victoria recalled reading *Northanger Abbey* with pleasure to "dear Albert," the deluxe dedication copy of *Emma* that had been presented to her great-uncle, the prince regent, in 1815 was relegated during her reign to the servants' library, where it seems to have remained, unread, for decades. The copy probably owes its present state of good preservation to the double neglect it found below stairs, where, as Roger Fulford remarked to the Jane Austen Society in 1957, "we may be thankful that John Brown's tastes were more for the cupboard than the bookshelf—the whiskey bottle rather than the novel."[5]

Alfred, Lord Tennyson was a great admirer of Austen, and perhaps the first person to satirize his devotion, saying to his host on a visit to Lyme Regis, "Don't talk to me of the Duke of Monmouth—show me the place where Louisa Musgrove fell!" On another occasion he expressed his gratitude that so little was known about the author's life, thanking "God Almighty . . . that there were no letters preserved either of Shakespeare's or Jane Austen's, that they had not been ripped open like pigs."[6]

The Austen family had no intention of exposing their aunt to such scrutiny, of course—in fact, had no intention of engaging with the public at all. They were a widely dispersed clan, thanks to the number of children and grandchildren descending from the Austen brothers (twenty-three nephews and nieces were alive at the time of Cassandra's death), and no one member of it had control over Aunt Jane's papers, memory, or intellectual property. Cassandra had left the most precious and intimate manuscripts—the letters—to Fanny Knight, but James's three children, James Edward Austen-Leigh, Caroline Austen, and their half sister, Anna Lefroy, had manuscript items too and made copies, which they passed around among them.

But even these close siblings weren't aware of the extent of the whole archive or what their cousin had at her disposal. "Lady Knatchbull has a whole short story they were wishing years ago to make public," Caroline reported to her brother in the 1860s, possibly referring to "Lady Susan," "but [they] were discouraged by others—& I hope the desire has passed away."[7]

The question whether or not there was "an estate of Jane Austen" didn't occur to anyone until it was tested. The publication in 1850 of a novel, *The Younger Sister*, by Frank Austen's daughter Catherine Anne Hubback, caused a certain amount of consternation in the family, for it picked up and worked on the plot and characters of "The Watsons," the fragmentary novel (not titled by Jane) that had been in the possession of Caroline Austen since 1845. Catherine Anne Hubback had been born in Chawton in 1818, so she never knew Jane, but she did know Cassandra well and probably looked over the fragment, along with other papers, many times in her youth. It is perfectly possible that Catherine Anne was encouraged by Aunt Cassandra to use it as a practice piece, just as James's children seem to have been encouraged in earlier years to make free with the incomplete parts of Jane's juvenilia. Anna Austen wrote a continuation of her aunt's story "Evelyn" in "Volume the Third" (it is signed with her married initials, so must postdate 1814), and one editor has suggested that James Edward's additions to the same volume could have been made as late as 1829.

"The Watsons" was, at any rate, so familiar to Catherine Anne Hubback that she must have either made a copy of it during Cassandra's lifetime or simply remembered it from frequent reading, like a fulfillment of Jane's pointed joke in 1799 about Martha Lloyd having read "First Impressions" so often that "she means to publish it from Memory, & one more perusal must enable her to do it."[8] The opening chapters of *The Younger Sister* replicate names, characters, and the basic family situation of Jane's manuscript closely, and Catherine Anne's borrowings seem to have been limited only by the brevity of the original. No wonder it riled her older cousins, the only other people who knew about the unfinished story. They were probably also taken aback by the dedication of Catherine Anne's book, "To the Memory of her

Aunt / THE LATE MISS AUSTEN." It was quite a bold move, laying claim to an aunt Mrs. Hubback had never known and whose work she was silently recycling. The interesting relation managed to slip into the title pages of her later novels too, like a form of product endorsement: "Life and Its Lessons / By Mrs Hubback / Niece of Miss Austen."

Catherine Anne Hubback's circumstances go a little way to excuse her behavior. She had married a barrister when she was twenty-four and had three sons by him, but when her husband suffered a breakdown only a few years later, Catherine Anne was put in the almost impossible position, for a middle-class woman of the time, of having to support herself and her children. She proved as resourceful and resilient a parent as her father Frank had always been and turned to novel writing, producing nine perfectly original novels after *The Younger Sister*, and later immigrating to America to join two of her sons. But even if her circumstances were generally known in the family, there wasn't much sympathy for her. Anna Lefroy, who, as a woman widowed young and left with a young family to support, might have been expected to be the most understanding, was convinced that her cousin had managed to purloin not only "The Watsons" but "Sanditon" during Aunt Cassandra's lifetime, and thought her "pretty sure to make use of it as soon as she thinks she safely may."[9]

No one outside the family would have recognized the source material of *The Younger Sister*, of course, and there was still no thought, among James Austen's children, of publishing Jane's unfinished pieces or her juvenilia. Family members were still likely to give away a Jane Austen letter if asked nicely by individual enthusiasts; even requests that were rude or abrupt (as one from a Mechanics' Institute in Guernsey to James Edward Austen-Leigh) could be rewarded by the gift of an autograph at least, or a manuscript reckoned to be unimportant, cut into scraps. Frank Austen kindly sent a letter from Jane to Martha Lloyd (his second wife) to a daughter of the president of Harvard, Miss Eliza Quincy, who had made her interest in Austen's novels sound like a matter of significance for Anglo-American relations: "The sun, it is said, never sets on the dominions of the British Queen," she told Frank in 1852, "—but the classics of English Literature exercise a yet more permanent and extensive sway, recognised even by

those sturdy republicans, who disown allegiance to any sovereign—
except the sovereign people."[10] Frank was doubtless unprepared for a
continuing correspondence with Miss Quincy, but the subject had animated her profoundly. "The electric Telegraph of Genius annihilates
the barriers of Time, and Space," she told him of his sister on another
occasion,[11] an interestingly up-to-date analogy to apply to a writer
not often associated with new technology.

Apart from Jane and James, all the Austen siblings lived to great
ages; even their disabled brother, George, the next to die, reached
seventy-two. Cassandra followed him in 1845, Henry in 1850, Charles
and Edward in 1852, and Frank in 1865, at the venerable age of ninety-
one. While they were alive, there was no likelihood at all of any further information about Jane Austen being put before the public. The
"Biographical Notice" of 1818 and 1833 had said more than enough,
in their opinion.

The next generation, who by the 1860s were themselves getting old,
began to act in defense of their aunt's memory only when they felt it
had become vulnerable to misinterpretation. Mary Augusta Austen-
Leigh, who as James Edward's adult daughter was privy to plenty of
family gossip on the subject of the first biography, recalled that "as curiosity grew stronger, while the family remained silent, it was not unnatural that in the absence of definite information certain erroneous
ideas should be entertained, and some mistaken statements made re-
specting herself, her home, and her position and opportunities in life."[12]
One of these "erroneous ideas" was that Jane Austen had disliked children, another that she "was not fond of animals." More pertinently,
with the passage of time, memoirs, letters, and biographies of Austen's
near-contemporaries were emerging that began to affect public per-
ceptions of figures from the previous generation. The most influential
was undoubtedly Elizabeth Gaskell's best-selling *Life of Charlotte
Brontë* in 1857, written in the immediate aftermath of the novelist's
death. Not only did the biography present Brontë as the preeminent
female novelist of her age, but Gaskell's pacy and highly colored prose
made the book as good as a novel itself, and the sensational life story
she revealed—of the oppressed genius and her sisters trapped in their

father's gloomy moorland parsonage—had thrilled readers and quickly established a potent cult following.

*The Life of Charlotte Brontë* was published only ten years after the sensational debuts of the three Brontë sisters with *Jane Eyre*, *Wuthering Heights*, and *Agnes Grey*. These shocking novels, published under male pseudonyms but soon revealed to be the work of a parson's daughters, easily eclipsed Austen's steady but by no means universal renown. Worse for Austen's reputation, Gaskell's biography quoted letters of Charlotte Brontë that singled Austen out for far-reaching criticism. These were from the previous decade, when Brontë, in a private correspondence with G. H. Lewes, had challenged the critic's ardent advocacy (notably more ardent than his praise of *Jane Eyre*). Brontë made clear her dislike for Austen and the sort of writing she represented:

> Why do you like Miss Austen so very much? I am puzzled on that point. What induced you to say that you would have rather written "Pride and Prejudice," or "Tom Jones" than any of the Waverley Novels?
>
> I had not seen "Pride and Prejudice" till I read that sentence of yours, and then I got the book. And what did I find? An accurate, daguerreotyped portrait of a commonplace face; a carefully-fenced, highly-cultivated garden, with neat borders and delicate flowers; but no glance of a bright, vivid physiognomy, no open country, no fresh air, no blue hill, no bonny beck. I should hardly like to live with her ladies and gentlemen, in their elegant but confined houses.[13]

Lewes's reply has not survived, but can be understood from Brontë's next letter to him:

> You say I must familiarize my mind with the fact that "Miss Austen is not a poetess, has no 'sentiment' (you scornfully enclose the word in inverted commas), no eloquence, none of the ravishing enthusiasm of poetry,"—and then you add, I *must* "learn to acknowledge her as *one of the greatest artists, of the greatest painters of human character,* and one of the writers with the nicest sense of means to an end that ever lived."

The last point only will I ever acknowledge.
Can there be a great artist without poetry?[14]

The rhetorical question had an undeniable resonance. Austen
was certainly "without poetry"; she eschewed extravagant language,
heightened emotions, dramatic situations, and any but the sparest de-
scriptive passages. In Brontë's view (and Wordsworth's), and that of
many readers since, this disqualified her from a certain seriousness of
attention; she was in a different, much tamer, league—one concerned
with realism, restraint, and understatement, all of which the younger
novelist wished to challenge. Brontë was unwilling to consider that
Austen's rejection of "the poetic" was not merely a symptom of primness and went deeper than temperament, experience, and her nurture
in the Augustan age. Of the two writers, Austen could be said to display the more truly romantic sensibility; she saw the potency of "the
ravishing enthusiasm of poetry" and put all her least lively heroines,
Fanny Price, Charlotte Heywood, and Anne Elliot, in peril of its effects. When Sir Edward Denham in "Sanditon" attempts to enthuse
Charlotte about Scott, Wordsworth, Campbell, Montgomery, and
Burns (incidentally revealing how much of the new writing Austen
herself was acquainted with), Charlotte's reply starts priggishly but
ends feelingly: "I have read several of Burns's Poems with delight . . .
but I am not poetic enough to separate a Man's Poetry entirely from
his Character; & poor Burns's known Irregularities, greatly interrupt
my enjoyment of his Lines. I have difficulty depending on the *Truth*
of his Feelings as a Lover. I have not faith in the *sincerity* of the affections of a Man of his Description: He felt & he wrote & he forgot."[15]
A writer, or person, "with poetry" is never entirely to be trusted, the
author implies.

The flights, transports, deliberate eloquence, and enthusiasm associated with romanticism, its perpetrators, and consumers are all
treated with deep suspicion in Austen's novels, not just as a temporary
danger (if Marianne Dashwood had been a less appreciative reader of
Shakespeare, she might not have misread Willoughby) but as a sign
of a sort of spiritual incontinence that has to be guarded against. Only
Elizabeth Bennet and Emma Woodhouse are never in danger of read-

ing Burns or being entirely miserable. In *Persuasion*, Anne Elliot rec-
ommends "a larger allowance of prose in his daily study" to Captain
Benwick, like a literary high-fiber diet, and later in the book reflects
that "it was the misfortune of poetry to be seldom safely enjoyed by
those who enjoyed it completely; the strong feelings which alone
could estimate it truly were the very feelings which ought to taste it
but sparingly."

It is easy to guess how much Austen would have disapproved of
the high coloring and abandoned sensuality of the Brontë sisters'
novels. Nothing of the sort could be "safely enjoyed," so its possible
qualification for a kind of greatness would have struck her as impertinent. But in 1857, it was Brontë's view of Austen that was being
quoted so disadvantageously and at such length by Mrs. Gaskell, and
it was Austen's old-fashioned restraint and regulation that was being
brought to readers' notice and stuck in their minds: "[She] maybe *is*
sensible, real (more *real* than *true*)," Brontë concluded witheringly,
"but she cannot be great."[16]

The Austen family—or at least its most interested parties: Anna
Lefroy, James Edward Austen-Leigh, Caroline Austen, and Cassy Esten Austen—did not at first mobilize against the sporadic assaults on
their aunt's literary reputation. They probably didn't feel the need to
while an eloquent advocate such as G. H. Lewes was engaged on her
behalf (by the late 1850s he had published four articles, three-
quarters, that is, of all available criticism on Austen), but eventually
even Lewes began to lament the dearth of biographical information
about his favorite novelist: "Miss Austen has made herself known
without making herself public. There is no portrait of her in the shop
windows; indeed, no portrait of her at all."[17] Unlike Fanny Burney,
whose voluminous *Diaries and Letters*, published between 1842 and
1846, gave readers "biography, and to spare," or Brontë (who Lewes
rather maliciously suggested "will soon cease to find readers"), nothing was known about Austen beyond the simple facts of her simple
life, laid out by Henry Austen in his "Biographical Notice" of 1818.

Some commentators were coming to their own conclusions about
the author. Two unsigned articles in the *Englishwoman's Domestic Magazine* in 1866 (a monthly with an enormous readership) kept returning

to Austen's unattractive "coolness": "Jane Austen's heart was tender, but without sentiment, and her imagination sustained, but quite cool and comfortable."[18] "Her love is nothing more rash than a deep attachment based on esteem, a chastened affection which does not catch fire under a thousand a year." The writer went on to accuse Austen of having only an "elegant" morality, a lack of enthusiasm, ignorance of real life, and, worst of all, insufficient femininity: "Miss Austen's brain does not seem to have any maternal love for its children: it treats them somewhat like a man of the world."[19] The idea of excessive "coolness," with its close friends frigidity and death, hung around the subject, and even a long and praising chapter on Austen by Julia Kavanagh in *English Women of Letters* came around, in its summing-up, to Austen's "cold views of life."[20]

These, or similar, remarks in the press may have been in Caroline Austen's mind in 1869 when she expressed concern to her brother about "this vexed question between the Austens and the Public,"[21] and how to settle it. James Edward Austen-Leigh, heir to Scarlets, author of a monograph about the Vine Hunt, and retired vicar of Bray, had, according to his daughter Mary Augusta, "long declined" the suggestion that he should write a memoir of his aunt, though many friends "often begged him to undertake" it. He felt, very reasonably, that his own memories were too thin and that there was not enough documentary material to go on. Also, the public expectation of a literary biography was of a work that would enhance an already big reputation with similarly large-scale life events and revelations—such as Tom Moore's *Life of Byron* in 1830, or Lockhart's *Life of Scott*—or at least open up a view of the subject within a literary context, by publishing letters and diaries. As a biographical subject, Jane Austen held out no such opportunities, though that wouldn't have deterred Thomas Babington Macaulay, whose journal of 1854 shows him as entranced as ever: "Wonderful creature!" he wrote. "Worth all Dickens and Pliny together." Four years later, he was still wondering what to do with his admiration: "If I could get materials, I really would write a short life of that wonderful woman, and raise a little money to put up a monument to her in Winchester Cathedral."[22] Had he been granted his wish, Macaulay's phantom *Life and Letters of Jane Austen* would doubtless have "placed" Austen very memorably in her literary and historical context—which was exactly what her family felt was unnecessary, and, moreover, what they were utterly unqualified to do themselves.

James Edward Austen-Leigh couldn't have contemplated undertaking a biography without the active encouragement and full cooperation of his sister and half sister, both of whom had spent a great deal of time in their aunts' company; Anna lived with her grandparents and aunts at Steventon between the ages of two and four (after her mother's death), and Caroline was a frequent visitor to Chawton as a child, about fifteen years later. Jane had encouraged both, separately, with their juvenile writing, and each, naturally, believed that she had been the favorite niece.

Though Anna's early novel, which Jane read and commented on at length in 1814, seems to have been destroyed by her in the 1820s,[23] she later published another, called *Mary Hamilton*, and two children's books. Anna might have been thought a good choice as biographer, but the possibility doesn't seem to have been considered by her or anyone else. Her "Recollections of Aunt Jane," a manuscript of 1864, was addressed to James Edward in the form of a long letter, rather like a series of notes. "I am sorry that [the text] should be so meager & unsatisfactory," she wrote in her final paragraphs, "but if this attempt should incline others to do the same, even if no more, the contributions when put together may furnish a memorial of some value."[24] This indicates that in the early 1860s the family was thinking of compiling a rather informal memorial, possibly for purely home consumption, preserving the memories of people who had known Jane Austen personally before that generation died out. Even when Caroline Austen wrote her more elaborate and lengthy reminiscences in 1867, she made it clear they were written primarily for other family members, "and for my own gratification."[25]

By 1869, however, the project had changed completely. The siblings had now decided on a conventional memoir, for trade publication, synthesizing the available family reminiscences and written by James Edward, the current head of the family. The "vexed question between the Austens and the Public" would be answered, and duty done.

James Edward's *Memoir of Jane Austen*, composed and published with great dispatch in 1869, remains the main source of biographical information, incorporating family reminiscences, extracts from letters, and anecdotes about Austen's life as a writer, which, combined with Austen-Leigh's saccharine portrait of his aunt—"there was scarcely a charm in her most delightful characters that was not a true reflection of her own sweet temper and loving heart"—established at a stroke the highly popular and durable cult of Jane Austen's sweetness and gentility.

Correspondence between James Edward and his siblings about the proposed biography shows how keenly Anna and Caroline racked their brains for extra material, refined their stories, and encouraged their brother toward a speedy conclusion of his task. He certainly had his work cut out, trying to make Jane Austen's quiet life look interesting, and, unlike his late uncle Henry Austen, had relatively little intimate knowledge to draw on. Henry could have painted an extremely full portrait of the subject, had he wished; James Edward never. The epigraph he chose for his book, from a life of Christopher Columbus, suggests James Edward's own view of himself as biographer, launching out, with jaw set and teeth gritted, toward terra incognita: "He knew of no one but himself who was inclined to the work. This is no uncommon motive. A man sees something to be done, knows of no one who will do it but himself, and so is driven to the enterprise."[26]

James Edward had access to the handful of letters from his aunt to his sisters and himself but no sight of Fanny Knatchbull's hoard; he was able to see copies of "The Watsons" and "Sanditon," but not, at first, "Lady Susan"; the volumes of juvenilia (of which he owned "Volume the Third") were similarly dispersed. Frank Austen, the last of his generation, died in 1865, too late to be asked for material, and all the letters from Jane to Frank's first wife, Mary, which he had kept carefully all that time, were destroyed by one of his daughters soon after his death. Uncle Henry's store of letters had also been lost or thrown away. James Edward had no idea of the number of letters that had been left to Lady Knatchbull, and certainly no idea of their content. Anna Lefroy didn't even know of their existence until the memoir project was almost complete, having presumed "as a matter of course" that Aunt Cassandra had destroyed all such personal manuscripts.[27]

Caroline was an invaluable assistant, as she had—besides her own rich memories—plenty of stories about Jane from her parents (her mother, the former Mary Lloyd, had known the Austens from girlhood), and was well informed about memorabilia, sending James Edward a copy of a rather remarkable survival, George Austen's letter to Thomas Cadell, which had been bought in a sale of the publisher's papers by Tom Lefroy's nephew. This younger Tom Lefroy was married to Jemima, Anna Lefroy's daughter and great-niece of Jane, so he had plenty of reason to be interested in the letter, though it seems surprising that he even got to hear of the sale at a date when the concept of "Austen memorabilia" barely existed. His interest seems to have been quickened by conversations he had had with his ancient uncle, now the retired chief justice of Ireland, who told him that he had indeed been in love with Jane Austen in the 1790s, but that it had been "a boyish love."[28] This information was surely solicited from the old man rather than volunteered and wasn't passed on by the younger Tom to James Edward until *after* the publication of the *Memoir*. There is a suggestion here of the younger Tom Lefroy pursuing his own agenda, perhaps out of sheer curiosity. But until James Edward's *Memoir* was published, there were no clear channels into which such information could run. There was no "estate" and no single heir. Very many anecdotes and reminiscences about Austen must have been lost.

Gathering of material brought relatively little to light and makes one wonder at how quick Austen's family had been to throw away her letters. None survives from Jane to either parent, nor to James, Edward, or Henry (a great loss, one imagines, given Henry's liveliness and particular interest in the publication of the novels). Caroline Austen testified that her aunt "wrote very fully to her Brothers when they were at sea, and she corresponded with many others of her family,"[29] but only six letters to Frank himself remain, only one to Charles. No letters to her brothers' wives have survived; Fanny Sophia, Frank's youngest daughter, is known to have destroyed the letters from Jane to her mother, Mary Gibson, but what of the many intimate letters that Martha, her stepmother, must have received from the novelist, some of which must have still been around in the early 1850s when Frank sent the one to Miss Quincy as a keepsake? It shows Cassandra's hoarding of around ninety to herself as the act of pious commemoration it was, rather than the act of vandalism it is sometimes represented to be.

James Edward had been on a visit to the site of Steventon rectory (his own childhood home as well as that of Jane Austen), only to find "traces of former things . . . even more obliterated than I had expected. Even the terrace has been levelled, & its site is to be distinguished only by the finer turf on that place."[30] It was similarly tricky trying to find dates and documents: "I am sure you will do justice to what there is," Caroline wrote to him, "but I feel it must be a difficult task to dig up the materials, so carefully have they been buried out of our sight by the past generat[ion]."[31] She had suggestions for various bits of "stuffing" for the book—some of Jane's light verse could be included, perhaps, or some carefully chosen items from the juvenilia. Of these, she favored the more nonsensical writings, like "Evelyn," the longest and latest of the teenage Jane's sallies into the absurd (in which the obnoxious Mr. Gower is instantly given everything he wants by the strangers he lands on in the charmed village of the title). Caroline seems to have suggested "Evelyn" on grounds of its dissimilarity from the published novels. "Kitty's Bower" (the unfinished novel now generally referred to as "Catharine, or The Bower"), and the other fragments like it, she did not think should be used: "What I should deprecate is publishing any of the 'betweenities' when the nonsense was passing away, and before her wonderful talent had found it's [*sic*] proper channel."[32] Caroline also had definite views about which biographical details should be kept under wraps: the flirtation with Tom Lefroy, for instance, and the proposal from Harris Bigg-Wither. "I should not mind *telling* any body, at this distance of time," she wrote to her brother, "but printing and publishing seem to me very different from *talking* about the past."[33]

But what about Fanny Knatchbull, the niece who Anna acknowledged had known their aunt best and enjoyed "a great & affectionate intimacy" with her[34] and of whom Jane Austen herself had written so lovingly in 1808, "I am greatly pleased with your account of Fanny; I found her in the summer just what you describe, almost another Sister, & could not have supposed that a niece would ever have been so much to me. She is quite after one's own heart; give her my best Love, & tell her that I always think of her with pleasure"?[35]

As a source of intimate knowledge and possessor of the majority of Jane's surviving letters (including those lauding her own charms and dearness), why did Lady Knatchbull not contribute at all to the gathering of memoir material? Various members of the family approached her on James Edward's behalf but were met with delays and deferrals. In 1869 Fanny's sister Elizabeth Rice warned him not to wait for a sight of the letters, as there was virtually no chance of it. Lady Knatchbull, she said, was prone to giddiness and confusion, an impression of advancing senility confirmed by Fanny's daughter Louisa, who protested that her mother would have been only too delighted to assist James Edward ten years earlier, but it was too late now.

But at the same time as these petitions for help with the memoir were flying around the family, Lady Knatchbull wrote an infamous letter to another sister, Marianne, that shows more focus than confusion about the subject:

> Yes my love it is very true that Aunt Jane from various circumstances was not so *refined* as she ought to have been from her *talent* & if she had lived 50 years later she would have been in many respects more suitable to *our* more refined tastes. They were not rich & the people around with whom they chiefly mixed, were not at all high bred, or in short anything more than *mediocre* & *they* of course tho' superior in *mental powers* & *cultivation* were on the same level as far as *refinement* goes—[36]

If it hadn't been for her own father's elevation into the gentry, her mother's real gentility, and the influence of their wealth, Fanny believed her unfashionable and unsophisticated Hampshire aunts would have been "tho' not less clever & agreeable in themselves, very much below par as to good Society & its ways." As it was, they had enough of a struggle covering up their inherent "signs of 'common-ness.' "[37]

The sour snobbery of this could, of course, be a symptom of the failing mental powers that Lady Knatchbull's family hinted at but seems to reflect her views at the time of writing. No wonder, then, that she didn't want anyone to read Jane's letters or quote them in a published book. They would only confirm the dreaded "commonness" of the Hampshire Austens and her own close commerce with it in the 1800s and '10s. Anna Lefroy had a separate theory about the chill between the Hampshire and Kent Austens, believing that her uncle Edward's wife Elizabeth (who she felt was a bit of a philistine) had markedly preferred Cassandra to Jane and had passed on this prejudice to her children (of whom, of course, Lady Knatchbull was the eldest).[38]

Lady Knatchbull never remarked on the biography of her aunt, if she ever read it. But her motives for keeping Jane Austen's letters so thoroughly to herself were probably mixed, for when the old lady died in 1882, in her ninetieth year, her son found the supposedly lost "Lady Susan" and a box containing more than ninety of Jane's letters "fastened up carefully in separate packets" with Cassandra Austen's inscriptions, bequeathing them to Fanny. More surprisingly, the manuscripts were also inscribed in Lady Knatchbull's hand, as late as 1856, in words that displayed all her former fondness: "Letters from my dear Aunt Jane Austen, and two from aunt Cassandra after her decease." Like her aunt Cassandra, she had perhaps placed too high a value on these remaining letters either to share or to destroy them.

JANE AUSTEN IS NOW considered to be one of the most difficult and challenging of biographical subjects, second only to Shakespeare in terms of how little of the life is knowable and of what interest it is. The complexity of the novels, and the originality, intelligence, and vitality of the mind behind them, make many of Austen's admirers long for more evidence of her inner life; in its absence, they find fertile grounds for speculation. But for James Edward Austen-Leigh in the late 1860s, the agenda was very different: His aim was to point out the consistency between his subject's life and works, and the wholesomeness and harmlessness of both. James Edward's own realization that his aunt was a serious author had come very late, and he had little time to assimilate it before her death. His portrait of her reflects this, emphasizing her domestic life, duty to family, contentment, and piety as the norm, with her literary genius a happy surprise that disturbed neither herself nor others. He calls her "dear aunt Jane" in the very first sentence of his book and encourages the reader to adopt a similarly familiar viewpoint: "We did not think of her as being clever, still less as being famous; but we valued her as one always kind, sympathizing, and amusing."[39]

The tone of James Edward's biography was very close to Henry Austen's original "Biographical Notice," with the emphasis firmly on the eventless nature of the life in question, the subject's cheerful and unselfish disposition, and her well-balanced character: "There was in her nothing eccentric or angular, no ruggedness of temper; no singularity of manner; none of the morbid sensibility or exaggeration of feeling, which not unfrequently accompanies great talents," James Edward asserted,[40] in a passage notable for its relentless negativity. Perhaps he was thinking of his own father, James Austen, as an example of the "great talent" plagued by morbid sensibility. James Edward clearly was thinking of his father for much of this biography of his aunt, quoting verses by him (anonymously) to illustrate topographical points and introducing anecdotes of his time at Oxford. James Austen, "writer of the family" no more, haunts the book and its author.

James Edward painted a cheerful picture of family life at Steventon rectory, the intelligence and good humor of the parents, and their offspring's personal charms and professional achievements. His evasions were almost all conventional for the time (just as sensational revelations are now conventional in biography) and understandable, if not essential, in terms of family loyalty and discretion. He omitted Jane's brief engagement to Harris Bigg-Wither and the rumor that she had once had a "seaside romance" with a man who subsequently died; he felt free to make a passing reference to Jane's flirtation with Tom Lefroy only because Lefroy died, at age ninety-three, while the book was being written. Otherwise, he represented his aunt as having lived a life without romantic entanglements or longings and gave a resolutely surface view of her social self: "With all her neighbours in the village she was on friendly, though not on intimate, terms. She took a kindly interest in all their proceedings, and liked to hear about them. They often served for her amusement; but it was her own nonsense that gave zest to the gossip. She was as far as possible from being censorious or satirical."[41] This was an oblique parry to those who had criticized Austen's chilliness; elsewhere he tackled Charlotte Brontë's remarks about Austen's style by quoting a passage that can be read as defending both women's right to their own form of expression.

James Edward's portrait is more suggestive than specific about his aunt's character. Though he asserts in the first pages that "there was scarcely a charm in her most delightful characters that was not a true reflection of her own sweet temper and loving heart,"[42] he doesn't provide any examples of how exactly she might have resembled Emma Woodhouse or Lizzie Bennet, nor does he stray into the territory of whose imagination created the less delightful characters in the books. Of Archbishop Whately's conjecture that Fanny Price's unrequited love in *Mansfield Park* must have stemmed from experience, James Edward protests that any such suggestion is "wide of the mark" and that the worldly knowledge displayed in the books was "the intuitive perception of genius." His aunt loved her home, her family (particularly her sister), her God; indulged only "wholesome pleasures, duties and interests," and found the modest dimensions of Chawton Cottage perfectly "sufficient." Everything was *sufficient* for "Aunt Jane."

If Mrs. Gaskell's stylistic model for her *Life of Charlotte Brontë* was the romantic novel, that of James Edward's *Memoir of Jane Austen* was the form most familiar to him, the sermon. Thus he felt free to introduce into the biography scholarly digressions; quotations from scripture, classics, and critical authorities; and passages of deliberate, steadying dullness, in the time-honored pulpit mode. Some of this was the "stuffing" that Caroline had so accurately predicted would be necessary, such as the inclusion of bits of family memorabilia and letters; at other times the biographer seemed to stray rather far from his subject, as in his ruminations on dinner-table decorations in the early century and a lengthy reflection on the history of spinning. Even the personal reminiscences could seem rather beside the point—his emphasis, for example, on Jane Austen's manual dexterity: "None of us could throw spilikins in so perfect a circle, or take them off with so steady a hand. Her performances with cup and ball were marvellous." This isn't exactly how Jane Austen might have expected to be remembered, nor for her neat way with folding and sealing letter paper. But James Edward wanted to assure his readers that to Austen, such things were not peripheral, and no domestic duty or accomplishment suffered in the making of her novels. He gives the example of the handiwork of a "housewife" needle case Austen once sewed for his mother, Mary Lloyd, showing that "the same hand which painted so exquisitely with the pen could work as delicately with the needle."[43] Phew!

Just where Austen could be placed in terms of class was a major preoccupation of the whole book. Even in 1816, Walter Scott had remarked that Austen's "most distinguished characters do not rise greatly above well-bred country gentlemen and ladies; and those which are sketched with most originality and precision, belong to a class rather below that standard"[44]—the implication being that that was the class she knew best and belonged to. Fifty years later, the early decades of the century seemed coarse and bumptious to the affluent gentlefolk of mid-Victorian England, and the Hampshire Austens were obviously not immune to feelings that were similar, if less obnoxiously expressed, to Lady Knatchbull's about how the passage of time might have left their aunt's life open to socially disadvantageous interpretation. The Chawton ladies, with their donkey cart and chickens, their poky parlors and homemade caps, were something for the nieces and nephews to look back on with a certain fond embarrassment rather than pride, and James Edward included in his book many passages on changing manners that were clearly intended to head off any misjudgment of the family as vulgar or poor: the fact that the Austens grew their own potatoes, for example, and furnished their home in a way that "would appear to us lamentably scanty." Even Anna expressed some surprise when she remembered the "cheap-looking carpet" and "cheaply papered walls" of Steventon rectory, and James Edward thought the lack of cornices there and "naked simplicity" of a few exposed beams adequate explanation to an audience of 1870 why the house "has since been considered unworthy of being the rectory house of a family living."[45]

The ground bass of apology and uncertainty can be heard even in James Edward's description of the part of Hampshire in which Austen was born and raised: "The features are small rather than plain . . . the hills are not bold, nor the valleys deep; and though it is sufficiently well clothed with woods and hedgerows, yet the poverty of the soil in most places prevents the timber from attaining a large size. Still it has its beauties."[46] He felt that the few extracts from his aunt's letters required apology too: "There is in them no notice of politics or public events; scarcely any discussions on literature, or other subjects of general interest . . . the reader must be warned not to expect too much from them."[47] Austen-Leigh certainly could not be accused of overselling his product, though his hesitance, so clearly genuine, may have contributed more to his book's effect than if he had adopted the role of an enthusiast. His qualified praises, underwhelming assertions, and multiple negatives left plenty of room for readers to supply their own enthusiasm, even love, for the subject.

Pivotal to the appeal of the life was the family's account of how this meek paragon had produced her books: working in the common sitting room, "subject to all sorts of casual interruptions," "she wrote upon small sheets of paper which could easily be put away, or covered with a piece of blotting paper." The swing door creaked, but our author, in an isolated exhibition of self-interest, "objected to having this little inconvenience remedied, because it gave her notice when anyone was coming." If any member of the family disturbed her writing, as James Edward guesses they all must have done, they were never aware of it through "any signs of impatience or irritability in the writer."[48] The passage in Caroline Austen's manuscript, "My Aunt Jane Austen," from which James Edward was deriving much of this, is far less certain about the nature of the writing that was going on: "My Aunt must have spent much time in writing—her desk lived in the drawing room. I often saw her writing letters on it, and I believe she wrote much of her Novels in the same way—sitting with her family, when they were quite alone; but *I* never saw any manuscript of *that* sort, in progress."[49] These qualifications to the evidence of "how Austen wrote" were all obliterated in the retelling.

The other cornerstone of the future Austen legend was the extreme of self-deprecating modesty suggested in Austen's remark about her "little bit of Ivory." This phrase, already publicized in Henry Austen's "Biographical Notice," and originally from a letter of Jane Austen to James Edward himself, seems to have been coined with the half-desire to set the reader's teeth on edge. The context of the letter is important: Austen had been bolstering the young James Edward's self-esteem in the kindest manner imaginable, congratulating him on his passage out of Winchester College, joking about their shared occupation (novel writing), and sympathizing with the young man for having mislaid two and a half chapters of his work in progress. The metaphors seem to get rather mixed at this point, as Austen jokes that she can't be suspected of stealing the chapters, even though "two strong twigs & a half towards a Nest of my own, would have been something": "What should I do with your strong, manly, spirited Sketches, full of Variety and Glow?—How could I possibly join them on to the little bit (two Inches wide) of Ivory on which I work with so fine a Brush, as produces little effect after much labour?"[50] What did she mean? It couldn't have been simple modesty, for this degree of modesty, or flattery, from the author of *Sense and Sensibility*, *Pride and Prejudice*, *Mansfield Park*, and *Emma* (just out that month) toward her eighteen-year-old novice-writer nephew would have been false indeed. Was she suddenly struck with one of those frequent anxious thoughts in the later letters about the sustainability of her gift and the degree of "labour" it required? Or had her auntly benevolence simply run its course in this paragraph and introduced a little bit of irony, letting her nephew understand that they were chalk and cheese?

The problematic phrase has led a much happier life detached from its context, signifying Austen's confession to limitations of scale. No matter that the "little bit of Ivory" had a literal as well as a metaphorical meaning (portable notebooks of the late eighteenth century were made from thin sheets of horn or ivory, two inches wide, which were wiped clean for reuse); the metaphor is what has stuck in readers' minds, evoking miniature painting, dedication to craftsmanship,

doggedness, and painstaking expertise. Austen appears to be anticipating the criticism most often leveled at her in later years that she was
too small scale, and inviting sentimental admiration, or at least forgive-
ness, for that characteristic instead.

Everything in James Edward's portrait confirms this sense of
Austen knowing and loving her boundaries: "She was always very
careful not to meddle with matters she did not understand," he wrote.
"She never touched upon politics, law, or medicine, subjects which
some novel writers have ventured on rather too boldly."[51] The story of
the prince regent's patronage is told as the apogee of Austen's success,
and edited parts of the correspondence with Rev. Clarke were reproduced to emphasize Austen's civility and restraint. The "Plan of a
Novel" is also partly reproduced, though Austen-Leigh's editing of it
and Rev. Clarke's letters take much of the sting out of the satire. "I
doubt whether it would be possible to mention any other author of note,
whose personal obscurity was so complete," James Edward marveled
in conclusion. "Jane Austen lived in entire seclusion from the literary
world: neither by correspondence, nor by personal intercourse was
she known to any contemporary authors. It is probable that she never
was in company with any person whose talents or whose celebrity
equalled her own; so that her powers never could have been sharp-
ened by collision with superior intellect, nor her imagination aided by
their casual suggestions."[52] No collision, no collusion: "Whatever she
produced was a genuine home-made article." Austen's writing was
domestic, personal, crafted, small scale, and quintessentially female.

James Edward Austen-Leigh was not actively seeking to set his
aunt up as a feminine ideal, but that was the channel into which his
thoughts (the thoughts of a clergyman as well as a nephew) naturally
ran. His book was undertaken for defensive reasons; it sought to answer "vexatious" questions about Austen that had already arisen in public debate and nip any further questions in the bud. One of the central
(unspoken) questions was that of the propriety of a decent woman
being a professional writer at all, a question Robert Southey had answered roundly in 1836 in a letter to Charlotte Brontë: "Literature
cannot be the business of a woman's life; & it ought not to be."[53] Mrs.
Gaskell had worked hard, in her biography of Brontë, to overlay the

"unladylike" image of the author that many readers had deduced from the novels with a counterbalancing angel, a victim of circumstances and rough company; she emphasized the Currer Bell / Charlotte Brontë divide as a way of dramatizing the tension in Brontë between her artist self and her private life. Austen-Leigh implicitly denied the possibility of any such division existing in his aunt's case. He emphasized her unity of mind, her imperturbability, the seamless segues from creativity to domesticity. It was really no bother at all, having an artistic temperament. Nice, even.

His book was finished and at the printers when the late Mary Russell Mitford's letters were published, revealing Mitford's mother's opinion of Austen having been "a husband-hunting butterfly" in her youth, and the unnamed friend's later portrait of Austen as the "poker of whom everybody was afraid." These images could hardly have seemed more at odds with the picture being prepared by Austen-Leigh, who appended a postscript vigorously refuting Miss Mitford's "misrepresentation of my aunt's manners" and discrediting the remarks on the grounds that they were merely hearsay.

Miss Mitford's was not the only unlovable portrait of Jane Austen in need of adjustment. Everyone agreed that the biography ought to contain an image of the subject, but there were only Cassandra's two sketches available, both owned by Charles Austen's daughter, Cassy Esten Austen, and neither were considered of any value. The faceless "bonnet" watercolor was hardly suitable; neither was the unattractive half-finished full-face drawing. Anna was not the only member of the family who thought this picture "hideously unlike" her aunt. A painting was commissioned from a Mr. Andrews of Maidenhead to bring Cassandra's sketch up to an acceptable level of pulchritude, and the result was a pastel-colored image of a chubby, vacant-looking young woman with huge eyes and pink cheeks. As required, it was significantly unlike the original: the subject's clothes were tidied up, with a concertinaed frill appearing around the cap to frame the face; her slumped posture was rectified, the folded arms (so expressive of the sitter's mood) unfolded, and the right eye brought down level with the left and rotated to a less cubist angle. Even the chair that this new "Jane Austen" was sitting on got a makeover, from a simple straight-backed affair to something more polished and substantial, with a decorative curve.

When she saw the result, Cassy Esten Austen remarked, "It is a very pleasing, sweet face,—tho', I confess, to not thinking it *much* like the original;—but that, the public will not be able to detect."[54] Still, it was "very much superior to any thing that could have been expected from the sketch it was taken from." Andrews's painting has not been reproduced often (it is used on the cover of *Collected Poems and Verse of the Austen Family*); for use as the frontispiece to the *Memoir* it had to be engraved, and it is the stippled engraving—by the firm of Lizars—that has been endlessly reprinted, copied, parodied, improved, and which was the first (and for many years the only) authorized image of Jane Austen to be offered to public gaze. Lizars's engraving was very like the Andrews painting, but not identical. The eyes were if anything even bigger, but the expression was not quite so bovine. Now Austen looked slightly uncomfortable rather than just stupid. Cassandra's picture had made her look tetchy. The only thing all three portraits have in common is the same representation of the number, position, and direction of the curls of brown hair emerging from under the subject's headgear. One senses Cassandra's gratitude for them—so much easier to do than eyes or a mouth—and Andrews's and Lizars's similar relief in having something noncommittal to copy. In terms of what Austen actually looked like, they are just about all we can cling to.

The resulting picture was thought perfectly fit for purpose, however. "The portrait is better than I expected," Caroline wrote when the first edition of the *Memoir* reached her, "—as considering its early date, and that it has lately passed through the hands of painter and engraver—I did not reckon upon finding *any* likeness—but there is a *look* which I recognize as *hers*—and though the general resemblance is *not* strong, yet as it represents a pleasant countenance it is *so* far a truth—& I am not dissatisfied with it."[55] It certainly worked like a charm on the reviewer in the *Spectator*:

> It is a great comfort to us to have so complete a verification of the theory we have always cherished—that Miss Austen's personal char-

acter was a sort of medium between the heroine of *Pride and Preju-dice*, Elizabeth Bennet, and the heroine of *Persuasion*, Anne Elliot. . . . The portrait prefixed to the volume—a very remarkable portrait—entirely bears out this double likeness to Anne Elliot and Elizabeth Bennet. It is a small head, with very sweet lively eyes, and a fullness about the face which seems to speak of health and spirit, but the air of high breeding and gentleness of nature is deeply impressed upon it. It is refinement, playfulness, and alertness, rather than depth of intellect, which the face seems to express.[56]

Mr. Andrews and Messrs. Lizars had done their job well.

When the *Memoir* was published, "a singular change took place" in the public's attention to Austen.[57] It wasn't just that the book attracted dozens of articles, notices, and reviews and quickly sold out its first edition of one thousand copies, but the subject seemed to fire readers' imaginations to an extraordinary extent. "Perhaps never before has so small a volume attracted so much attention!" Caroline Austen remarked.[58] James Edward began to get correspondence from all over England and America from people who had been affected by the portrait of his aunt. "These letters afforded him much pleasure and not a little surprise," his daughter recalled later. "Until that period he had not realized to how large a number of readers, and in what a high degree, the Aunt to whom he as a boy and a young man had been so warmly attached, had also become a living, though an unseen friend."[59] Well, she was *their* aunt, too, now.

Much to the family's surprise, there was demand not only for an immediate reprint but for more information, especially about Austen's juvenile writing and her unpublished works, which had been mentioned only in passing by James Edward. The rapidly produced second edition included a significant amount of extra material: the tiny play *The Mystery*, more letters (including the one to Martha that had been saved by being given away to Miss Quincy, the American enthusiast), the whole of "The Watsons" (named thus at its first appearance by James Edward), a paraphrase of "Sanditon," and the cancelled chapters of *Persuasion* and "Lady Susan." This last was not from the original, still in Lady Knatchbull's possession, but from a copy made by one of the cousins. James Edward's text wasn't adjusted to accommodate this editorial U-turn, and on the subject of Jane Austen's "betweenities" still read: "It would seem as if she were first taking note of all the faults to be avoided, and curiously considering how she ought not to write before she attempted to put forth her strength in the right direction. The family have, rightly, I think, declined to let these early works be published."[60]

Still, there were limits to what the family was prepared to reveal. Lord Stanhope, who had read Henry Austen's "Biographical Notice" of 1818 carefully enough to remember the mention of some verses "replete with fancy and vigour" that Jane Austen had written on her deathbed, wrote to Bentley asking why James Edward Austen-Leigh had not even referred to them in the *Memoir*. The truth was that the family felt these lines were too frivolous to be broadcast as a last work:

> *When Winchester races first took their beginning*
> *It is said the good people forgot their old Saint*
> *Not applying at all for the leave of St Swithin*
> *And that William of Wykham's approval was faint*[61]

Caroline Austen was annoyed that Lord Stanhope was "raising a hue & cry" about the poem: "Tho' there are no reasons *ethical* or orthodox against the publication of these stanzas, there are reasons of taste—I never thought there was much point in them—they were good enough for a passing thought, but if she had lived she would probably soon have torn them up." This is probably very true, and it is easy to see how the family felt the light tone of the verses "would read badly as amongst the few details given, of the closing scene."[62] But its truth was becoming irrelevant, for, as Caroline understood well, there was a sort of Pandora's box effect under way: "Nobody felt any curiosity about [the verses] *then* [when Henry Austen alluded to them in 1818]—but see what it is to have a growing posthumous reputation! we cannot keep any thing to ourselves *now*, it seems."[63]

The family was waking up to the fact that Aunt Jane's ephemera, if not of any obvious importance to them, were of great interest to readers and publishers and that "an unabated interest is still taken in every particular that can be told about her," as James Edward said in the preface to the second edition of his book. Bentley reissued all Austen's novels in 1870, then brought out a lavish collected edition in 1882, on special, weighty paper, with many "extras" (including the *Memoir*, now treated as a key text), calling it "The Steventon Edition." A burst of other editions followed, from deluxe and copiously illustrated to a sixpenny series; by 1892, you could buy a Jane Austen novel in dozens of formats, including a set that stretched out the oeuvre to ten volumes and was reprinted five times in as many years.

The *Memoir* was almost universally welcomed as a comforting verification of what readers had hoped, that Jane Austen's humor and irony, unlike that of later Victorian novelists, arose from a contented mind and life "of perfect calm." "It is always a pleasure to know that any popular writer *was* what he or she 'must have been,'" R. H. Hutton wrote in the *Spectator*,[64] in a neat example of a circular argument. Anne Thackeray was just as convinced that Austen's life had been "touching, sweet and peaceful" and that her character shared "the harmlessness of a dove."[65] "As we turn from the story of Jane Austen's life to her books again, we feel more than ever that she, too, was one of these true friends who belong to us inalienably—simple, wise, contented, living in others, one of those whom we seem to have a right to love."

But the *Memoir* also prompted thoughtful readers to question the likeliness of James Edward Austen-Leigh's portrait, set against the works. In a long and critically searching essay in 1870, Richard Simpson objected that it was wrong to see Austen as a miniaturist rather than a social critic and skilled ironist, and the novelist Margaret Oliphant complained that Austen-Leigh had completely overlooked "the fine vein of feminine cynicism which pervades his aunt's mind." In a pointed comment on the biographer's generally apologetic tone, she also blamed him for seeming "half-ashamed to have it known that [Jane Austen] was not just a young lady like the others, doing her embroidery."[66] Two distinct camps were forming, one containing readers like Mrs. Oliphant, who were keen to celebrate Austen's mental distinctiveness and artistry, the other—much, much bigger—of those who took comfort in such an artist being *just like the rest of us*.

Public interest in Austen's life was stirred further by the publication of the letters that Cassandra had left to Fanny Knight, which on her death in 1882 passed to her son, Edward Knatchbull-Hugessen, Lord Brabourne. Within two years, Brabourne had got them into print in a handsome two-volume edition, published by Bentley and with a dedication to Queen Victoria (despite her carelessness of *Emma*). Lord Brabourne clearly had no scruples about printing his great-aunt's private correspondence; James Edward Austen-Leigh, Anna Lefroy, and Caroline Austen had all died in the previous decade, so they never discovered how much had been withheld from them by Fanny Knatchbull.

Though it was still very much a book produced by the family and took liberties with the text (removing possible coarseness, for example), Brabourne's edition was unusual for presenting Austen as a legitimate subject for curiosity and speculation. This was very different from the approach of James Edward Austen-Leigh, who only ten years earlier had been so keen to reveal less, not more, than he had discovered about his aunt. Brabourne relied heavily on "stuffing," providing a lengthy biographical and critical introduction (at 111 pages, not far short of James Edward's whole book) and filling his notes with details of genealogies and county gossip that may have proved invaluable to later editors but which did not impress contemporary readers much. Mrs. Humphry Ward, reviewing the book in *Macmillan's Magazine*, laid into Brabourne not just for being criminally boring, ponderous, and "wandering" as editor but for choosing to publish Austen's letters at all: "The virtue of literary reticence is fast becoming extinct," she wrote. "We have almost indeed forgotten that it is a virtue at all."[67]

The next generation of Austens, Austen-Leighs, Knights, Lefroys, and Hubbacks were numerous, had no personal knowledge of Jane Austen, and were naturally less concerned about issues of privacy or propriety as time went on. The manuscripts and relics that had been dispersed far and wide among them began to acquire potential monetary value, and soon after the publication of the *Letters*, Lord Brabourne had no qualms about getting rid of the originals. He did so singly at first, perhaps to test the market. "I have no doubt I can let you have another letter of Jane Austen for £5," he wrote to a dealer in 1891. "Most of these letters are signed only 'J.A' altho' they are undoubtedly genuine, & I would willingly add a written statement that I know them to be so." He reported that the only manuscript he possessed was "Lady Susan," which the author had given to "her favourite niece," his mother (not exactly true—Cassandra had given it), and that he was thinking of including it in a Sotheby's sale, "unless I shall be previously tempted by a private offer."[68]

The frontispiece to volume one of the *Letters* was a photograph of a full-length portrait of a young girl, bearing the legend "Portrait of Jane Austen by Zoffany." It belonged to a cousin of Brabourne, the Reverend John Morland Rice, and had been given to him by a friend, Thomas Harding Newman, who had it from his stepmother, who in turn had been given the portrait by a cousin of Jane Austen, Colonel Thomas Austen of Kippington in Kent. When Colonel Austen made the gift in 1817, he told Mrs. Harding Newman that the subject was the young Jane Austen, having inherited it with the contents of his mother's house; so "family tradition" about the identification was strong.[69]

The portrait was accepted at face value for many years and after its first publication in 1882 was reproduced and copied almost as widely as were images derived from the 1870 Cassandra/Andrews portrait. Of the two, it is the far more attractive picture, but many recent commentators have cast doubt on the identification, mostly on grounds of costume and the lack of any documentary evidence or references to such a painting being made. On the latest attempt to sell it as "a portrait of Jane Austen," in the spring of 2007, it failed to reach its reserve price and was withdrawn. None of these issues clouded the first appearance of the portrait in print in 1882, however, and its ownership on the *Letters* side of the family rather accentuated the sense of two camps forming, each with equal claim to be the heirs of the author, but not entirely in tune with each other. And whoever the Rice Portrait is of, it has been accepted as a portrait of the young

Jane Austen for such a long time now as to form part of her iconography by association.

JAMES EDWARD AUSTEN-LEIGH HAD told the story in his *Memoir* of how the verger of Winchester Cathedral in the 1860s, puzzled by the number of people who wanted to know the whereabouts of "Jane Austen's tomb," had asked a visitor, "Pray, Sir, can you tell me whether there was anything particular about that lady?" It was the last date at which such ignorance would be excusable.

In the few years between the publication of his book and his death, James Edward Austen-Leigh used some of the proceeds from the *Memoir* to have a memorial tablet erected in the aisle of Winchester Cathedral as a sort of vertical postscript to the black marble slab of Jane's gravestone, and, presumably, as a help to those lost tourists. "Jane Austen / known to many by her writings," it began, clarifying the gravestone's reticence. By the turn of the century, an anonymous writer in the *Church Quarterly Review* remarked that "in 1870 the love for [Austen's] writings was the possession of a select but limited circle, [but] in 1900 every man of intellectual pretensions either likes to read her books or thinks it necessary to apologize if he does not."[70] The *Memoir* may have been intended to resolve "the vexed question between the Austens and the Public," but in fact James Edward and his sisters had opened the floodgates to speculation and curiosity about their aunt. She was public property and on her way to becoming a national treasure.

# CHAPTER 5

# Divine Jane

THE NOVELIST MARGARET OLIPHANT MADE SEVERAL SHREWD remarks in her review of Austen-Leigh's *Memoir* in 1870, at the very beginning of the burgeoning of Austen's fame. Austen-Leigh had sought to impress readers with his aunt's personal and professional modesty; his (unsurprising) view was that she had not got her due during her lifetime. Mrs. Oliphant wondered rather how the author had subsequently achieved wider recognition: "To the general public ... it is scarcely to be expected that books so calm and cold and keen, and making so little claim upon their sympathy, would ever be popular." She was surely right in thinking that Austen's novels, as novels, were unlikely candidates for mass consumption and global fame, that there was a great deal about them, in fact, that was uncompromising and pokerishly unbending, that their surface satisfactions hid other agendas, too privately interesting to the author to impel her to point them out. But Mrs. Oliphant was also right that such considerations would make very little difference to the growth of Austen's popularity. The widening audience was not for the novels so much as for the novels in combination with "Miss Austen" and, increasingly, "Jane."

Several new biographies of Austen appeared in the 1880s and '90s, all heavily derivative of the *Memoir*, and in 1883 a Harvard under-graduate won a prize for his dissertation on Austen's novels, the first time the author had been studied in the academy. Another American, Oscar Fay Adams (a friend of the poet James Russell Lowell), was the only one of the new biographers who attempted to do some original research and was the first to travel around the sites significant to Austen in England, taking photographs as he went (reproduced in the second edition of his book). Most of his rivals in the field were interested only in recasting the published material to their own taste: Sarah Tytler, the first "unofficial" biographer, filled her book with résumés of the novels, while Sarah Fanny Malden made what she could of the romantic episodes in Austen's life, including the shadowy "seaside ro-mance" and a completely apocryphal story, promulgated by Sir Fran-cis Doyle in the 1880s, of how Austen had once been engaged to a naval officer (à la *Persuasion*) and had been due to meet him on a walking tour of Switzerland with her father and sister when news came of his death: "The story adds that the young officer had over-walked himself, and became so alarmingly ill on his way that he had been carried to a cottage, where he lay for many days between life and death, incapable of communicating with the outer world until just before his death, when he rallied sufficiently to give the Austens' ad-dress to those who were nursing him."[1] . . . and so forth, and so on, a complete fiction. Even Adams, with his quasi-scientific approach, felt the need for a softening process to go on, stating his aim as "to place [Austen] before the world as the winsome, delightful woman that she really was, and thus to dispel the unattractive, not to say forbidding, mental picture that so many have formed of her."[2]

In 1885, Jane Austen made it into the *Dictionary of National Bi-ography*, an honor not granted to Elizabeth Inchbald or Charlotte Smith. The article was written by Leslie Stephen, the editor of the project, who kept his account brief and brisk, outlining Austen's life, career, and critical reception without deviating into the admiration "even to fanaticism" that he noted "of innumerable readers." His em-phasis is on scale: her understanding of "the precise limits of her own powers" (cue the "little bit of Ivory") and how, within her tiny world, she is "flawless." His characterization, derived from the only readily available sources, Austen-Leigh's *Memoir* and Brabourne's *Letters* (which Stephen judges "trivial" and affording "no new facts"), follows them in lauding her most mediocre accomplishments—"[She] could sing a few simple old songs in a sweet voice, and was remarkably dextrous with her needle"—and thinking her art "unconscious." But Stephen's coolly appraising tone, that of the men's-club cabal that ran London literary life in the 1880s and '90s, and his pivotal position in that influential society, admitted Austen, like a guest on the Savile's annual ladies' night, to a different locus of appreciation. As James Edward Austen-Leigh had noted of his aunt's preeminent popularity among a group of "well-known literary men" gathered at a country house, she appeared to have "the power of attracting powerful minds."[3]

It was important to Austen's growing status that she was open to such "discovery" and that it could be made to reflect flatteringly on the discoverer. James Edward Austen-Leigh's view of who appreciated Jane Austen best during her lifetime had been an emphatic restatement of what his father had written, that "to her family alone / Her real & genuine worth was known." Reflecting on "how coldly her works were first received, and how few readers had any appreciation of their peculiar merits,"[4] James Edward claimed all the credit of perspicacity for the family: "If they had known that we, in our secret thoughts, classed her with Madame d'Arblay or Miss Edgeworth, or even with some other novel writers of the day whose names are now scarcely remembered, they would have considered it an amusing instance of family conceit":

To the multitude her works appeared tame and commonplace, poor in colouring and sadly deficient in incident and interest. It is true that we were sometimes cheered by hearing that a different verdict had been pronounced by more competent judges; we were told how some great statesman or distinguished poet held these works in high estimation; we had the satisfaction of believing that they were most admired by the best judges, and comforted ourselves with Horace's "satis est Equitem mihi plaudere." So much was this the case, that one of the ablest men of my acquaintance said, in that kind of jest which has much earnest in it, that he had established it in his own mind, as a new test of ability, whether people *could* or *could not* appreciate Miss Austen's merits.[5]

This idea (generated by Austen-Leigh's friend R. H. Cheney) of Austen appreciation being some kind of "test" or benchmark of taste and intellect had irresistible appeal and featured prominently in many reviews of the *Memoir*. But the whole passage, with its insistence on "we and they," was the strongest possible foundation for a literary cult emerging around Austen that addressed the club mentality rather than the subject's actual achievements. Rather like a reversal of the Groucho Marx quip, "I don't want to join a club that will accept me as a member," the idea of a society of Austen appreciators self-selected for their superior discrimination held out a way to join a band of people linked by complacency over their own taste. Her snob value was guaranteed by this formula, and by 1894, George Saintsbury was confident that "a fondness for Miss Austen" could be considered "itself a patent of exemption from any possible charge of vulgarity."[6]

As this supposedly exclusive interest spread, Mrs. Oliphant's wonder "that books so calm and cold and keen . . . would ever be popular" was borne out by the books themselves having to adapt to the requirements of a mass market. Just as "Jane Austen" had become "Jane," the texts on their own no longer seemed suitable vehicles for what could be read into them, and late-nineteenth-century, post-*Memoir* editions of Austen increasingly introduced illustrations—however poor or inappropriate—as decoration and to some extent *distraction* from the novel in hand. Austen's characters had inspired such widespread affection by this date that there was a craving to give them a concrete shape, to "fix" the best-loved of them in the public mind's eye, in the way that modern film and television versions of the novels vie with one another through more and more ingenious or desperate casting to get just the "right" Emma Woodhouse or Elizabeth Bennet or Anne Elliot, or the right one for the audience of the moment. After a number of pre-Raphaelite-style illustrated editions in the 1870s and '80s (the Routledge *Emma* has an interestingly Ford Madox Brown–ish look), the 1890s saw a burst of incontinently decorated versions, from those by Edmund H. Garrett for the American market to Chris Hammond's pen-and-ink pictures for George Allen, and the brothers C. E. and H. M. Brock's separate sets of pictures for Macmillan and Dent. All tended toward sentimental caricature, and there was no attempt at historical accuracy—one reviewer in 1903 complained with justice that the J. M. Dent illustrations made the characters "look rather as if they were dressed up for acting in their poke-bonnets, short waists, high stocks, and pantaloons."[7]

The 1894 Allen and Macmillan edition of *Pride and Prejudice*, with 160 illustrations by Hugh Thomson, showed what commercial potential was locked into the presentation of Austen's novels. Thomson didn't just impose his own mark on everything in the book (he even redrew the lettering of the title page) but redrew the boundaries between the author's ownership of a text and an interpreter's, abducting *Pride and Prejudice* into the land of kitsch. It was an instant success: Thomson's super-fussy fine pencil work, the blandly interchangeable faces he gave to all the "attractive" females (whose heads are much smaller than anyone else's), and the exaggerated physiognomies of the "comic" characters proved immensely popular; the edition sold 11,500 copies in its first year and was reprinted countless times until the middle of the following century. These were far higher sales than any previous edition of the novel and earned more money for the illustrator than the author or her estate had ever seen.[8] Though not universally admired (E. M. Forster called them "lamentable"), Thomson's drawings have acquired a "classic" status of their own, and an extensive set of printers' first proofs from his *Pride and Prejudice* hang now in the sanctum of all things Austen, the Jane Austen House Museum, as if they represent an officially sanctioned way to visualize the story.

The edition that was so stuffed with Thomson's decorations was also notable for a preface, by George Saintsbury, which revealed the spectacle of a respected critic and academic indulging in sentimental reverie about Austen's characters and confiding that Elizabeth Bennet was at the top of his list of fictional heroines that "no man of taste and spirit" could help falling in love with and wanting to marry.[9] In the distinction he drew (pace Walt Whitman) between "loving by allowance" and "loving with personal love," Saintsbury let slip a new word:

> In the case of the not very numerous authors who are the objects of the personal affection, it brings a curious consequence with it. There is much more difference as to their best work than in the case of those others who are loved "by allowance," by convention, and because it is felt to be the right and proper thing to love them. And in the sect—fairly large and yet unusually choice—of Austenians or Janites, there would probably be found partisans of the claim to primacy of almost every one of the novels.[10]

Janites, or "Janeites" as the spelling was adapted, now had a name and a banner under which to rally.

Leslie Stephen had commented acidly as early as 1876, "I never . . . knew a person thoroughly deaf to humour who did not worship Miss Austen. [Hers] seems to be the very type of that kind of humour which charms one large class of amiable persons; and Austenolatry is perhaps the most intolerant and dogmatic of literary creeds."[11] The coining of the term "Janeite" by Saintsbury in 1894 showed how widespread and mainstream Austen fandom had become by then, far surpassing the sentimental cult of any other writer. Several influential middlebrow commentators seemed to have entirely lost their heads over the female paragon who had emerged from the biography; Austen Dobson and Richard Brimley Johnson both gushed about her charm, and E. V. Lucas was delighted to see the spirit of criticism "disconcerted and defeated in the presence of the 'divine chit-chat' of this little lady."[12] Lucas said there was "no middle way" with Austen; you either idolized or ignored her, a formula that easily modulated from an argument about taste to a statement of belief. The American novelist and critic W. D. Howells, himself an ardent Janeite, remarked in 1890 on the transition that was taking place: "The story of 'Pride and Prejudice' has of late years become known to a constantly, almost rapidly, increasing cult, as it must be called, for the readers of Jane Austen are hardly ever less than her adorers: she is a passion and a creed, if not quite a religion."[13]

Religious imagery began to appear everywhere, from Austen's books being frequently described as "sacred" and "immortal" and her name "hallowed," to a passage in *Persuasion* being called "one of the very sacred things of literature."[14] Howells was the first to name the author "the divine Jane,"[15] and though he meant it semisatirically, the sobriquet gained immediate currency. In 1900, the Earl of Iddesleigh proposed a magazine entirely devoted to Jane Austen and, in an article titled brazenly "The Legend of St Jane," talked of his "worship" at various "sacred spots." By the early years of the new century even the distinguished academic A. C. Bradley felt free to presume when he lectured to a group of Cambridge undergraduates "that, like myself, you belong to the faithful"[16] and that "the faithful enjoy comparing notes," while Saintsbury, who was professor of English literature at Edinburgh, had by 1913 disintegrated to the point of declaring himself proud to be "an Austen Friar, a knight (or at least a squire) of the order of St Jane."[17]

A cult needs relics, pilgrims, a priesthood, a shrine. Austen's first home in Steventon had been demolished in the 1820s, and her last, the cottage at Chawton, was in use as estate workers' tenements and bore little resemblance to the house the author had known. Winchester was the only readily accessible pilgrimage site in the 1890s, and Americans were the first palmers; they laid flowers on the gravestone in the cathedral and wandered up and down College Street, trying to identify the house where Jane Austen had died. Octavius Le Croix, proprietor of the College Street confectionery shop, was so annoyed at being asked by tourists whether or not his was the right building that he petitioned his landlords, Winchester College, to put up a tablet on the outside. "They never buy anything and they waste my time," the disgruntled trader complained to a housemaster's wife. However, a few months later he was asking for the sign to be removed again. The Americans had been silenced, but now he had a new lot of time wasters in the shop, local people asking who Jane Austen was.[18]

Local people might well have been puzzled by the Austen memorial stained-glass window that was installed in Winchester Cathedral in 1900, paid for by public subscription at the suggestion of Austen's American biographer, Oscar Fay Adams. The artist, C. E. Kempe, was not, of course, allowed to represent Austen herself or her creations in the cathedral's glass (however much some Janeites might have dreamed of it), but seems to have been hard pressed to find suitable alternative imagery. His design is so cryptically allusive as to be virtually meaningless: two rows of three figures, including David with his harp, St. John, his gospel open at "In the beginning was the Word" (in Latin); and several of the children of Korah, mentioned in 2 Chronicles 19–20 as spontaneous and joyful praisers of the Lord. If it weren't for a barely legible inscription at the bottom of one panel (in Latin) that translates, "Remember in the Lord Jane Austen / who died July 18th, A.D. 1817," I doubt that anyone would guess what or whom the window commemorates. The presence of St. Augustine at the head is meant to be a big clue, as one guide tells us: "His name, in its abbreviated form, is St Austin."[19] How much better it would have been if church authority and precedent had allowed Kempe to include among the sons of Korah Mrs. Elton with her "apparatus of happiness," the strawberry trug and rustic hat, or Lady Bertram and Pug: both so instantly recognizable.

Rudyard Kipling, a fervent Janeite, regarded Winchester as "the holiest place in England" after Stratford[20] and used to go out of his way to pass through the town on journeys down country. A rollicking quatrain that he published in the 1920s could have provided the cult of Austen, had they sought one, with the words for an anthem, and the nation with an alternative patron saint:

> *Jane lies in Winchester—blessed be her shade!*
> *Praise the Lord for making her, and her for all she made!*
> *And while the stones of Winchester, or Milsom Street, remain,*
> *Glory, love, and honour unto England's Jane!*

Janeites have never fought shy of blasphemous suggestions. David Rhydderch, in 1932, only half-jokingly, compared the author's emergence from "long eclipse" with that of another inspired virgin, the newly canonized Joan of Arc: "Beside her tomb in Winchester, her name is writ on brass; and above, a Latin inscription beneath the harps of David in stained glass points her worth. The Maid of Orleans already looks down upon us; and the day is not far distant when the 'Divine Jane' like patience on a monument smiling at fame, will keep her company."[21]

THE CULT OF DIVINE Jane provoked some violent reactions, none more so than Mark Twain's. Twain found English literary taste and tradition oppressive, and Austen represented the worst of it to him; he thought her "impossible" not just in literary terms, but socially and politically. Ralph Waldo Emerson had had a similarly strong antipathy, accusing Jane Austen of being "sterile in artistic invention, imprisoned in the wretched conventions of English society, without genius, wit, or knowledge of the world."[22] No "3 or 4 Families in a Country Village" or little bits of Ivory for him! Like Emerson, Twain loathed what he perceived as Austen's artificiality and English spinster passionlessness, dismissing her characters as a bunch of "Presbyterians." "I often want to criticize Jane Austen, but her books madden me so that I can't conceal my frenzy from the reader; and therefore I have to stop every time I begin," he wrote to Joseph Twitchell. "Every time I read 'Pride and Prejudice' I want to dig her up and hit her over the skull with her own shin-bone."[23]

Twain didn't encounter Austen's novels under very auspicious circumstances. During his grueling world lecture tour of 1895–96, conducted to raise some quick cash after the bankruptcy in 1894 of his publishing firm, Webster & Co., Twain read *The Vicar of Wakefield* and "some of Jane Austen" on the boat between Wellington and Sydney, and thought them both "thoroughly artificial."[24] A few weeks later, on the long haul from Sydney to Ceylon, he found "the best library I have seen in a ship yet," though that wasn't saying much, as the usual suspects were staring out at him: "I must read that devilish Vicar of Wakefield again. Also Jane Austen."[25] The experience proved decisive, for on the next ship, from Madras to Mauritius, he was relieved to find there was no Austen on board: "Just that one omission alone would make a fairly good library out of a library that hadn't a book in it."[26]

Twain never tired of railing against Austen or (apparently) returning, aghast, to her novels. "Whenever I take up Pride and Prejudice or

Sense and Sensibility, I feel like a barkeeper entering the kingdom of heaven. I know what his sensations would be and his private comments. He would not find the place to his taste, and he would probably say so." This characteristically epigrammatic opener is from an essay on Jane Austen that Twain never published in his lifetime. But Twain took his antipathy to Austen so seriously one can't help seeing it as an inflated response to the "Presbyterianism" he saw in her and his settled dislike of the English. Passing through India on his 1896 tour, between one Austen novel and another, Twain had been disgusted by the British army's refusal to acknowledge the danger to troops of contracting syphilis, of which he witnessed many bad cases. "Then those 70,000 young men go home and marry fresh young English girls and transmit a heritage of disease to their children and grand children," Twain wrote in his diary. "England is the home of pious cant."[27]

The strength of Twain's feelings against Austen was also partly in reaction to those of his friend W. D. Howells, who had become something of a one-man Austenolatry machine. As editor in chief of the *Atlantic Monthly* in the 1870s and editorial writer for *Harper's Monthly* in the following years, Howells kept his fulsome praise of Austen ever before the public. Twain goaded him with letters claiming that he could just about read Poe's prose if he was paid to, but not Jane Austin's [*sic*]: "Jane is entirely impossible. It seems a great pity to me that they allowed her to die a natural death!"[28] Howells said later that Austen was Twain's "prime abhorrence," but that "he forbore withering me with his scorn, apparently because we had been friends so long, and he more pitied than hated me for my bad taste."[29] Perhaps, like the argument between G. H. Lewes and Charlotte Brontë in the 1840s, and like the antipathy that F. R. Leavis felt toward Lord David Cecil a century later, the difference between Twain and Howells was another example of what Ian Watt has called "the total impasse between different personalities which the subject of Jane Austen so perennially provokes."[30]

AUSTEN'S MOST ARDENT FANS and most dispassionate critics in the late nineteenth century were American, including the writer who was later called Austen's literary "son" and heir, Henry James. James knew George Pellew, the young Harvard man who had written the first thesis on Austen, and in a letter to him, with characteristically deferential politeness, referred to the author as "the delightful Jane."[31] His public articulations about Austen aired a much more subtle and discriminating view. In his essay "The Lesson of Balzac," first published in 1905, James conceded that Austen was "one of those of the shelved and safe, for all time," but, like the Brontës (the industry around whom appalled him), she had entered a zone of unreal and disproportionate attention: "This tide has risen high on the opposite shore, the shore of appreciation—risen rather higher, I think, than the high-water mark, the highest, of her intrinsic merit and interest; though I grant indeed— as a point to be made—that we are dealing here in some degree with the tides so freely driven up, beyond their mere logical reach, by the stiff breeze of the commercial."[32]

James's convoluted expression here, and insistence on there being a degree of Austen appreciation that is "merely logical," and others that rise above the author's "intrinsic merit and interest" seems sniffy and ungenerous, but his underlying point was in defense of this—and any—author against forces that prevent him or her from being read in ways that are untrammeled by commerce and celebrity. Overvaluation, he believed, does no one any good, and his chilliest remarks are reserved for that distorting agent, "the special bookselling spirit":

> an eager, active, interfering force which has a great many confusions of apparent value, a great many wild and wandering estimates, to answer for. For these distinctly mechanical and overdone reactions, of course, the critical spirit, even in its most relaxed mood, is not responsible. Responsible, rather, is the body of publishers, editors, illustrators, producers of the pleasant twaddle of magazines; who have found their "dear," our dear, everybody's dear, Jane so infinitely to their material purpose, so amenable to pretty reproduction in every variety of what is called tasteful, and in what seemingly proves to be saleable, form.[33]

James was writing before the dawn of the Jane Austen tote bag and T-shirt, of course, and the salability he refers to was limited to print versions of Austen's novels, magazine fillers, and a very few stage productions. Nevertheless, "pleasant twaddle" about Austen was becoming unavoidable; as Sarah Fanny Malden had remarked in 1889, "those who do appreciate her novels will think no praise too high for them, while those who do not, will marvel at the infatuation of her admirers; for no one ever cares moderately for Jane Austen's works."[34]

The idea that Austen had divided the reading nation was echoed by R. H. Hutton the following year: "It cannot be denied that for a very considerable number of remarkably able men, Miss Austen wields no spell at all, though for those over whom she does wield a spell, she wields a spell of quite curious force." His analysis of Austen's charm addressed the issue of "smallness" as a deliberate choice on the part of the author, which chimes, or fails to, with her readers' temperaments. Austen's artistry, Hutton claimed,

> is a selection of all that is most superficially interesting in human life, of all that is most easily appreciated without going very deep, and an exclusion of all that it takes real wear and tear of spirit to enter thoroughly into. . . . It was hardly possible to find a finer sieve, a more effective strainer for artistic material than such a mind as this, and the result was something exquisitely interesting and attractive to those who liked the fastidious selection of social elements which such a mind instinctively made for itself, and intolerably uninteresting and unattractive to those who loved to brood over the larger enterprises, the deeper passions, the weightier responsibilities, the more massive interests at which Miss Austen hardly glanced except to convince herself that she must leave them to the care of others.[35]

It is Austen's ability to intrigue "remarkably able men," even "statesmen and thinkers," that encouraged Hutton to conclude that what was coming through Austen's "fine feminine sieve" was not simply pap. He pictures those able men turning gratefully from the cares of the real world to Austen's parallel universe, where she had created for the reader "a social world . . . relieved of the bitterest elements and infinitely more entertaining, . . . which rivets the attention without wearying it, and makes life appear far less dreary and burdensome, though also far less laborious, eager, and anxious than it really is." In this delicately altered reality, one could find the most extravagant form of escape.

Had any female writer ever had quite this effect before? "The power of attracting powerful minds" was what James Edward Austen-Leigh had also marveled at, and his friend R. H. Cheney (of "the test") had been "one of the ablest men." None of the factors usually despised in women's literature—the absence of big themes, the love stories, the thoroughly domestic focus—seems to have stood in the way of their appreciation, for they took comfort in perceiving a controlling intelligence behind it: discriminating, generous, critical, and humorous—a "powerful mind" itself. Cultural conservatives took this as evidence, not that women might have greater potential than was usually assumed, but that Austen was some sort of exception, almost an honorary man.

It was no accident that Austen's appeal was recognized by this group during a period of rising feminism and that her verbal restraint and quiet life began to be held up as examples of what the specter of the 1890s "New Woman" was threatening to overthrow. The growing number of educated, independent (but poor) unmarried women in society was a new and worrying phenomenon, a challenge to male dominance of the professions, a threat to sound government if they succeeded in getting the vote, an affront to every traditional value. The birth rate was falling, home life was suffering, and the world was beginning to turn upside down. Jane Austen came in very handily here as a model of a high-achieving woman in an unreformed society who seemed to have been perfectly happy with her lot, who, far from complaining about the conditions of her own existence or the rights of women generally, beamed her cheerful, contented disposition on all and sundry and quietly got on with writing her charming books. If a great writer could cause so little disturbance and make so few demands domestically and professionally, what need ordinary women of any special treatment?

George Saintsbury made the comparison explicit in his preface to *Pride and Prejudice*, where he praised Elizabeth Bennet as having "nothing offensive, nothing *viraginous*, nothing for the 'New Woman' about her, [who] has by nature what the best modern (not 'new') women have by education and experience, a perfect freedom from the idea that all men may bully her if they choose, and that most will run away with her if they can."[36] Elizabeth is a model for all times, not just her own, "not in the least 'impudent and mannish grown.'" "Mannish," a favorite term of abuse toward late-nineteenth-century feminists, is a word Saintsbury used earlier in his essay to distinguish Austen's genius, in which he felt there was "though nothing mannish, much that was masculine." It was an interesting distinction: "mannish" viragos on one side and "masculine" Austen ("somewhat like a man of the world" as the *Englishwoman's Domestic Magazine* had suggested back in 1866) on the other.

But Austen could also be held up as an example by the opposite camp. In her essays and feminist journalism, Millicent Fawcett promoted Austen to independent young women of the working and lower middle class as "an encouragement to them to be reminded how much good work had been done in various ways by women."[37] For once, "work" didn't mean the sewing that had featured so prominently in Leslie Stephen's *DNB* article and that was feebly echoed by E. V. Lucas in his entry on Austen for the eleventh edition of the *Encyclopedia Britannica*: "During her placid life Miss Austen never allowed her literary work to interfere with her domestic duties: sewing much and admirably, keeping house, writing many letters and reading aloud."[38] Fawcett was the first person to treat Austen as a producer of "good work," a devoted sister and a "thoroughly womanly" woman,[39] and addressed her remarks to those very "bachelor girls" who were regularly vilified in the press as unnatural and *oddish*. Descriptions of this demographic turn up time and again phrases that could easily apply to Jane Austen herself, from her "oddish" "bachelor" status and independent earning capacity to the "sharp and critical common sense" that Freud found characteristic of his earliest hysteria patients (see his description of "Anna O" and her "powerful intellect" in *Studies on Hysteria*). And not just the author but her creations: The *Yellow Book*'s condemnatory image of women who "attempt to take the initiative, particularly in marriage, or attempt to assert themselves emotionally"[40] could be aimed exactly at Emma Woodhouse or George Saintsbury's intended, Lizzie Bennet.

*Jane Austen's dramatization of scenes from Samuel Richardson's* Sir
Charles Grandison, *showing her habit of working in a series of small,
hand-folded booklets.*

Jane's father, the Reverend George Austen, who did the most to encourage her early writing.

The letter which Jane's father sent to the publisher Thomas Cadell on 1 November 1797, offering him "First Impressions." Someone at the office has written "declined by Return of Post" along the top.

*The publisher John Murray at about the date when he took Jane Austen onto his prestigious list.*

*A royalty check from Murray to "Miss Jane Austin" for £38 18s 1d earned on sales of* Emma *in 1816.*

*Austen's persistent adviser, the Reverend James Stanier Clarke, in a pastel by John Russell dating from the 1790s.*

Jane's brother Henry in the 1820s. He acted as her agent during her lifetime and literary executor after her death.

Cassandra Austen in middle age, after the death of her beloved sister.

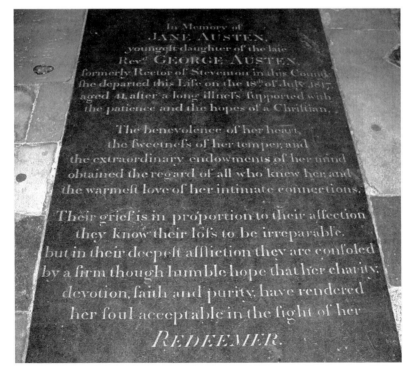

Jane Austen's gravestone in Winchester Cathedral, which omits to mention her writing.

*The publisher Richard Bentley, whose interest in Austen saved the author from years of neglect.*

*The title page of Richard Bentley's 1833 edition of* Sense and Sensibility, *which got Jane Austen back into print in England from the first time since her death.*

SENSE AND SENSIBILITY,

A NOVEL,

BY

JANE AUSTEN.

*Marianne, suddenly awakened by some accidental noise in the house, started hastily up, and with feverish wildness, cried out "Is mamma coming!"*

LONDON:
RICHARD BENTLEY,
(LATE COLBURN & BENTLEY,)
CUMMING, DUBLIN.—BELL & BRADFUTE, EDINBURGH
GALIGNANI, PARIS.
1833.

*Jane's first biographer, her nephew James Edward Austen-Leigh, at around the date of the* Memoir's *publication, 1870.*

*Austen's devoted editor and champion Robert William Chapman in 1949, toward the end of his scholarly work on the author.*

*The house in Chawton, Hampshire, that was Jane Austen's home from 1809 until her death in 1817; a photograph taken in 1902, when the property still belonged to the Knight estate and was divided into three separate dwellings.*

*Dorothy Darnell, founder of the Jane Austen Society* (second right), *with T. E. Carpenter* (right) *outside Chawton Cottage in the late 1940s.*

The "horrid scratch" of Jane by Cassandra, made circa 1810, that her nephew and nieces thought too ugly to put before the public.

A watercolor makeover of the same picture, commissioned from James Andrews in 1869 to create a more attractive image of the author.

Andrews's picture engraved by the firm of Lizars for publication in the Memoir of Jane Austen— "Divine Jane" emerges.

*Another version of Cassandra's sketch from an 1873 publication by an unknown artist, known as the "Wedding-Ring Portrait" for its whimsical addition to the subject's ring finger.*

*A silhouette, said to be of Jane Austen, very similar (but not identical) to the one bought by the National Portrait Gallery on R. W. Chapman's advice in 1948. It could be evidence of a small souvenir industry around Austen starting up in the mid- to late-nineteenth century.*

*Mr. and Mrs. Bennet drawn by Hugh Thomson for the 1894 edition of* Pride and Prejudice. *The illustrations were judged "lamentable" by E. M. Forster, but gave a huge boost to Austen's sales.*

*Félix Vallotton's woodcut portrait of Jane Austen for the* Revue Blanche, *which accompanied the serialization of Félix Fénéon's* Catherine Morland *in 1898.*

*Maximilien Luce's lithograph of the writer and anarchist Félix Fénéon awaiting trial in Mazas Prison in 1894. One of the books on his desk could be* Northanger Abbey, *which he was translating into French.*

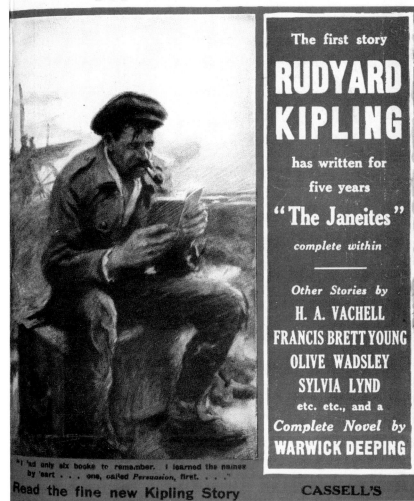

The cover of the magazine which first published Rudyard Kipling's story "The Janeites" in 1924, showing Humberstall reading Persuasion at the edges of the battlefield.

*Girl magazine's version of Jane Austen's early writing career in an issue from 1954, drawn by Eric Dadswell.*

Jane Austen
1775 ~ 1975

Jane Austen's House, Chawton

FIRST DAY COVER

*The Royal Mail commemorative stamps issued to celebrate the bicentenary of Jane Austen's birth in 1975, showing Mr. Darcy, Emma, and Mr. Woodhouse, Catherine Morland, and Henry and Mary Crawford.*

*Greer Garson and Laurence Olivier as Elizabeth Bennet and Darcy (with Frieda Inescort as Miss Bingley) indulge in a little target practice in Robert Z. Leonard's 1940 production of* Pride and Prejudice.

*James McAvoy and Anne Hathaway as Tom Lefroy and Jane Austen decided that their elopement is too fictional to proceed. A still from the 2007 bio-pic,* Becoming Jane.

*Jane Austen hits the big time in 1995:* Entertainment Weekly's *amusing
send-up of the "Austen-mania" effect.*

George Gissing, the author of the 1890s antifeminist best seller *The Odd Women*, thought Austen's novels "very healthy" and recommended them earnestly to his sister as part of a course of self-improvement.[41] Both Austen-Leigh's *Memoir* and Jane Austen's novels were favorites for family reading circles and were considered eminently "safe" for girls. Actual girls showed a degree of skepticism about the relevance of Austen to their lives at the turn of the new century. In an article for *Temple Bar* in 1892 called "A Girl's Opinion on Jane Austen" (presumably solicited from the young author to test the Zeitgeist), Edith Edlmann protested that Austen's warmest admirers were found "not so much among other young people, as among savants and men of letters." It was this "constant affection of the few and cultured [that] still keeps her in the niche of the temple of fame." Emma Woodhouse only becomes bearable, Edlmann believed, "somewhere about chapter fifty, but we think, on the whole, that it was a pity Knightley didn't marry Miss Bates":

> We may congratulate ourselves that we live in the days when High Schools, Extension Lectures, Magazine Clubs and lawn-tennis have superseded sentiment, sensibility, hysterics and mutual confidences. Such *Schwärmerei* we now leave to our German sisters. We also hope that the young lady who could describe herself as "doatingly fond of music, and my friends say I am not devoid of taste" is as obsolete as the atrocities she committed in water-colours, and the fringe and sofa cushions she worked in worsted and beads.[42]

The savants and clubmen, and the ladies who sewed, were all welcome to her.

IN THE LAST YEARS of the nineteenth century, two "Odd" but not entirely "New" women, the sisters Constance and Ellen Hill, packed their notebooks and pencils and hired an old-fashioned chaise (of the kind they believed the author might have ridden in) in order to go in search of "Austen-land," as they whimsically called it. They were collecting material for a new kind of book on Jane Austen, one that involved prolonged personal involvement, close research, and imaginative engagement. Constance wrote the text, and Ellen drew the pictures, a formula they later employed in similar books on Fanny Burney and Maria Edgeworth.

Starting at Steventon, the sisters traveled to Reading, Bath, Lyme Regis, Southampton, Stoneleigh Abbey, Chawton, Godmersham, and Winchester, poking into any building that had a connection with the author and pursuing any descendants of the family willing to speak to them or show them documents and relics. Constance Hill was much more dogged in her researches than anyone had been before, and although her book is horribly gushing and emotional, she captured some interesting information from sources that were just on the brink of disappearing. In Steventon, they happened upon a Wordsworthian "old man leaning on a garden gate" who turned out to be a member of the Littleworth family, son of one of Jane Austen's goddaughters and also related to the Austen ladies' manservant William (he who had accompanied the dog, Link, to and from the dairy at Chawton House). He told them that the pump from the former washhouse was the only remnant of the Austens' home, but that when he was a boy, bricks and rubble from the demolition still littered the field. In Basingstoke, they located the former county ballroom in a building adjacent to the Angel Inn, degraded in function to a hay loft, but still just recognizable as "a reception room of importance; . . . when we push aside the litter beneath our feet, the fine even planking of a dancing-floor appears."[43] Constance Hill was keen to emphasize the magical aspects of these discoveries, with sudden revelations, miraculous beams of light, and inexplicable coincidence all playing their part.

Ellen Hill's contribution to the book was significant, as the many line drawings she made had an essentially documentary purpose, for all their incipient tweeness. Ellen Hill drew as many objects and buildings as she could from life and reconstructed other images from prints, or (as in the case of the hay loft/ballroom) from an imaginative projection of her own. The vignettes at the ends of chapters were architectural details of stair rails or fireplaces or doorways in buildings that Austen would have known, some of which no longer existed. As a result, although it looks and reads a bit like a children's book, *Jane*

*Austen, Her Homes and Her Friends* contains valuable extra atoms of Austen information and marked the first "heritage" approach to Austen biography.

Part of the appeal of Janeism was its ingrained Englishness, which for cultural and linguistic reasons slowed the dissemination of her works in the non-anglophone world. The few translations that had appeared in the early years, into French, German, Spanish, and Swedish, came and went, and there was a lone Danish translation of *Sense and Sensibility* in midcentury by the Catholic propagandist Carl Karup. Bentley copublished his Standard Novels versions with the Parisian firm Galignani in the 1830s, and the German publisher Tauchnitz included Austen in their British Authors series in the 1860s and '70s, but her presence abroad wasn't backed up by any critical recognition. Politically and ideologically, Austen was unattractive to the anglophobic Danes and the eastern European nations, and the French were inclined to think of her as a "puritan."[44] Sir Walter Scott and his big bow-wow strain was more the thing, and Scott's popularity abroad left little room for other British authors and continued long after his star began to wane at home.

Xenophobic Janeites could take comfort in the thought that Austen's humor was so delicate and gossamer and all that—so finely ironized that no translation could reproduce it; even the best translation ensured that the essential "Jane" remained where she had always remained in life, in England. They would not have been pleased to discover one of the oddest corners into which Austen penetrated in the last decade of the century, the anarchist cells of Paris. Cells in two senses: Félix Fénéon, poet, essayist, and bomber, was both a member of a tight-knit group of political extremists and an inmate of the Mazas prison for four months. It was there that he came upon Jane Austen.

Fénéon, an influential promoter of Postimpressionist art (a term he coined), earned his living as a clerk at the War Ministry in Paris but led a double life as an anarchist. He was an associate of several notorious figures: François Claudius Koenigstein, known as "Ravachol," the terrorist martyr who was guillotined for attempting to blow up two judges in 1892; Émile Henry, another bomber who ended up on the guillotine; and Laurent Tailhade, who was injured in a bombing at the Café Foyot the following year and who said memorably after the event, *"Qu'importe l'acte, si le geste est beau?"* (What does the act matter, if the gesture is noble?). Fénéon was one of those suspected of planting the Café Foyot device, and when his office at the Ministry was searched, the police found ten detonators and a vial of mercury. The suspect claimed that they had belonged to his late father, but this didn't prevent his arrest under new legislation against association of malefactors, and he was sent to prison to await trial. The papers made a great deal of this *"arrestation sensationnelle"* of the civil servant and intellectual, and, quizzed by reporters, Fénéon's friend Stéphane Mallarmé didn't help by claiming "there are no better detonators than his articles."

The show trial of thirty suspected anarchists took months to prepare, during which time Fénéon was kept in solitary confinement at Mazas. Probably the worst aspect of his incarceration was that he was refused access to periodicals or books from outside, due to the political nature of his crime, and had to rely on the prison library, in which the only works of literature (considered innocuous, as they were by women) were some novels of George Sand and a book called *Northanger Abbey* by a dead Englishwoman. The book's "pithy style and keen insights on human nature"[45] charmed Fénéon, who recognized in the author a sort of fellow traveler, who could expose middle-class manners and mores with a few deft strokes, to devastating satirical effect. Perhaps like a buried bomb itself, *Northanger Abbey* had detonated in the mind of a very receptive reader. Fénéon's friend, the American poet Stuart Merrill, was permitted to bring a dictionary into the prison, and the inmate sat down to make a translation. Unlike the poems and treatises written by another anarchist detainee, Charles Chatel, Fénéon's translation was not thought to be inflammatory and escaped confiscation.

At the "Trial of the Thirty," which opened in August 1894, Fénéon ran rings around the judge and prosecutor with his calm, insolent wit—an example is when the judge accused him of surrounding himself with the known anarchists Cohen and Lavel, and Fénéon replied, "You can't surround yourself with two people. You need at least three."[46] Perhaps he had been honing his "pithy style" on that of

Jane Austen; certainly Mallarmé, called as a witness, testified that "he is above using anything, other than literature, to express his thoughts." The case ended with acquittal for everyone except three burglars, and Fénéon, kicked out of his job at the War Office, became editorial secretary of the influential literary magazine *La Revue blanche*.

Over the next four years, Fénéon finished and "meticulously refined" his translation of *Northanger Abbey*,[47] aided by his friend, the English poet John Gray, Oscar Wilde's former lover and the man who was thought to be the model for fiction's arch-aesthete, Dorian Gray. Wilde himself was languishing in Reading Gaol at exactly the same time, and, in an odd coincidence, dreamed of providing a better stock of books for the "poor imprisoned fellows I live with" that would include "about a dozen good novels. Stevenson's, some of Thackeray . . . Jane Austen (none here)."[48] Austen seemed a good choice for those in extremis. Across the Channel, Fénéon's *Catherine Morland* was published in serial form in the *Revue blanche* in 1898, the first French translation to replicate rather than simply exploit Austen's text, reproducing as nearly as possible the elegant cadences and comical end-stops of her prose: "*Personne qui ait jamais vu Catherine Morland dans son enfance ne l'aurait supposée née pour être une héroïne,*" he begins, clearly relishing the passages, such as the defense of the novel in chapter 5, where Austen's authorial voice comes through most clearly:

> *Las! Si l'héroïne d'un roman n'est pas patronnée par l'héroïne d'un autre roman, de qui pourra-t-elle attendre protection et égards? Laissons aux rédacteurs de revues le soin d'incriminer toute effusion d'imagination et de déplorer, sur un mode marmiteux, les riens qui font maintenant gémir les presses. Ne désertons pas notre propre cause. Nous sommes une caste fort décriée.*

The issue before the serialization began, an article on Austen appeared in *La Revue blanche* by Fénéon's friend and colleague Théodore Duret. It assumed that the reader had no knowledge of her at all and relied for its few biographical details not on the *Memoir*, but on Henry's 1832 "Biographical Notice" that prefaced all the early editions of *Northanger Abbey*. Duret promoted the idea of Austen as an isolated, natural genius, *"développée spontanément, sur elle-même"* (developed spontaneously on her own), and also stressed her precocity, an impression immensely enhanced by the woodcut that accompanied the article, derived from the Rice Portrait, which made Austen look more alert and knowing than the subject of the painting, but every bit as young. The artist, Félix Vallotton, was well known in avant-garde periodicals of the day for his striking expressionist style, though his subjects were usually political and contemporary: police brutality, anarchist protests, and street scuffles.

Duret's accompanying article was a significant piece of criticism, and not only because it singled out aspects of Austen's craft that hadn't been noticed before, but because being "taken up" in Paris by the *Revue blanche* gave Austen the imprimatur of an exclusive and demanding intellectual elite. Duret and Fénéon were at the heart of the French avant-garde. Fénéon himself, apart from being Georges Seurat's first and most enthusiastic promoter, was also the first publisher of James Joyce in French. His associates at the *Revue blanche*, and its successor, the *Nouvelle revue française*, included Mallarmé, Édouard Vuillard, Henri de Toulouse-Lautrec, and André Gide, who later wrote of Austen, "her horizon is limited, a little empty, but what delicacy in her delineation of feelings! Jane Austen may not be animated by any mighty demon, but on the other hand, what unfailing, what sure understanding of others."[49] Politically, Austen appealed to Fénéon as a critic of the bourgeoisie; intellectually, she represented a stringent antiromanticism. Like her *Yellow Book*–ish makeover by Monsieur Vallotton (so much classier than the insipid transformation effected by Andrews and Lizars in 1869), Austen was here taking her place among the cosmopolitan, multicultural icons that appealed most to the artists and intellectuals shaping the coming age.

THE AUSTEN FAMILY, IN its many branches, continued to exert a strong influence on how the author was presented to the public, and in the generation following James Edward Austen-Leigh and his sisters produced a flurry of books on their illustrious great- and great-great-aunt. Catherine Anne Hubback's son, John, collaborating with his daughter Edith in 1906, shifted the biographical focus to "Jane Austen's sailor brothers" in a book of that title. It included the previously unpublished letters from Jane to Frank and Charles, a remarkable photograph of Frank in his old age, and the first publication of Cassandra's original sketch of Jane. The history of Frank's and Charles's naval careers—which touched on Trafalgar and the siege of Corunna—was a salutary reminder that life in the Austen family during the Napoleonic Wars wasn't all spillikins and satin stitch.

Mary Augusta Austen-Leigh followed up a 1911 monograph about her father, James Edward, with *Personal Aspects of Jane Austen* in 1920, which revisited a great deal of the material in the *Memoir of Jane Austen* and added to the biographical stock by printing extracts from Jane's marginalia in Goldsmith's *History of England*, the Steventon schoolroom copy of which had passed down to her. Mary Augusta used her authority as a blood relative of the subject to enforce what had previously been surmises; she insisted that Cassandra Austen "kept only those [letters] which she considered so totally devoid of general interest that it was impossible anyone should, at any time, contemplate their publication" and quibbled with a critical biography published in France, Léonie Villard's *Jane Austen: sa vie et son œuvre*,[50] over the degree and intensity of Jane Austen's religious feelings. On the whole, though, Mary Augusta favored leniency toward the interloper, seeing it as a patriotic motive not to pursue her criticisms too far "at the present time, when a strong desire is felt that the bonds between our nearest Ally and ourselves should be drawn closer, those formed by a mutual study of each other's literature can hardly be neglected."[51] This wasn't fanciful; the proliferation of translations of Austen into French in the interwar period (and another big postwar surge in the late 1940s) was second only to the wave of interest following the Austen film adaptations of the 1990s.

Mary Augusta's book seems retrogressive compared with the biography published seven years earlier by her brother, William, and nephew Richard Arthur Austen-Leigh, a well-known scholar of King's College Cambridge. *Jane Austen: Her Life and Letters, A Family Record* rather turned James Edward's method on its head by seeking to be as documentary, factual, and unsentimental as possible, using family authority in the service of biographical accuracy, not to court popularity. Some sort of example was needed of "rational" appreciation of Austen when even professors of English, such as A. C. Bradley, could be found swooning over the author and her creations, saying of Lizzie Bennet, "I was meant to fall in love with her, and I do."[52] Richard Arthur Austen-Leigh took the "scientific" approach even further with the publication of *Austen Papers 1704–1856* in 1942, a fascinating dossier (if rather stark, in literary terms) of family letters, accounts, wills, and contracts. Such documentation was obviously more valuable as a means to understanding Jane Austen in the twentieth century than praise of her dexterity and vague surmises about her niceness; but it's interesting that the movement away from "dear aunt Jane" started in the family and was aimed not at the general reader but at the critical establishment.

BY THE TIME OF the Great War, "Jane" had come to represent qualities that not only defined a sorely threatened English culture but held out the means to repair it. Books were one of very few solaces for men at the front; they were easily acquired from home through the efficient Field Postal Service and constituted one of the quickest means of escape. Paul Fussell, in *The Great War and Modern Memory*, has written about the popularity of eighteenth-century authors among soldiers in the trenches; their books offered "an oasis of reasonableness and normality, a place one could crawl into for a few moments' respite."[53] Edmund Blunden acknowledged that the copy of Edward Young's *Night Thoughts* that he had with him at Passchendaele "kept me from despair"—"I felt the benefit of this grave, intellectual voice, speaking out of a profound eighteenth-century calm"—and Alec Waugh felt similarly grateful in the same battle to have just received a copy of Matthew Prior's poems. The effect was two-edged: Augustan writing comfortingly recalled an age of rationality, distant composure, and preindustrial calm, while the act of reading it in the grotesque context of trench warfare, facing mortal danger, generated its own kind of nihilist comedy. As Paul Fussell remarked, "The gross inappropriateness of certain books was part of their value," citing Geoffrey Keynes's choice of Courtney and Smith's *Bibliography of Samuel Johnson* between bursts of fire at Ypres.

Austen was prime among the texts that went to war, and the trenches were full of Janeites. It is not known whether Siegfried Sassoon had with him any of his extraordinary Austen collection, but he owned a rare copy of *Emma* (one of only four surviving of the 1816 edition pirated in Philadelphia), a first edition of *Northanger Abbey* and *Persuasion*, and early editions of the other novels, all of which had belonged to Harris Bigg-Wither's sister, Elizabeth.[54] Perhaps he felt, like Austen's future editor and scholarly champion, Robert William Chapman, that "to handle a first edition again" in the theater of war could re-create the sense of home.

At the outbreak of the war, Chapman had taken with him on active service three editions of James Boswell's *Journal of a Tour of the Hebrides* to collate, a task that he hoped would help block out the realities of life as a temporary gunner with the Royal Garrison Artillery in Salonika. "Upright in his stifling burrow,"[55] surrounded by the sights and sounds of modern warfare, the cultivated life Chapman had left behind in Oxford came back to him more in the form of hallucinations than memories:

> The graces of civilisation and the delights of learning are far from me now. But my nomadic and semi-barbarous existence is still solaced by a few good books; and the best odes of Horace, the best things in Boswell or Elia, often awake memories of Attic nights. Memories and visions in which gleaming mahogany and old morocco are seen darkling in a haze of smoke, and an old man in his big chair by the fire draws forth, for my pleasure and his, the hoarded treasures of his rich old mind.[56]

The scholarly Chapman was subsisting on literary scraps, reading an Alfred Austin anthology over and over again and poring over his copies of Boswell "in the hope of finding a corruption in the text." "If there still be any Gentlemen of England," he wrote in Macedonia, "who sit at home in ease, and hop like elderly sparrows from shelf to shelf of their well-appointed libraries, tell them they do not know what a book can be."[57] Though Johnson and Boswell had been his main scholarly interests before the war, by the end of his term of active service, Chapman had begun to make notes for a school edition of *Emma*. The edition was never finished but provided much-needed entertainment and distraction for the lonely bookworm. His notes show him calculating the distances between Hartfield and Randalls, Hartfield and Donwell, and Highbury and London, not just as if they were all equally real places that he could map, but as if he could travel to that world and inhabit it.[58]

The therapeutic potential of Austen's novels in wartime was recognized on a wider scale when they were chosen as "salubrious reading for the wounded" and prescribed as an aid to convalescence for the most severely shell-shocked soldiers. Thus *Pride and Prejudice*, *Emma*, and *Sense and Sensibility* appeared at the top of a graded "Fever-Chart" drawn up for use in military hospitals by an Oxford don exempted from military service, H. F. Brett-Smith, a history fellow at Oriel College and author of the slim volume *Poems of the North* (1912). In this way, Austen's novels can be said to have seen active service themselves, and it is odd to think of how many damaged and dying men in field hospitals and convalescent homes might have swum in and out of consciousness to the sound or the memory of the words of "Divine Jane."[59]

Austen's symbolic significance in the minds of distressed English servicemen at the front was given its most elaborate expression in Rudyard Kipling's story of the trenches, "The Janeites," written in 1924. The edition of *The Story-Teller* in which it first appeared had as cover illustration a picture of a soldier sitting on a box in a battlefield, engrossed in reading an Austen novel. The legend next to it was " 'THE JANEITES' . . . The first story RUDYARD KIPLING has written for five years." Kipling's strange narrative, like several others in the 1926 collection *Debits and Credits* where it was published, has a frame-narrative set in an imaginary Freemason's lodge, "Lodge Faith and Works, 5837" (the author was a Freemason from his youth and founder of two lodges connected with the War Graves Commission). A group of Masons who are cleaning the regalia of their lodge one Saturday in 1920 get into conversation about their experiences in the trenches. Humberstall is a shell-shocked ex–private soldier, discharged in 1917 "after the dump went up at Eatables," who returned to the front voluntarily in preference to staying at home with his agitated womenfolk—"Not for *me* thank you! till the war was over."[60] He recalls the officers whom he served as mess waiter on this second trip to the trenches—Hammick, a former divorce lawyer, and his friend Mosse, a private detective—and how, when Humberstall overheard them conversing about "Jane," he was struck by their change of tone: "She was the only woman I ever 'eard 'em say a good word for. 'Cordin' to them Jane was a nonesuch. *I* didn't know then she was a Society."[61]

Humberstall begins to attend to what they are saying about "Jane" only after a new officer, ignored at first by Hammick and Mosse, reacts to the name with delight: "No sooner 'ad Gander passed that remark than they both shook 'ands with the young squirt across the table an' called for the port back again. It was a password, all right! Then they went at it about Jane—all three, regardless of rank." Another time, when the three officers are lamenting the fact that "Jane" died barren, Macklin, Humberstall's immediate superior, interrupts them with a fifteen-minute lecture on how she did leave lawful issue "in the shape o' one son; and 'is name was Enery James." Amazed at how Macklin gets away with this insubordination, Humberstall bribes him to reveal the "Jane" secret, and is told the password, "Tilneys and trap-doors." When Humberstall uses this phrase in the hearing of an officer, the effect is immediate: He looks at him "through and through" and silently hands over half a dozen Turkish cigarettes.

In order to maintain the flow of patronage, Humberstall pays Macklin for a crash course in "Jane," who, he finds, was a real person, "a little old maid 'oo'd written 'alf a dozen books about a hundred years ago. 'Twasn't as if there was anythin' to 'em, either. *I* know. I had to read 'em." Though Humberstall has to have the books drummed into him and feels that " 'er characters was no *use*! They was only just like people you run across any day," Austen is seen working in him surreptitiously: He soon feels completely familiar with her characters and names four of the guns after them: the Reverend Collins, Miss Bates (a noisy one), General Tilney, and "Lady

Catherine de Bugg." Though Lady Catherine buries Mosse when the position is bombed, and Humberstall is the only Janeite to survive, his knowledge does turn out to be of use, after all; overheard by a nurse semi-raving about Miss Bates, he gets treatment that, it is clear, would have been denied him otherwise: "'Do you know what you're sayin'?' she says, an' slings her bony arm round me to get me off the ground. 'Course I do,' I says, 'an' if you knew Jane you'd know too.' 'That's enough,' says she. 'You're comin' on this train if I have to kill a brigadier for you.'"[62] "There's no one to touch Jane when you're in a tight place," Humberstall concludes. "Gawd bless 'er, whoever she was."

Rudyard Kipling was himself "in a tight place" when he wrote "The Janeites," convalescing on the Riviera from a stomach operation. His chronic gastric pain dated from the loss of his only son, John, in the second battle of Loos in 1916; since then Kipling had devoted himself to writing a memorial history of John's regiment, *The Irish Guards in the Great War.* "The Janeites" marked his return to health, his return to fiction writing, and a new creative phase. As with the scheme of reading provided by H. F. Brett-Smith, "Jane" was showing her curative powers. His story places a love of Austen and her works among different kinds of mutually beneficial social networks: the Masons, of course, but even the war itself, as Humberstall remarks: "In lots o' ways this war has been a public noosance, as one might say, but there's no denyin' it 'elps you slip through life easier. The dairyman's son 'ad done time on Jordan with camels. So he stood us rum an' milk."[63] "Jane" allows the soldiers, in their extremity, to slip easier not just through life, but through death too, amused, comforted, and prepared for any irony—even that of being crushed by a gun named after Lady Catherine de Bourgh.

Not everyone found that "Jane" survived the war with them. When the future novelist L. P. Hartley went up to Balliol in 1915, one of the friends he made among the very thinned-out undergraduate population included Aldous Huxley, later Austen's first screen adaptor. On return to Oxford after two years' home service in the Royal Garrison Artillery, Hartley met another Janeite, the elegant, brilliant Lord David Cecil, with whom he fell deeply and closetedly in love. Cecil's great admiration for and knowledge of Austen spurred on Hartley to try to like the author as well as he could, but in a talk given many years later to the Jane Austen Society (called "Jane Austen and the Abyss"), Hartley related how his feelings for Austen fell off:

> The War came, and as Gunner Hartley I went into the Army, which had its rules and regulations, indeed, but not such as I understood, nor do I think Jane Austen would have understood them, for civilised living had gone by the board. Although I never went overseas, Army life did seem at the beginning a kind of Abyss; a chaos without signposts or landmarks, in which dread and bewilderment reigned. I think that during that time my confidence in Jane Austen as an interpreter of life must have been severely shaken, and though I read some escapist literature, I did not return to her.[64]

It is interesting to see someone not finding Jane Austen a comfort at all, but quite out of key with modern life and unable to answer the needs of a changed world. Undoubtedly, there was a conflation in Hartley's mind between Austen and her charming advocate Cecil (the man who was later often spoken of as Austen's spiritual heir), and the disappointment he felt in the novelist can be seen as a deflection of his painfully chagrined feelings toward the critic, whose engagement to Rachel MacCarthy in 1931 came as one of the most unpleasant shocks of Hartley's life. But Hartley's negative feelings about Austen didn't go away; he later said that he believed Kafka's depiction of consciousness as neurotic and fragmented was "closer to the truth than Jane Austen's" and came to favor fantasy as "a normal medium for Englishmen in our time," enabling them "to escape what they faced"[65]— whatever that might be.

THE FIRST CENTENARY OF Austen's death fell during the war but might not have been marked publicly at all had it not been for the efforts of the devoted Hill sisters, Constance and Ellen, who took it upon themselves to raise funds for the erection of a plaque on the side of Chawton Cottage and the gift of a "Young People's Library" in the author's memory to Steventon village school. This seems to have been more a one-bookcase affair than a whole room, but it delighted Miss Constance Hill. "How sweet the Schoolroom looked with its merry nosegays of country flowers—and the dear children's bright faces," she wrote in thanks to the Manor House, "so in keeping with dear Jane Austen and her life in the simple Parsonage that it was like a beautiful poem!"[66]

At the modest ceremony for unveiling the plaque at Chawton Cottage, Constance Hill had been even further transported: "We, her grateful readers from far and near, were standing on the very spot where Jane sat at her little mahogany desk and brought into being the gentle Fanny Price, the spirited Emma, and the sweet Anne Elliot."[67] A "little company of devotees" listened as Sir Frederick Pollock made a short speech about how it was now possible to record the final judgment on Austen and read a letter from W. D. Howells that reflected on the happy condition of being one of Austen's fans: "She has always been a family cult with us. . . . We talk of her as if she were our living friend, and I do not believe her elect and genial spirit resents our freedom; she must know it is from our grateful love of her."[68]

Howells made a distinction between writers such as Michel de Montaigne, Charles Lamb, and George Borrow, who had "taken the world into their confidence by disclosing themselves," and Austen, who "had commanded our affection because she could not help it, and we had canonised her in her home, as it were, by force."[69] The home in which Austen had been "canonised" was still very much an imaginary one—not the actual house at Chawton, still owned by the Knight family and in use as estate tenements. No one has recorded what the tenants thought of having Ellen Hill's plaque fixed to their outside wall or how they maintained the author's former residence at this date, if they had been aware of its literary significance before the Hills came along. The centennial celebrations at Chawton, so thinly attended, hardly impacted on the life of the village, unlike the mobbing of the Brontë sisters' home village, Haworth, twenty years earlier when the first Brontë Museum had opened, attracting ten thousand visitors to the emergent literary shrine in the summer of 1895 alone.

The fact that the party gathered at Chawton had nothing more substantial to hear than the sentimental effusion of the absent American critic, and that Ellen Hill's Arts-and-Craftsy commemorative plaque had been paid for by "Anglo-American friends," hints at the negligence of the home nation to recognize Austen's significance up to this point. Nowadays, there are whole sections of UK travel guides devoted to "Jane Austen Country" and a sign welcomes you to it when you cross the eastern county boundaries between Hampshire and Berkshire, but in 1917 there was little identification of the writer with a specific part of England. "Jane Austen Country" was rural, certainly, green, pleasant, quiet, and resolutely southern (unlike the wild, windswept, hilltop north country so topographically suitable to the Brontës' kind of writing and sensibilities), but its potency resided in remaining amorphous, and if it had a significant location, one would have had to say it was *in the past* rather than at any coordinates on a map. Ellen Hill had grasped this in her illustration to *Jane Austen: Her Homes and Her Friends* of an old-fashioned fingerpost at a rural junction, reading "To Austen-Land," though she might easily have added an identical pointer in every direction.

The recent film treatments of Austen's novels have gleefully realized the idyll and ideal of England that forms the background to Austen's selectively realistic love stories. It doesn't manifest itself very often in the books, but then it doesn't have to: it is implicit in the author's deep conservatism (deep as in background, as well as profound). She can be devastatingly, minutely realistic about individuals, but society as a whole, or rather the nation that contains it, is exempt from analysis, from cynicism, and from irony. Her eruptions of feeling about it don't disturb the novels for long, but are powerful.

In the early novels, it perhaps shows only in the picturesque passages about the country near Pemberley in *Pride and Prejudice*, but it emerges strongly in the critique of "improvement" in *Mansfield Park*, the sympathy shown in *Persuasion* for sailors dying "in a foreign field," longing for home, and the passage in *Emma* where the strawberry-picking party (a mock-idyll presided over by ultra-bourgeois Mrs. Elton) looks across the Donwell estate to the meadows, river, and farm:

"It was a sweet view—sweet to the eye and the mind. English verdure, English culture, English comfort, seen under a sun bright, without being oppressive."[70]

The sense of how deeply Austen was in tune with "English culture, English comfort" became much stronger during and after the Great War, as the reporting of the centenary celebration foreshadowed. The *Daily Telegraph* mused wistfully on the far removal of Austen's quiet corner of the English countryside "from the present world-conflict," and rejoiced that her themes and method were also worlds away from that of the neurotic moderns: "She needed none of the maddening problems which vex and torment the souls of so many of our modern novelists." Austen could teach these perverse authors a thing or two about how to be a patriotic writer in wartime:

> There is no sound of war in her pages, though she had sailor brothers of distinction, and she lived through the Napoleonic era. All is placid in her Hampshire villages; and the main business of life is to marry off marriageable daughters to eligible young men. But as that produced first-class comedy, we profess ourselves thoroughly satisfied, and gladly take this opportunity of laying—even in the midst of this monstrous upheaval—a little token of our abiding gratitude on her grave in Winchester Cathedral.[71]

Placidity was, of course, much to be wished for, and Austen could provide a placid new postwar world with images of how things had been and could be again: "peaceful sheltered villages and wooded, gently sloping hills carpeted in spring with primrose and anemone, its lanes winding between high hazel hedges that opened now and then to disclose airy Constablesque vistas of sky and distant downland," as Lord David Cecil described it.[72] In 1922, A. B. Walkley wrote of Austen's novels as a place to live, a refuge, even perhaps a convalescent home: "This house of rest, built and endowed by Jane Austen, becomes for those who have once felt the peace of it a second home."[73]

To others, she seemed part of the damage, not the cure. With his very different but no less passionate view of postwar England, D. H.

Lawrence singled out Austen as one of the bad old elements that ought to be washed away:

> In the old England, the curious blood-connection held the classes to-gether. The squires might be arrogant, violent, bullying and unjust, yet in some ways they were at one with the people, part of the same blood-stream. We feel it in Defoe or Fielding. And then, in the mean Jane Austen, it is gone. Already this old maid typifies "person-ality" instead of "character", the sharp knowing in apartness, instead of knowing in togetherness, and she is, to my feeling, thoroughly unpleasant, English in the bad, mean, snobbish sense of the word, just as Fielding is English in the good generous sense.[74]

BEFORE THE GREAT WAR, Robert William Chapman had been a lexi-cographer and editor at the Clarendon Press in Oxford, working on the *New English Dictionary* and a revision of Liddell and Scott's standard Latin grammar, but during his four long years of service he conceived a more significant kind of cultural custodianship, declaring that "to re-store, and maintain in its integrity, the text of our great writers is a pi-ous duty." His job became a vocation, and (inspired by his wife, as we shall see) the writer he turned to as the most deserving of his devotion and skill was Jane Austen. Chapman's Clarendon edition of Austen's novels, published in 1923, was the first complete scholarly edition of any English novelist, employing techniques transposed wholesale from editing of Greek and Latin texts, and giving Austen a unique sta-tus in the new discipline of English Literature and beyond. The seri-ousness with which Chapman treated Austen and her works—so necessary after the depredations of "Janeism"—was pivotal to her estab-lishment as a classic author in the twentieth century.

Chapman was the son of an Episcopalian vicar, born and brought up in Perthshire, who came to Oxford as an undergraduate and spent most of the rest of his life in the city, first at Oriel College, where he was a prize scholar in classics, later at the University Press. Oddly enough for a man who became obsessed with book collecting, he ad-mitted that, as an undergraduate, "I doubt if I knew very well what a folio was," and that it was only the antiquarian interests of the young woman he was to marry that kick-started his career as a collector.[75] This young woman, Katharine Metcalfe, who Chapman excitedly recalled "had bought an *Arcadia* in folio while yet a schoolgirl,"[76] might be said to have been a bit of a collector's item herself. When Chapman met her in 1912, she had taken a first at Lady Margaret Hall and had just started work as a tutor in English at Somerville. She had also embarked on an ambitious project, encouraged by the critic Sir Walter Raleigh (first professor of English literature at Oxford), to undertake a new, textually accurate, edition of *Pride and Prejudice*, of which she had the loan of a first edition.

Metcalfe's *Pride and Prejudice*, published in the year she and Chapman met, was the first to treat Austen's work as a text rather than a story. The typesetting and page layout (including the antiquarian touch of catchwords at the turn of the page) was handsome and sober, there was a substantial introduction, giving an overview of Austen's life and works, and appendices explaining matters of social history, domestic life, and language in the Regency period. There was also a brief chronology of Austen's works and the places she had lived in, a selection of quotes from critics, and textual notes. These were the most significant of Metcalfe's innovations; though the textual variants were very few (no original manuscript, of course, existing), she was the first person to acknowledge that they might be worth recording.[77]

Metcalfe effected "Chapman's real introduction to Jane Austen," as Margaret Lane later wrote in a roundup of his illustrious career. As the couple fell in love, they planned a jointly edited complete works of Austen, using Metcalfe's *Pride and Prejudice* as the model and first volume. Following their marriage in 1913, in line with the university employment regulations of the time, Metcalfe had to give up her fellowship at Somerville, and her career as a don was "briskly cut short."[78] Her freelance career as an editor continued, though; her handwriting is all over the Chapman archives, and in 1923, four months before the publication of her husband's chef d'œuvre, Oxford University Press published a separate edition by her of *Northanger Abbey*, a very odd duplication of effort from one household on one subject from one publisher.[79] Like her 1912 *Pride and Prejudice*, Metcalfe's text of *Northanger Abbey* was incorporated into the Clarendon edition; not that either was recognizable in the new packaging, for, remarkably enough, Chapman didn't mention his wife's contribution to the project anywhere in the published volumes. His description of her *Pride and Prejudice* in his *Bibliography of Jane Austen*, published forty years later, doesn't go far toward rectifying the oversight: "This unassuming edition is equipped with a perceptive introduction and notes, and anticipates the textual rigours of the next item"—"the next item" being Chapman's own *Novels of Jane Austen*.[80] *Anticipates*, not *inspired*. It is only thanks to later scholars such as David Gilson and Kathryn Sutherland that Metcalfe's work has been properly acknowledged at all.

Chapman's landmark edition of Austen was published in five volumes in 1923. It is not clear whether he always envisioned the project going on, as it did, another thirty years, to include all Austen's extant writing and his own bibliography and edition of the Austen-Leigh *Memoir*; in the 1920s he had ruled out the juvenilia as suitable material for publishing, though he felt "Lady Susan," "The Watsons," and "Sanditon" worth his attentions. Through his avidity and busyness on behalf of the dead author and her descendants almost as much as through his scholarship, Chapman quickly became the ultimate authority on his subject. All through the 1920s, he was busy tracking down Austen manuscripts and encouraging the Bodleian and the British Library to buy as many of them as possible. The first twelve pages of "The Watsons" had been generously donated to a Red Cross sale by W. Austen-Leigh in 1915 and bought by Lady Ludlow, who lent them to Chapman. Lady Ludlow subsequently sold her twelve pages to a bookseller who cataloged them in 1925 for £385, "a monstrous price," according to the scholar. He borrowed the rest of the manuscript from L. A. Austen-Leigh and his three sisters, who didn't want to sell. "It is in my safe at the moment," Chapman wrote to a Miss Greene in 1925, evidently pleased at being curator of so much Austen material, if only temporarily.[81]

In 1922, while Chapman's Clarendon edition was still unpublished, an attractive edition of "Volume the Second," the original of which was still in Francis Austen's family, was brought out by Chatto and Windus under the title *Love and Freindship*. The book had an introduction by G. K. Chesterton, who made an ardent case for Austen's place in the great tradition of the very best English burlesque writing, and was decorated with Cassandra's appealing watercolor illustrations to "The History of England" as endpapers. Coming out just after Daisy Ashford's super-selling *The Young Visiters* (and sharing the same publisher as well as the same endearingly juvenile misspelling), *Love and Freindship* had considerable impact both as a publishing phenomenon and as an exposé of Austen's young character, "the discovery of an inspiration," as Chesterton put it. The inventive and irreverent author of "Volume the Second" appeared as the opposite of the restrained, secretly smiling aunt promulgated by the *Memoir*; as Augustine Birrell said in the *Times*, "We found ourselves simply revelling in the revelation . . . made to us of the 'Elementary Jane.' "[82]

One reviewer failed to revel, and that was Chapman himself, writing anonymously in the *Times Literary Supplement*, "We should be sorry to have been responsible for this publication." While conceding that there was in *Love and Freindship* "now and then a sentence one would be sorry to have missed," he thought the act of publishing it amounted to an act of "espionage or exhumation."[83] Chapman had read the private correspondence between Austen-Leigh and his sisters about Jane Austen's "betweenities" and undoubtedly felt he was toeing the family line over their unsuitability for publication, but there was raw professional jealousy in his antipathy too. Chesterton had bested him and scored a hit with a text Chapman didn't—at that time—consider part of the official Austen canon. When he tracked down the manuscript of "Volume the First" in 1932, however, and persuaded the Bodleian to buy it, he wasted no time editing that work himself and eventually published editions of all the juvenilia.

One of Chapman's talents was for inspiring awe among his colleagues at the Clarendon Press. Elizabeth Jenkins, a future biographer of Jane Austen, recalled a man "so critical and austere that it was an alarming experience to receive his opinions, though a wholesome one,"[84] and his colleague Bywater remembered the "chill glance of recognition and dispraise" Chapman habitually cast over the wares of

Oxford booksellers and antiquarians. John Gore said of Chapman's Austen editions, "They will never be superseded as authorities. He put into them all his scholarship, years of research and a strictness in the sifting of evidence worthy of a Lord Chief Justice." Gore made it sound as if Austen ought also to have been a bit in awe of her twentieth-century editor and grateful for his attentions: "I often wonder what [she] would have felt if she could have foreseen that every word of almost every sentence she scribbled down at odd moments on her little desk at Chawton Cottage would one day be examined and tested, as through a microscope, by a great scholar."

Chapman's work *has* been superseded, though, as all such scholarship will be in time, and has had its critics. David Gilson has very politely pointed out that Chapman recorded "by no means all" the differences between editions of Austen's books published in her lifetime,[85] and Chapman's bibliography of Jane Austen has been picked out by Richard Howard as an example of selective and prescriptive editing. Howard notes that Chapman omitted from his bibliography the kinds of essays that, in Chapman's opinion, Jane Austen would not have understood. Howard characterized the process thus:

> To Chapman, Austen would turn over in her grave if she heard scholars describe her novels in terms alien to her apprehension, the apparatus of literary history and textual scholarship, to say nothing of post-structural interpretation, being regarded as likely to misrepresent her enterprise. To Chapman, Jane Austen is in the canon not because of her social vision or her artistry, but because she had the good fortune to be able and the good taste to be willing to record the elegant manners of her time. Hence with inexorable circularity, Chapman's edition of Austen creates the author it presumes, and the history it desires, a graceful monument to country life in Regency England, inveterately given to graciousness and tranquillity.[86]

Even in the presentation of Austen's texts by Chapman, the way was paved to full-scale "consumption" of Austen as a multifaceted literary-historical product. The illustrations to *The Novels of Jane Austen*—of carriages, dress, dancing steps—introduced quantities of extra information that was generic rather than specific to Austen. There were, of course, no vulgar representations, à la Hugh Thomson, of Elizabeth overhearing Darcy at the Meryton assembly or Mr. Elton proposing in the carriage; there were no homely pencil drawings of Steventon rectory derived from a niece's notebook but instead were decorous views of the Pump Room and plates from Ackermann's Repository. Chapman's editions removed Austen from her own particular life story and attached her to the age she lived in—specifically its genteeler aspects. There was no attempt to illustrate the less attractive clothes, houses, or activities within the novels' scope. Thus the editing carried aspects of the Janeite delusion into criticism by stressing Austen's difference from other authors—her special case status. No one rushed to copy Chapman's method for other authors, because it wasn't appropriate. There were no appendixes about donkeys or illustrations of orphanages or convict ships in editions of Dickens. Austen was being treated like a cultural package: educational, in unchallenging ways, and reliably, cleanly, entertaining.

For all his austerity and intimidation of underlings, Chapman's feelings about his subject were strong, emotional, and possessive. His excitability in correspondence with those to whom he felt he could unbend is marked, and he clearly relished his custodianship of the choice items passing in and out of his little safe, as well as things in the Bodleian whose purchase he had overseen (such as "Volume the First," which he kept at home for several months to work on[87]). He was, in his way, quite an operator and once cornered the great American collector J. Pierpont Morgan in the smoking room of a liner mid-Atlantic and came to an agreement with him by which Chapman gained access to Morgan's extraordinary holdings of Austen letters in return for first refusal (as if Morgan would refuse!) of any manuscripts that Chapman found for the British Museum that were passed over. That was good enough for the collector. "All I ask are the crumbs from the rich man's table," he told Chapman, with distracting simplicity.

Nor was the unbending scholar immune to sentimentality about Austen. In his bibliography (of all places) Chapman refers to Virginia Woolf's dictum about Austen not being able to be caught in the act of greatness, the soggiest thing she ever said on the subject, as "the golden sentence."[88] And he echoed Woolf's sentiment, in both senses, in his introduction to the *Letters* in 1932, claiming a magical element to Austen's art of characterization: "I cannot be mistaken in the belief that, in their several degrees, [the people in *Jane Austen's Letters*] are alive. How they are brought to life, without quotation and almost without description, may be perceived but can hardly be explained."[89] For all his classicism, mandarin airs, and unparalleled recall of "the lapses of lesser scholars," Robert William Chapman could be as un- or even anticritical as the next man.

# CHAPTER 6

# Canon and Canonization

In 1890, Jane Austen's first professional academic biographer, the historian Goldwin Smith, had shone the light of his scholarly mind on his subject only to report that there was nothing in Austen to illuminate: "There is no hidden meaning in her; no philosophy beneath the surface for profound scrutiny to bring to light; nothing calling in any way for elaborate interpretation," he wrote.[1] Her characters were "genteel idlers" and "vapid," and the books—it was part of their charm—needed no commentary: "Some think that they see a difference between the early and the later novels. It is natural to look for such a difference, but for ourselves we must confess we see it not." In the same year, the reviewer John Mackinnon Robinson took Smith to task for not appreciating Austen's modernity and "art-concealing art," but agreed that Austen was hardly a fit subject for a whole critical book, implying that Smith's own was pretty redundant: "It is impossible, indeed, to write a book on Jane Austen: you must not write treatises on miniatures."[2]

So, as it began, Austen criticism made a principled attempt to shut itself down. Pleasure and business don't mix, and there seemed to be no work to be done on such a delightful author, who wrote so clearly and simply, and who was so small scale. Scale had been the most frequently discussed issue, where Austen had been discussed critically at all; some, such as Thomas Carlyle, felt that her refusal to tackle large themes automatically excluded her from the ranks of the great novelists, while advocates such as G. H. Lewes lauded Austen's careful self-regulation as the means to "perfect" art: "She does not touch those profounder and more impassioned chords which vibrate to the heart's core—never ascends to its grand or heroic movements, nor descends to its deeper throes and agonies; but in all she attempts she is uniformly and completely successful."[3]

As soon as the "little bit of Ivory" was inserted into the discourse, no one could get enough of "miniature" and "fine brush strokes" analogies, using them to account for Austen's skill in terms of control, female niceness, and wisdom about her own limits. This view of Austen's art required nothing of the reader but a willingness to be delighted, as one might be in the presence of a superior conjuror. The manual dexterity that James Edward Austen-Leigh had harped on in the *Memoir* became intimately associated with Austen's writing skill, as if she practiced the latter as a form of cottage craft. Choosing not to inquire into "how she did it" could thus be made into a compliment to the author, as in this centenary newspaper tribute: "So delicate were the touches of the miniaturist that they defy analysis with the same challenge as threads of gossamer."[4] She really had thought of everything!

Another way to "defy" analysis was to promote Austen as an accidental artist, working unconsciously or instinctively. Henry James, who never liked to see immanence analyzed, likened her to "the brown thrush who tells his story from the garden bough."[5] "The key to Jane Austen's fortune with posterity," he wrote, in "The Lesson of Balzac," "has been in part the extraordinary grace of her facility, in part of her unconsciousness." James went on to picture the author musing over her workbasket while her unconscious did its trick, "and her dropped stitches, of these pardonable, of these precious moments, were afterwards picked up as little touches of human truth, little glimpses of steady vision, little master-strokes of imagination." Little, little, *little*. By 1928, Rebecca West had heard enough of such opinions to complain, "Really, it is time this comic patronage of Jane Austen ceased."[6]

The perception of Austen's novels existing in a zone beyond literary criticism added hugely to their popular appeal. As Brian Southam has remarked, it was attractive to know that a great writer "could be enjoyable, and could be spoken of affectionately as a friend, as well as revered as a genius." Austen's adoption by the educational establishment would not have followed very naturally if the academy hadn't been stuffed with Janeites during the early years of the new century, just as the discipline of English literature was being introduced to British universities (it had been taught in America for several decades already). George Saintsbury in Edinburgh, A. C. Bradley in Liverpool, and Sir Walter Raleigh at Oxford all ensured that as soon as the canon existed, their favorite was not just in it but held a special position. This was in marked contrast to writers like Sir Walter Scott and Fanny Burney, who hadn't stood the test of time, or not the test of that time, at any rate.

There was another reason for Austen's easy passage into English literature courses: English was considered a "soft" subject, suitable for the increasing number of women students who aspired to university education (even if they weren't yet allowed to earn degrees), and Austen's novels were some of the least inappropriate works of fiction for unmarried women to read and discuss with the older men who taught them. As Leslie Stephen had said in detraction, there was nothing in the novels "that would prevent them from being given by a clergyman to his daughter as a birthday present."[7] Writing to Robert William Chapman in 1917, Professor Walter Raleigh (formerly the teacher of Katharine Metcalfe) took comfort in what he saw as Austen's laughable ignorance about worldly matters: "She knows a lot, and I believe she knows what she doesn't know. At least, I shouldn't like to believe that she thought she knew anything about married people or young men."[8] Raleigh implies that a valuable status quo was thus preserved between the sexes: Austen "knows what she doesn't know," and, best of all, keeps it to herself. No one wanted wise virgins—whether authors or students—to be too *knowing*.

Once Austen began to appear on syllabi and lecture lists, the comparisons with Shakespeare dried up almost immediately. Macaulay, whom Henry James called Austen's "first slightly ponderous amoroso,"[9] had led the way with his startling claim in 1843, "Shakspeare [*sic*] has had neither equal nor second. But among the writers who . . . have approached nearest to the manner of the great master, we have no hesitation in placing Jane Austen."[10] G. H. Lewes followed Macaulay's lead in 1847 by calling Austen a "prose Shakespeare" on account of her "marvellous dramatic power." Both men, in attempting to give a suitable impression of their admiration for Austen to readers who hardly shared it in the 1840s, grabbed at the Bard for emphasis, but the comparison was barely tenable. Those who tried to expand the analogy (including Richard Simpson in 1872 and the Shakespeare scholar A. C. Bradley in 1911) stressed Austen's "Shakespearian" creation of character and ear for dialogue, though Miss Bates and Mrs. Allen—the two characters Bradley singled out—could be just as convincingly described as "Chaucerian" or "Burneyan." A feeble poem by Rudyard Kipling titled "Jane's Marriage" (which he appended to his story "The Janeites") places Austen in company with Shakespeare and the world's other great storytellers but doesn't take its own compliment to the author very seriously:

*Jane went to Paradise:*
*That was only fair.*
*Good Sir Walter followed her,*
*And armed her up the stair.*
*Henry and Tobias,*
*And Miguel of Spain*
*Stood with Shakespeare at the top*
*To welcome Jane.*

The true connection between Austen and Shakespeare lay in their popularity, accessibility, and impact on readers' affections. Leslie Stephen had satirized this in his invention of the term "Austenolatry" in the 1870s, in imitation of "Bardolatry"—that commercially led, nationalistically flavored, anti-intellectual idealization of the poet that burgeoned in the later eighteenth century, almost entirely at the hands of one man, David Garrick. James Edward Austen-Leigh had been the unlikely impresario of his aunt's own similarly rocketing fame. Long after their own time, both Shakespeare and Jane Austen had managed to find a popular audience and appeal to them over the heads of an interpretive elite.

WHEN ARNOLD BENNETT SAID of the Janeites in 1927, "They are nearly all fanatics. They will not listen. If anybody 'went for' Jane, anything might happen to him. He would assuredly be called on to resign from his clubs,"[11] his personification of the Janeite as a metropolitan clubman acknowledged the same truth as Virginia Woolf's joke that "there are twenty-five elderly gentlemen living in the neighbourhood of London who resent any slight upon [Jane Austen's] genius as if it were an insult to the chastity of their Aunts."[12] They may both have been alluding to the Janeite cabal that ran the Royal Society of Literature at the time, so solipsistically Janeite, in fact, that when one of their number, H. W. Garrod, did "go for" Jane, in his 1928 lecture "Jane Austen: A Depreciation" (in response to another fellow's gushing tribute), his criticisms of Austen were, apparently, conceived in the spirit of playful opposition, "written without thought of publication, for a pleasant occasion, and in lightness of heart."[13] And though his remarks were waspish (Garrod questioned the manliness of male Janeites, in thrall to "a mere slip of a girl"), the context was cozy.

"Janeism" had spread far beyond the control of twenty-five elderly gentlemen, however. There were books of quotations, Christmas compilations, articles in *Country Life* and the *Lady*, as well as in *Notes & Queries* and the *Times Literary Supplement*, continuations of "Sanditon" and "The Watsons," sequels to *Pride and Prejudice, Sense and Sensibility, Mansfield Park*, and *Emma*. No discussion of country houses, riding habits, Bath, silhouettes, or embroidery could pass, it seemed, without mentioning her name, and she was cooed over and sentimentalized, travestied and elaborated upon quite regardless of what was being said about her in Clubland. In his preface to the "Georgian edition" of

Austen's novels in 1931, John Bailey remarked on "the extraordinary spread" of her cult and how odd it was that readers' sense of intimacy with the author seemed to increase with the passage of time, rather than the opposite. Katherine Mansfield put something like the same point more wittily: "The truth is that every true admirer of the novels cherishes the happy thought that he alone—reading between the lines—has become the secret friend of their author."[14]

Jane Austen was in vogue because her period was in vogue as well. The revival of Regency style in domestic architecture in the years following the Great War, especially in small-scale suburban homes, meant that a whole generation of English men and women were raised in miniature houses that strove to resemble Pemberley. The classical portico, filtered through its English Regency renderings, had become, ironically, a symbol of modernity, and architectural streamlining (so necessary when space was short) marked a decisive move away from the fuss, clutter, and untenable size of Victorian homes. Novels were shorter in the new century; biographies were too, after Lytton Strachey, and Jane Austen's life and works, which seemed restrained and tidy by comparison with the "breeding plots" of the big Victorian family sagas, fitted in very nicely with the style of the times.

The modernists had little to say in praise of Austen; she was more the preserve of the Bloomsbury Group. Leslie Stephen, who had praised Austen so faintly in the *Dictionary of National Biography*, changed his mind about the author as time went by, and—as Carrington and Lytton Strachey also intended—turned to her novels for comfort on his deathbed. His daughter Virginia Woolf proved a highly sympathetic and penetrating critic of Austen. The publication of *Love and Freindship* in 1922 had fascinated her, with its revelation of the fifteen-year-old Austen "laughing, in her corner, at the world," and Woolf had no trouble squaring this interestingly subversive figure with the writer of the letters and the familiar novels: "Charming but perpendicular, loved at home but feared by strangers, biting of tongue but tender of heart—these contrasts are by no means incompatible, and when we turn to the novels we shall find ourselves stumbling there too over the same complexities in the writer."[15] Far from being constricted in a space two inches wide, "Whatever [Austen] writes is finished and turned and set in its relation, not to the parsonage, but to the universe."

But there was unease among the literati about how to distinguish their own forms of Austen appreciation both from those of her "adorers" and from the hoi polloi. In an interview late in his life, E. M. Forster (a much more obvious "heir to Austen" than Henry James) named Austen, along with Proust, as the author from whom he had learned most, especially about "the possibilities of domestic humour."[16] In the 1920s, however, he could only express his admiration satirically, claiming he shared "the fatuous expression and airs of personal immunity" and "primal stupor" of the die-hard Austen fan: "I am a Jane Austenite, and therefore slightly imbecile about Jane Austen. . . . She is my favourite author! I read and re-read, the mouth open and the mind closed. Shut up in measureless content, I greet her by the name of most kind hostess, while criticism slumbers."[17]

Criticism didn't slumber, of course: Forster was reviewing Chapman's 1923 Clarendon edition of *The Novels of Jane Austen*, and had adopted this self-parodic tone to provide cover for a critique of Chapman's enterprise in which he seemed to give credit to Chapman's scholarship ("Even his textual criticism helps") while amply illustrating its pedantry. According to Forster, Chapman's minute attention to certain background detail in the novels might have "woken the Jane Austenite up" ever so slightly and exposed Austen's texts to "contact with the life of facts," but the books "continue to live their own wonderful internal life" regardless of both fans and critics.

The sense that several distinct groups of interested parties had emerged, each invested in a different view of "Jane Austen," became even clearer in 1932 when Chapman published his two-volume *Jane Austen's Letters to Her Sister Cassandra and Others*, a book that crowned twenty years of work. Forster was not the only commentator to be consternated; it turned out that Lord Brabourne's partial and inaccurate 1884 *Letters* had, in fact, been pretty representative of the material as a whole, and that Chapman's editing, far from rescuing Austen from accusations of dullness and triviality, enforced those impressions. Forster was disappointed to find that Austen's most personal writing "had not the magic that outlasts ink" and that no number of footnotes about coach timetables and bank accounts could revive its essential meaning: "Cassandra understood, her niece Fanny Knight understood, the Austen Leighs and Lord Brabourne had some conception—but we students of to-day, unrelated to her by blood, what part have we in this family talk, and whose triviality do we expose but our own?"[18]

A number of other critics found the unliterariness of Austen's letters positively irritating: Garrod described them as "a desert of trivialities punctuated by occasional clever malice," while Harold Nicolson thought them "trivial and dull," the work of a mind "like a very small, sharp pair of scissors. . . . She emerges diminished." As Mary Lascelles noted, there was an air of triumph among these anti-Austenites at the discovery that "the writer of the celebrated novels was no better than anyone else and rather less likeable than most."[19] Chapman's printing for the first time of passages that the family had hitherto suppressed, such as Austen's remarks about the Misses Debary's bad breath and the gratuitously unpleasant joke about Mrs. Hall's stillbirth being the result of "happening to look at her husband" exposed a lack of taste and feeling that no one had previously supposed possible of dear Aunt Jane. No matter that the novels contain exactly consonant passages of ill humor (such as the brutal critique of Mrs. Musgrove's "large fat sighings" over her good-for-nothing dead son in *Persuasion*, and Emma's heartless wit against Miss Bates at the Box Hill picnic); this was the woman in propria persona. Though Austen's popular image skipped ahead along a primrose path, blithely detached from texts or textuality, among the reading class, Chapman was responsible for the sharpest readjustment in Jane Austen's reputation in living memory.

THE FIRST DECADES OF the twentieth century saw significant movements of the Austen papers, manuscripts, and memorabilia out of family hands and into those of collectors and collections, many of them American. Chapman had thought £385 a "monstrous price" for twelve pages of "The Watsons" in 1925; one can guess what he thought eight years later, when Walter M. Hill of Chicago bought the manuscript of "Lady Susan" (which had passed from Lord Brabourne to Lord Rosebery in 1892) for $8,812 at a Sotheby's sale, or when the same buyer paid £1,000 for a single Austen letter.

A particularly valuable stash of treasures containing letters, the memoranda about the novels' dates of composition, Cassandra's sketch of Jane, and the amber crosses bought for the sisters by their brother, had descended via Charles Austen to three of his granddaughters, who sold most of the items off in the 1920s, using Chapman as their intermediary. The manuscript items went mostly to the British Museum and J. Pierpont Morgan, but the crosses, and Jane's letter about them, were bought by a young Yale graduate student, Charles Beecher Hogan. In a correspondence with Chapman, the director of the National Portrait Gallery, Henry Hake, who at the time was trying to find a decent likeness of Jane Austen to purchase for the Gallery, was told that Hogan's purchases were "nothing to your purpose."[20] Yet Hake was curious enough to inquire about the young collector from a correspondent in Connecticut, who reported that Hogan was an assistant in the reference department of the Yale library. "He is in, I should say, his middle twenties & I shd. think was on the impecunious side." Two months later, Hake's friend sent a newspaper cutting announcing Hogan's forthcoming marriage to Miss Carolyn Crosby of Minneapolis, "one of America's wealthiest heiresses," with the wry note added, "'Impecunious' no longer!" Jane and Cassandra's amber crosses became a wedding present to Hogan's wealthy bride.

In the rapidly rising market for Austen manuscripts and memorabilia, Hake hoped that some hitherto unknown portrait of Jane Austen might now come to light, but his search was long and unrewarding. He had seen a reproduction of the Andrews portrait but didn't seem to know that it was derived from a different picture; similarly, he believed the Rice Portrait to be exactly what the caption in Brabourne's edition of the *Letters* claimed, "Jane Austen by Zoffany." Hake approached the Hubbacks and Rices with a view to buying the picture for the nation, but the family, though willing to consider a copy being made, didn't want to part with it at that date.

When Hake asked Chapman's advice about images of Austen, the scholar blew cold on the Rice Portrait. "I never feel happy about this picture, and I know that R.A.A-L [James Edward's grandson, Richard Austen-Leigh] is very sceptical."[21] Hake transferred his attention to the possibility of other images existing in the family and enlisted the help of Frank Austen's grandson, eighty-eight-year-old John Hubback, to make inquiries on his behalf. A week later Hubback confirmed that the family had no knowledge of any "original portrait of Jane Austen in her maturity, that can be accounted a trustworthy likeness. . . . All those round-eyed prints or sketches, such as that in 'Lady Susan' or in the Memoir by J. E. Austen Leigh are admittedly very touched up."[22] He was convinced that the Andrews picture was "a made-up affair from some other drawing," but, remarkably enough, claimed not to know the sketch it was derived from, though Cassandra's drawing had been reproduced in his own book, *Jane Austen's Sailor Brothers*, in 1906. None of Cassy Esten Austen's descendants, who had owned the sketch until their sale of manuscripts and relics in 1920, seemed to remember the picture either or make the connection between it and the Andrews/Lizars doll. In 1932, the Andrews picture was still in the family, owned by Lois Austen-Leigh, of "Sanditon" in Aldeburgh.[23]

Even Chapman seemed ignorant on this score. He told Hake that there was "a horrid little sketch (head) by Cassandra reproduced *somewhere*. This cannot be of any importance." Chapman was about to publish, as a frontispiece to his edition of *Jane Austen's Letters* in 1932, the "bonnet" picture by Cassandra, now acknowledged as the only unequivocally authentic picture of Jane Austen. Chapman told Hake that this too was "nothing to your purpose"—a favorite phrase—"because it gives only the back of the sitter's head."[24] So Hake made no further inquiries about the image, and it remains in the possession of Austen descendants to this day.

Twelve years after Hake's initial inquiries, the gallery purchased, on Chapman's encouragement, a silhouette that had been found in a second edition of *Mansfield Park*, with the handwritten inscription "L'aimable Jane." It was thin grounds for an identification with Jane Austen, and the item is seldom exhibited (it has been cataloged by the National Portrait Gallery as "uncertain" and "possibly by Mrs Collins, c.1801"), but, in 1948, Chapman held out the hope that it might "start speculation and lead to discoveries" if he used it in one of his Clarendon volumes. "All the other candidates have been reproduced, some *ad nauseam*," he wrote to Hake, "and I think the shade deserves a run for its money."[25] The idea that there could be *candidates* and *competition* involved in establishing an authentic image of Jane Austen was surprising, as Chapman's remarks about Austen icons often were. In his book *Jane Austen: Facts and Problems*, he described the "bonnet" watercolor as "the graceful outline of a seated lady," when most observers would remark on its utter lack of gracefulness, dumpy body, and clumsily misaligned limbs. "It has nothing inconsistent with what is known of Jane Austen's figure," Chapman concluded, presumably not meaning to sound ungallant.[26]

In 1945, Elizabeth Jenkins tracked down "the Cassandra scribble," as Hake referred to it in a memo, in the inventory of Frederick Lovering of St. Austell, whose estate was up for sale. Hake, though obviously not very impressed by the quality of the item, understood its importance and was quick to secure the purchase. It has been on display at the National Portrait Gallery ever since. Though it can't be absolutely authenticated, it has become the ur-image of Austen and all the more precious for being so rare, fragile, and faint.

Another small watercolor has been put forward in subsequent years as a portrait of Austen: a rather glamorously dressed full-length figure, allegedly painted by the hapless Rev. James Stanier Clarke, the prince regent's librarian. Like the silhouette, its claims to authenticity are weak, but the fact that it gets mentioned at all in discussions of Austen iconography shows how desperate people are for a suitably attractive image of our best-loved novelist. A 2007 article in the *New York Times*, titled "Pretty Words, Jane; Would That You Were Too," expresses this wishfulness in rather extreme terms: "The dreary spinster of the Cassandra sketch isn't anyone we recognize."

This raises the question of how we would "recognize" Jane Austen, with only Cassandra's drawings and various conflicting written testimonies to go on. In the two generations following hers, the family couldn't even agree on the color of Jane's hair and described it variously as "fair," but also "light brunette," "black," and "neither light nor dark." The lock of hair that is now on display at the Jane Austen House Museum isn't much help on this score, having faded over time to a pale, sandy tone. Even between 1949 and 1971, it was thought to have faded so much that the Jane Austen Society committee decided to have some maintenance work done. They sent in an expert from the giant chemical group Unilever to examine the lock, and his conclusion was that within the last three months of Austen's life, her hair had not been brushed or combed much, a dismal reminder of the exigencies of the sickbed.[27] Subsequently, the hair coloring firm Elida was employed to restore "the original colour" of the hair—whatever they imagined that was—but the sample today is again extremely pale, so perhaps it's time for another posthumous hair job.

There was more agreement among the nephews and nieces about intangible attributes of their aunt's appearance, such as "liveliness" and the brightness of her eyes. James Edward Austen-Leigh had struggled to evoke her "very attractive" person; light, firm step; and "whole appearance expressive of health and animation." But this was not much more forthcoming than Henry Austen's description in his original "Biographical Notice," where he avoided the vulgarity of referring directly to his beloved sister's looks by saying, "Of personal attractions she possessed a considerable share. Her stature was that of true elegance. It could not have been increased without exceeding the middle height. Her carriage and deportment were quiet yet graceful. Her features were separately good." Even Henry, who knew his sister so well, couldn't settle to one consistent description and altered the wording in 1833 to "her stature rather exceeded the middle height," dropping the phrase about "true elegance." Since "stature" was really the only physical attribute he was discussing in the first place, the change was very odd. Had Jane grown? One of the few things that can be surmised from Austen's own evidence is that she must have been taller than average. She refers to her height several times in the *Letters*, ordering flat-heeled shoes and instructing Cassandra to buy two lengths of muslin, "one longer than the other—it is for a tall woman. Seven yards for my mother, seven yards and a half for me."[28]

The curl, if not the color, of her hair, is also documented in the *Letters*. As early as 1798, when she was only twenty-two, Austen rejoiced in being able to adopt the convenience of wearing a muslin cap in the evenings and "saving a world of torment as to hair-dressing": "My long hair is always plaited up out of sight, and my short hair curls well enough to want no papering."[29] Clearly, she was not a vain young woman, nor even particularly "well-turned-out." The most imaginary aspect of the many imaginary portraits of Austen that have appeared over the decades (thoroughly documented by Deirdre Le Faye in the *Jane Austen Society Report* for 2007) must be conspicuous elegance of dress.

Without a good and flattering image of the author, taken from life and documented as being reasonably like, people will continue to find ingenious alternatives. In the 1960s, a direct descendant of one of Austen's brothers, Mrs. Diana Shervington, was said to bear such a "strong family likeness . . . to the sketch of Jane Austen" (a dubious distinction!) that it was felt very appropriate to make a photographic record of her, in Chawton Cottage, wearing a pelisse believed to have belonged to the novelist that had been handed down in the family to a great-grand-niece, a Mrs. Jenkyns. Unfortunately, Mrs. Shervington was the wrong size for the pelisse, so when she was pictured gazing thoughtfully into the lid of her great-great-great-aunt's workbox, the costume she was wearing had to be provided by a theatrical hire firm. However, the pelisse fitted a great-great-great-grand-niece, who posed by a window in Chawton Cottage. The concept was, presumably, that the combination of garment, descendant, house, and photographic verisimilitude would work a mild magic and allow us to "see" Jane Austen. Miss Jenkyns's face, not being the one with the supposed resemblance, was turned away from the camera, so in a way the committee's objective was achieved as well as it could have been, for the picture does inadvertently recall that only verifiable image of Jane Austen, the one of her in a pelisse and bonnet, out of doors on a summer day, with her back to the viewer.

JUST AS AUSTEN'S NOVELS had appealed strongly as candidates for illustration in the last years of the nineteenth century, so it was only a matter of time in the twentieth before the film industry would turn to them, too. Classic novels were powerfully fashionable in Hollywood in the 1930s and '40s: *David Copperfield, Oliver Twist,* and *Wuthering Heights* all became big box-office hits, and though Austen's books lacked the drama and sensationalism of Dickens and the Brontës, they had perfect credentials for light romantic comedy. *Pride and Prejudice* had emerged as the "representative" Austen novel; there had been stage adaptations—one by A. A. Milne in 1936—one-act plays, and "scenes" for amateur and school performances. The book seemed to lend itself to dramatization more readily than the other Austen texts (there was only one attempt at adapting scenes from *Mansfield Park* for stage performance, and none whatsoever of *Persuasion*). With its strong female lead, handsome hero, witty dialogue, and "screwball" comic minor characters, it was an easy choice for Hollywood. After an initial plan by Irving Thalberg to produce a film version starring his wife, Norma Shearer, and Clark Gable, the project went ahead from MGM in 1939 with a different cast and directed by Robert Z. Leonard.

When the war broke out, many of the British expats in Hollywood had wondered whether or not to return home, but they were encouraged not to by a cable from the ambassador, Lord Lothian, who pointed out that "the continuing production of films with a strong British tone is one of the best and subtlest forms of British propaganda."[30] Leonard's 1940 *Pride and Prejudice* certainly had a "strong British tone." Bringing Austen's beloved novel to the screen for the first time and stuffed with British actors and accents, it both fed off and enhanced the cachet of British culture and tradition at a time when both were under threat.

Aldous Huxley was working on the script in November 1939, in an airless cubicle on the MGM lot in Hollywood. In a letter to Eugene Saxton, he described it as "an odd, cross-word puzzle job. One tries to do one's best for Jane Austen; but actually the very fact of transforming the book into a picture must necessarily alter its whole quality in a profound way.... The insistence upon the story as opposed to the diffuse irony which the story is designed to contain, is a major falsification of Miss Austen."[31] Huxley's scruples about the adaptation didn't count for anything, it hardly needs mentioning; the producers insisted on simplifying the plot, dropping parts of the dialogue that were "too literary," and inserting odd bits of new material. Huxley could hardly keep up with the transformations that the director demanded for "Pee and Pee," as he was soon calling it, and complained to Grace Hubble, "I barely stopped my director from having Bennet fight a duel with Wickham!"[32]

"The story" was conveyed mostly intact (with some significant deviations: Lady Catherine de Bourgh is made to relent her meanness and give Darcy and Elizabeth's match her blessing) and the emphasis was firmly on the archness of Elizabeth Bennet, as played by Greer Garson, and the comic potential of characters such as Mrs. Bennet, Mary Bennet, and Mr. Collins. Whether it was Aldous Huxley or his cowriter Jane Murfin who penned phrases such as "There's no one as dignified as a mummy" [Elizabeth] and "Shall we not call it quits and start again?" [Darcy] is not recorded. Both utterances occur in an invented scene where the characters do a little target practice with bows and arrows at a garden party: fictions within fiction.

One completely arbitrary change was of the period of the action, which Leonard moved on forty years from that of the book, to justify more elaborate costumes. Edith Head, the designer, influenced by her colleague Walter Plunkett's costumes for *Gone with the Wind*, felt that the fashions of 1815 didn't afford her enough scope. The resulting dresses were fantastically extravagant; the Bennet women hardly fit in the milliner's shop of the opening scene, they are wearing such huge hats and crinolines, and when Darcy and Elizabeth sit together on a bench, it is not pride nor prejudice that seems to keep them apart, so much as their clothes.

The finished film had the comforting, theatrical look of many movies of the time, shot almost entirely in the studio, with painted backdrops suggesting the views from a terrace or through a window. The titles emphasized this staginess, by featuring lists of dramatis personae, but no actors' names—"Those living at Meryton Village," "Those living at Longbourn," etc.—and opening with a sort of verbal curtain: "It happened in OLD ENGLAND." The fact that it was an American production of a British classic gently reflected the relation of the Allies in the war and the heritage that both countries were jointly defending. Audiences on both sides of the Atlantic could feel nostalgic for a period when the British army and navy beat off the threat of invasion while genteel life went on at home uninterrupted and the landed classes could meet and mate in peace. The one overt reference in the screenplay to a battle is inserted to indicate the imagined new historical period: Mrs. Bennet greets the information that Bingley has £5,000 a year with "That's the most heartening piece of news since the battle of Waterloo!" but some other lines were slipped in to reflect the wartime situation of 1940 too. In the assembly scene, Elizabeth remarks to Charlotte Lucas, "Oh why is England cursed with so many more women than men?" And, as Karen Morley, the actress who played Charlotte Lucas, later recalled, the whole cast was preoccupied during filming with the news from Europe of Adolf Hitler's advance through the Netherlands and Belgium.

Greer Garson went on from her role as Lizzie Bennet to play Mrs. Miniver in the patriotic weepie of that name that was a runaway success for William Wyler and MGM in 1942. The association—as between Laurence Olivier's roles as Darcy in 1940 and Henry V in 1944—was probably not deliberate and may never have been acknowledged, but it is exactly the sort of connection—of one middle-class English heroine with another, and with a beautiful actress; of a great interpreter of Shakespeare with Austen's proudest gentleman and the nation's most valiant king—that works most powerfully in the collective unconscious. There is something viral about fame: heartless, predatory, proliferating. The first film of *Pride and Prejudice* may not have affected Jane Austen's literary standing one jot but impressed millions of people with a complex sense of her importance.

A STRANGE SATIRIC NOVEL of 1938, *The Impregnable Women*, by Eric Linklater, not only predicted the coming European war and London being "annihilated" by airborne bombs, but depicted the prime minister of this near-future England retreating after an international conference for a period of solitude in the company of Jane Austen: "When he woke up he refused to see anyone till six o'clock, because he was reading *Pride and Prejudice*."[33] Something oddly similar happened in real life in 1943 when Winston Churchill, then minister of defense, arrived in Tunisia in early December on his way to the conference at which he, Franklin D. Roosevelt, and Joseph Stalin were going to plan their final strategy against Hitler and set dates for Operation Overlord. The minister was already voiceless and feverish and soon developed pneumonia. By the end of the month, he was confined to bed in great discomfort, as he recalled in his memoir:

> Fever flickered in and out. I lived on my theme of the war, and it was like being transported out of oneself. The doctors tried to keep the work away from my bedside, but I defied them. They kept on saying, "Don't work, don't worry"; to such an extent that I decided to read a novel. I had long ago read Jane Austen's Sense and Sensibility, and now I thought I would have Pride and Prejudice. Sarah read it to me beautifully from the foot of the bed. I had always thought that it would be better than its rival. What calm lives they had, those people! No worries about the French Revolution, or the crashing struggle of the Napoleonic wars. Only manners controlling natural passion so far as they could, together with cultured explanations of any mischances.[34]

This recalls R. H. Hutton's remark in 1890 about Austen's novels having such charm for "statesmen and thinkers" on account of their quality of being "like enough to the real world to be for a time eagerly lived in."[35] It is strange to think of the planning of D-day beginning with this respite among the "calm lives" of Longbourn and Meryton, a powerful reminder of an idyllic England governed by manners and cultured explanations. A 1930s biographer of Austen, Beatrice Kean Seymour, had written, "In a society which has enthroned the machine-gun and carried it aloft even into the quiet heavens, there will always be men and women—Escapist or not, as you please—who will turn to [Jane Austen's] novels with an unending sense of relief and thankfulness." But, as Churchill was painfully aware, the calm depicted in *Pride and Prejudice* was no longer retrievable on the home front.

Back in bomb-shattered London, the film and stage heartthrob Robert Donat was preparing to take his touring company around the country with a production of *Emma*, starring the young Anna Neagle. It was to be "a wonderful tonic for the hard-pressed provinces which had suffered greatly from enemy bombing."[36] Rugby, Glasgow, Manchester, and Bristol all got their dose of Highbury; Bristol even got two, as there was a rival *Emma* on stage there already when the Donat troupe arrived. Perhaps some elements of the "national" themes in *Emma* that Lionel Trilling later identified made that novel particularly appealing during the war. "It seemed to me . . . perfect escapist entertainment," the leading lady recalled later. "For a couple of hours, anyway, our audiences could leave behind the horrors of the mid-20th century for the leisurely calm of the early 19th."[37] The London run of the play opened at the St. James's Theatre on February 6, 1945, just before a new wave of doodlebug bombing began. The theater attempted to save the show by starting as early as possible, to avoid the raids, as Neagle recalled:

> There was no doubt that the V-2s were bad for business. One matinee, when the theatre was packed with ladies (mainly elderly), there was a tremendous crash, a V-2 rocket had actually landed not far from the theatre. Everything rocked. Mr Weston, one of the characters in the play, burst on to the stage crying, "Oh, a terrible thing has happened, my love." "What is it, my love?" his wife asked in alarm.
>
> "A catastrophe. Someone has broken into the turkey house. Not a turkey left!"
>
> A momentary pause—then a roar of laughter swept through the theatre. . . . We learned later that we had, in fact, had a lucky escape.[38]

THE WAR YEARS ALSO saw the formation of the first literary society devoted to Jane Austen, which was to become one of the most well-organized and serious institutions of its kind, eventually spawning subsidiaries all around the world. The Jane Austen Society lagged some way behind the Brontë Society, founded in 1894, which had proved such an amazing innovation in author worship, with its huge crowd-pulling potential and the thriving museum at Haworth. Austen's club started very modestly, with just a handful of enthusiasts gathering in the home of the founder, Miss Dorothy Darnell. She had chanced to drive through Chawton one time and thought she recognized the house at the corner. Inquiring of the Automobile Association man on road duty if it had been Jane Austen's house, he replied rather irritably, "Yes—she's the plague of my life!"[39]

At the period when Miss Darnell first drove by, in the 1930s, Chawton Cottage was still owned by the Knight estate and divided into three parts, as it had been after Cassandra Austen's death, when the contents of the cottage had been dispersed. The corner rooms housed Chawton Village Library (a development that would have amused Jane), but there was no one left in the village who could say how the rooms of the original building had been disposed. Darnell's vision of restoration therefore involved not just trying to buy and repair the building but to reinvent the structure, layout, and contents of the interior.

Darnell displayed an intense, proprietorial watchfulness over the welfare of the property. She got to know, for instance, when one of the old Austen fireplaces ended up among nettles on the local blacksmith's scrap heap, "wrenched out," in the report's emotional language, to make way for a gas fire. She got Hugh Curtis, curator of the Curtis Museum in Alton (and a direct descendant of Jane Austen's Alton apothecary), to take the fireplace into protective custody until such time as she could return it to its rightful situation. The incident proved a spur to the small group of like-minded enthusiasts, which included Darnell, her sister, Elizabeth Jenkins, and the newly co-opted Mr. Curtis, to form a committee and launch the Society, specifically "to promote or procure the acquisition of the residence of Jane Austen, at Chawton in Hampshire, as a national memorial to the novelist."[40]

The Society's first objective, to persuade the Knight estate to sell the property, was gained with remarkable ease, even though the current owner, Major Edward Knight, was on wartime active service. However, the price he was asking for the freehold—£3,000—was entirely beyond the Society's means, and they had to resign themselves to a long-term, possibly endless, campaign of fund-raising, as they saved up a trickle of half-crown subscriptions and waited for word of mouth to spread awareness of a national treasure under threat from neglect.

It was a difficult time to be trying to elicit large donations from individuals or institutions, when everyone was so preoccupied and impoverished by the war and before the National Trust had extended its remit to such projects (the first writer's house it took over was Beatrix Potter's in 1943, and that only because she had willed it to them), but salvation came from a local gentleman, T. Edward Carpenter, who in 1947 offered to buy Chawton Cottage outright and vest it in a trust for the benefit of the nation. Carpenter was so thorough in his generosity that he was also prepared to buy property in Alton to rehouse the sitting tenants and went on, in the words of the brief obituary in the Society's *Report* for 1970, to make the "upkeep, improvement and enrichment" of the house his life's work. He also restored the graves of Cassandra Austen and her mother in the parish churchyard and was ready to step in promptly whenever a relic emergency occurred. In the mid-1950s, a keen-eyed Austenite spotted a miniature of George Austen's sister, Philadelphia Hancock, for sale in a New Bond Street shop and reported it to Carpenter, who paid "a somewhat high price" in order to save the piece for the house. His devotion to the cause paid off, as the seller, a descendant of Francis Austen, was moved not only to reimburse him but to donate the miniature to the Austen Trust.

Perhaps people recognized another layer to Carpenter's enthusiasm for memorializing Austen. Carpenter and his wife had lost their twenty-two-year-old son, Lieutenant John Philip Carpenter of the First Battalion East Surrey Regiment, on active service in Italy in 1944 and undertook the purchase and restoration of Chawton Cottage as a memorial to him as well as to its famous former resident. Much of Carpenter's indefatigable energy on behalf of the museum, and that of his wife—a deeply knowledgeable Janeite—was a form of displaced grieving for their own posterity. Austen presented herself quite naturally as a healing agent for these scars of war, and her charming former home, lovingly restored over the years to as close a version as possible of its 1809 self as funds and imagination would allow, was a simple and effective material reminder of all the things that young British soldiers had died for: peace, order, freedom, gentility, and beauty.

Dorothy Darnell threw herself into the saving of Chawton Cottage with true zealotry, making extensive inquiries in the village and among the Austen descendants to discover the nature and whereabouts of any Austen memorabilia, furniture, et cetera, and all available local traditions and gossip about the family and their home. Though it seemed, as Elizabeth Jenkins said later, "as if nothing would ever come to light,"[41] Darnell's instinct proved right: a table that had been bought by a neighbor from the sale of Cassandra's effects in 1845 came back down the road to the cottage, as did the flagstones from the kitchen floor, which had been removed to form a path in the Dower House garden. Once the museum was established, it became the natural focus of interest in Austen and in time would exercise a remarkable pull on the heartstrings and consciences of those people who were in possession of Austen relics.

As those relics lost personal significance in the family, they gained in monetary value in the market. J. Pierpont Morgan and Charles Hogan had been early beneficiaries, picking up what are now thought of as priceless treasures for perfectly affordable prices. Another avid American collector was Mrs. Alberta Hirschheimer Burke, wife of Henry Gershon Burke, a successful lawyer and accountant. Together the couple acquired an unmatched collection of Austen material, including first editions of all the novels, manuscript letters, memorabilia, rare editions (Siegfried Sassoon's first U.S. edition of *Emma* among them), and more than one thousand books by and about Austen; her eventual bequest of much of this material to the Morgan Library in New York has made that the most valuable Austen archive in the world. In 1948 Mrs. Burke bought several items from the Sotheby's sale of Frederick Lovering's collection (sold by Charles Austen's family in the 1920s). They included the letters by Cassandra to Anne Sharp and Fanny Knight describing Jane's last illness and death, and a lock of Jane's hair given by Cassandra to Harriet Palmer, Charles Austen's sister-in-law and later second wife.

Mrs. Burke didn't enjoy her purchase of the lock of hair long, however. She and her husband were among the earliest members of the Jane Austen Society, and it was at the 1949 meeting at Chawton that Mrs. Burke made a dramatic presentation, apparently acting on the spur of the moment. T. Edward Carpenter, who had also bought items at the Sotheby's sale but had been outbid for the hair, was making a speech about his disappointment and lamenting the loss of the relic to foreign shores, when Mrs. Burke interrupted him from the audience, announced that she was the purchaser, and that she would present the item to the museum. "This dramatic moment will be well remembered by those present,"[42] the Society reported, understandably amazed by Mrs. Burke's generosity.

The scene was reprised twenty-six years later, with Charles Beecher Hogan in the role of surprise benefactor. As well as conducting valuable private scholarship on Austen,[43] Hogan had pursued a long and successful career as an Austen collector since his early acquisition of Jane and Cassandra's amber crosses for his heiress bride in 1933. His collection, most of which went to the Beinecke Library at Yale on his death in 1983, included a first edition of *Sense and Sensibility* and a set of first editions of the novels formerly belonging to Edward Knight (which Hogan bequeathed to the Jane Austen Society). This generous Janeite had said as far back as 1966 that he intended to leave the amber crosses to the Society (albeit they were, strictly speaking, his wife's to give, not his), but on the occasion of addressing the Annual General Meeting at Chawton House in 1974, surprised everyone by producing the necklaces and making the gift there and then. The crosses were "received with delight and considerable emotion by those present."[44]

As with Mrs. Burke and the lock of hair, the suddenness of the gift and the theatricality of announcing it at Chawton House in front of the assembled membership of the Jane Austen Society suggests religious parallels: a donor, a relic, a priesthood, a congregation, a sacred place. The answer to prayer. On both occasions, members wept for joy at the return of the hallowed objects to their rightful place.

Despite these generous gifts, there was a sense of slight desperation at the relative ease with which Americans, with their money and hunger for cultural emblems, could acquire Austen memorabilia and remove them from the country. It was a common complaint of the time that, through sheer dollar-power and craving, so many gems of

British heritage were ending up in the States. In the early 1970s, popular opinion was freshly offended by the sale of London Bridge and its removal to what was seen by many as an incongruous new home in Lake Havasu City, Arizona. Never mind that the 1825 structure was only the latest of many former bridges on that Thames site; its loss was treated like the loss of all of them. The country wasn't used to feeling the sharp end of cultural colonization, being the looted rather than the lootee. Ten years after the Hogan gift, T. Edward Carpenter's anxieties were still not wholly quieted, and he summed up the feelings of the Jane Austen Society and the country when he said of the large number of Austen letters that had ended up in North America, "They ought to be with us."[45]

A PROPERLY RESEARCHED BIOGRAPHY of Austen, by the novelist and former Clarendon Press employee Elizabeth Jenkins, did not appear until 1938. That book, and Mary Lascelles's classic study, *Jane Austen and Her Art* (1939), were part of a new Austen industry arising from Chapman's editorial work. Lascelles's intelligent speculation about Austen's conduct of her career and her analysis of Austen's style broke new ground critically and biographically. Far from believing that "everything worth saying on [the] subject had been said already," Lascelles positioned herself "at the beginning of the exciting 'how?' and 'why?' of analysis."[46] After Lascelles, no one questioned that Austen could bear comparison with the great novelists of the later nineteenth century—with Dickens, Dostoyevsky, James—and there was widespread recognition of her role in modernizing the novel. Her credentials as a classic author and cornerstone of the canon were confirmed; even "maverick" critics such as F. R. Leavis awarded Austen a pivotal position. "Jane Austen is the inaugurator of the great tradition of the English novel," Leavis declared in the opening chapter of his most famous book, "and by 'great tradition' I mean the tradition to which what is great in English fiction belongs."[47]

The new accent was on revisionism, the more surprising the better. The Communist poet and essayist Edgell Rickword placed Austen in his own "great tradition" of English writers alert to social change,

which included Charlotte Brontë, Matthew Arnold, Anthony Trollope, George Gissing, and Richard Jefferies. Rickword took the rarity
of Austen's "outbursts" in the novels as evidence of their significance,
seeing them not as slips but the tip of a very large iceberg. The scene
in *Emma*, for instance, when Jane Fairfax exclaims against the gov-
erness trade, he felt reversed the usual view of the author's intentions:
"It is very unusual for Jane Austen to refer to flesh. She must have intended to bring the protest home to the most obtuse."[48] David Daiches
went further than this, describing Austen's work as "Marxist before
Marx," a conclusion W. H. Auden had, in his own way, reached in
the 1930s in "Letter to Lord Byron," with this characterization of the
novelist as a beady-eyed monitor of the bottom line:

> *She was not an unshockable blue-stocking;*
> *If shades remain the characters they were,*
> *No doubt she still considers you as shocking.*
> *But tell Jane Austen, that is, if you dare,*
> *How much her novels are beloved down here.*
> *She wrote them for posterity, she said;*
> *'Twas rash, but by posterity she's read.*
>
> *You could not shock her more than she shocks me;*
> *Beside her Joyce seems innocent as grass.*
> *It makes me feel uncomfortable to see*
> *An English spinster of the middle-class*
> *Describe the amorous effects of "brass",*
> *Reveal so frankly and with such sobriety*
> *The economic basis of society.*[49]

Austen was beginning to be seen through the lens of alternative
ideologies and different disciplines; Geoffrey Gorer, an anthropologist,
was one of the first critics to apply Freudian analysis to Austen's novels, identifying a recurrent reversed Oedipal pattern of heroines who
actively dislike their mothers and marry men who stand in a paternal
relationship to them. The sudden abandonment of "her own myth,"
as he calls it, in *Persuasion*, with the mother-figure Lady Russell not

entirely blamed and a merciless portrait of Anne's father, indicated a hidden but significant personal change: "She had learned that, like all myths, it was eventually an enemy of life."[50]

The most dramatically revisionist view of Austen was put forward by the psychologist D. W. Harding in 1940 in his essay "Regulated Hatred," a piece of social as much as literary criticism, the very title of which was calculated to "wake the Jane Austenite up." Harding argued that Austen couldn't rightly be described as a satirist at all, as her objects were more personal and "more desperate" to find a way of living with her own critical attitudes. She was not seeking to entertain "a posterity of urbane gentlemen" with her writing but looking for "unobtrusive spiritual survival, without open conflict with the friendly people around her."[51]

Harding's subject was as much "the atmosphere surrounding her work" as the work itself, and he characterized it as "seriously misleading." Far from providing urbanity, calm, and genteel sensitivity, Harding found the novels and letters full of disturbing astringency that could only be enjoyed if deliberately misread. The popular impression of the author was therefore, in his opinion, utterly false, and its wide currency "an indication of Jane Austen's success in an essential part of her complex intention as a writer." "Her books," he wrote, "are, as she meant them to be, read and enjoyed by precisely the sort of people whom she disliked; she is a literary classic of the society which attitudes like hers, held widely enough, would undermine."[52]

Harding was not saying anything absolutely new—Mrs. Oliphant had remarked on Austen's cynicism seventy years earlier, and Reginald Farrer, in 1917, had remarked that "her present 'fans' do not know her place, and their antics would without doubt have excited Jane's lethal irony."[53] But Harding was saying it at greater length, and people were at last ready to hear it.

In the years after the war, Austen became subject-of-choice for all the most ambitious literary critics, the Everest glistening majestically in the distance, demanding to be attempted. Marvin Mudrick, Lionel Trilling, Ian Watt, Tony Tanner, A. Walton Litz, and Raymond Williams all wrote trenchantly about Austen; even Edmund

Wilson, who seemed unsure of his admiration, indulged "A Long Talk" about her. On the question of "smallness," Wilson chose to turn the telescope around the other way and wonder that the "spirit of classical comedy . . . should have embodied itself in England in the mind of a well-bred spinster, the daughter of a country clergyman, who never saw any more of the world than was made possible by short visits to London and a residence of a few years in Bath and who found her subjects mainly in the problems of young provincial girls looking for husbands." This was a point made differently by Q. D. Leavis in one of her remarkable essays on Austen for *Scrutiny* in the 1940s. Listing many extraordinary experiences of which Jane Austen had firsthand or close knowledge—fatal accidents, violent deaths, financial straits, prosecution by the law, public disgrace, sexual misconduct, war, revolution, bankruptcy, elopement, travel—Leavis remarked that "to ascribe the lack of dramatic incident in the novels to the author's humdrum experience and confined outlook is clearly wrong; the novels are limited in scope and subject by deliberate intention."[54]

Q. D. Leavis's "Critical Theory of Jane Austen's Writings" established a chronology that rejected the "two phases" theory, so beloved of sentimentalists. "The business of literary criticism is surely not to say 'Inspiration' and fall down and worship," she asserted tartly, "and in the case of Jane Austen it is certainly not entitled to take up such an unprofitable attitude."[55] It was no longer thought appropriate to flatter or patronize Austen. When Arnold Kettle returned to the issue of Austen's limitations in 1951, he accepted that "the silliest of all criticisms of Jane Austen is the one which blames her for not writing about the battle of Waterloo and the French Revolution. She wrote about what she understood and no artist can do more."[56]

"But did she understand enough?" he went on to ask. Perhaps there was, after all, something to "blame" Austen for—her unquestioning acceptance of the class society in which she grew up. The "sensitive values" recommended in *Emma*, Kettle contended, are applicable only to a minority, whose moral and social refinement is maintained entirely at the expense of other people. Is there not, he wondered, in the status quo underlying *Emma*, a complacency which renders "the hundred little in-complacencies" that the book promotes almost irrelevant?[57]

The Janeite torch was carried through this dark wood of new crit-icism by Lord David Cecil, the elegant old Etonian who had written in comfortably hyperbolic tone in 1931 that "There are those who do not like her; as there are those who do not like sunshine or unselfish-ness. But the very nervous defiance with which they shout their dis-satisfaction shows that they know they are a despised minority. All discriminating critics admire her books, most educated readers enjoy them; her fame, of all English novelists, is the most secure."[58]

Cecil was a committed Janeite, president of the Jane Austen Soci-ety, and public commentator on the author for more than forty years. His short biography, *A Portrait of Jane Austen*, published in 1978, was immediately popular and has never been out of print. As full of inac-curacies as it is, Cecil's beautiful prose, discriminating sensibility, and aristocratic charm (as well as the lavish production of the book, which had dozens of illustrations, many in color) made this the biography of choice for the general consumer of "all things Austen." Cecil's view of the world that Austen inhabited was wildly sentimental but beguil-ing. Take his description of "the green smiling landscape of field and woodland and leafy hedgerows" in which Austen grew up, a style to rival Thomas Gray: "with something at once homely and immemorial in the atmosphere emanating from its thatched villages, each centring around a grey old church, its interior enriched with sculptured monu-ments of successive generations of local landowners and set in a grassy churchyard populated by gravestones inscribed with the names of suc-cessive generations of their tenants."[59]

Cecil's biography linked Austen firmly with genteel, "smiling" southern landscapes like these: old parish churches, comfortable coun-try houses, and the most attractive aspects of Regency decor and archi-tecture; he praised Chippendale and Sheraton chairs, Wedgwood and Worcester cups—not because there is any evidence that Jane Austen ever sat on the one or raised the other to her lips but as examples of the "peculiar amenity" of life at the time, "provided one was born English and in sufficiently easy circumstances."[60] Quite a proviso. Anything excellent or pleasant of the period could be co-opted in this way to associate with the subject; Austen's novels, for example, are "artistic achievements of a Mozartian perfection."[61]

Cecil's heritage-heavy approach spoke powerfully to the masses of people beginning to take a somewhat proprietary interest in the huge range of stately homes and estates that opened to the public as tourist sights in the 1970s and '80s. The cash-strapped, denatured gentry of the postwar world, forced by a succession of popular governments' taxation strategies to open the doors of their ancestral homes to "the people," were regularly to be seen selling tickets of admission to their own drawing rooms on a Sunday afternoon, far more vivid examples of "living history" than the costumed actors one encounters at most heritage sites today.

David Cecil's book begins with a visit to such a property, and for a moment the reader might believe that he, like the rest of us, had been contemplating "the portraits of powdered and beruffled ladies and gentlemen staring down" from the ticket-holding side of a scalloped rope, but no: there "with . . . the tall windows open onto stretches of parkland hazy in the light of a fine September evening, my mother opened *Pride and Prejudice* and began to read it aloud to me." Son of the Marquess of Salisbury, grandson of the former prime minister, and with impeccable aristocratic pedigrees on both sides of his family, Lord David was, of course, part of that gorgeous landscape of privilege himself.

Fanny, Lady Knatchbull, would have been amazed to see how, more than a century after her death, Aunt Jane could be so strongly associated with refinement and class, and how many aristocratic and establishment figures considered her their favorite writer. There was an unusually high proportion of upper-class people on the committee of the Jane Austen Society from its very beginnings, when Robert William Chapman persuaded the seventh Duke of Wellington to be the first president, "the advantage of which, both socially and in the literary sphere, was very great," as Elizabeth Jenkins wrote later.[62] In the 1980s, Margaret Lane, Countess of Huntingdon, was thought "lovely to look at, and lovely to listen to" as president, and when an Austen aficionado was required for a TV quiz in 1957, Lady Cynthia Asquith was the one chosen.

The 150th anniversary commemoration of Austen's death, which took place in Chawton in 1967, was led by a group of impeccably traditional, conservative figures. The Duke of Wellington laid a wreath, the Tory leader Edward Heath ("an attentive reader" of the novels) made a short speech, Isobel Baillie sang, and the commentary on a film about the village was spoken by beloved wartime broadcaster Alvar Liddell. The committee that set up the festivities comprised two majors, one brigadier, and a Conservative Member of Parliament.[63]

Austen's attraction for the Tory establishment had much more to do with gentility, decorum, and maintaining the status quo than with literature. Sir Hugh Smiley was a well-loved member of the Jane Austen Society committee for thirty years and conducted its affairs "with military precision and a Guardsman's courteous efficiency";[64] his wife was also a long-serving committee member. The Smileys were represented, in an obituary of Sir Hugh, as offering direct links with Jane Austen's world: "Their house, with its lovely Regency furniture and its close connections with contemporary thought, is a reminder of how much of modern life can be lived among the beauty of Jane Austen's era."[65] But while Lady Smiley knew the novels of Jane Austen "almost by heart," the obituary had to admit that Sir Hugh "was renowned for claiming that he had not read Jane Austen's novels and didn't intend to."[66]

WHEN DAVID CECIL ANNOUNCED Austen's fame to be the "most secure . . . of all English novelists," he did so in the spirit of silencing any further debate with the remaining "despised minority" who disagreed with his conclusion. But the point at which Austen's status became unassailable in the second half of the last century was also the point at which Austen studies really began to take off. Critical activity, much of it originating across the Atlantic, focused increasingly on political, sociological, and historical elements in Austen's work. Not that any of these had been entirely absent before, but now they were systematized, with whole books emerging on single aspects of the ever-fertile subject.

D. W. Harding (and Marvin Mudrick in *Jane Austen: Irony as Defense and Discovery*, 1952) sparked the reinvention of Austen as an ironist of unplumbable depths open to multiple new interpretations and rereadings. She became a rich subject for feminist, postfeminist, and postmodernist commentators in the 1970s, '80s, and '90s, and the opening up of the female literary culture of the late eighteenth century as an area of research brought every aspect of Austen's work and life (especially its "uneventfulness") under scrutiny. References in the novels and letters to slavery, civil unrest, and war all began to be noticed, and the pragmatism that had shaped Austen's life, rather than being seen as a symptom of conservatism or complacency, began to look like a deliberate strategy that she had exploited to achieve a degree of autonomy and intellectual freedom.

One of the most influential Austen books of the 1970s, Marilyn Butler's *Jane Austen and the War of Ideas*, placed the novelist more thoroughly than ever before in her historical context—not that of Regency decor or Lord David's teacups, but of revolution and reform. Butler was partly following Alistair Duckworth (in *The Improvement of the Estate*, 1972) and Raymond Williams (in *The Country and the City*, 1973), whose discussions of Austen aligned her with forces of change and mobility during the Industrial Revolution. Butler demonstrated that rather than describing "an unfocused, idyllic, pre-industrialised village world," Austen's fiction was part of a conservative reaction to both the Jacobin novel and Jacobin politics. The book marked Austen's passage into the romantic movement, which had seemed to be going on independent of her, albeit she appeared there as a programmatic conservative. Terry Eagleton satirized the effect this had on the critical establishment: "The scandal of Butler's book was that it sheared coolly through decades of Trillingesque talk about Austen's 'tensions' and finely-tuned ambivalences and actually said that, well, when you get down to it, she's just a straight *Tory*. Nothing could be at once more obvious and impermissible."[67]

Austen's primness was also stripped away as critics began to recognize the worldliness of her "marriage plots" and her interest in sexual politics. Lionel Trilling, in one of several influential essays on Austen, credited her with provoking "male panic at a fictional world in which the masculine principle, although represented as admirable and necessary, is prescribed and controlled by a female mind," representing

Austen as perhaps the world's most influential and sexually manipu-
lative virgin. Austen was a gift to feminist theorists and provoked intense debate among them as to the nature and degree of her own
feminism. In their landmark study, *The Madwoman in the Attic: The
Woman Writer and the Nineteenth-Century Literary Imagination*, Sandra Gilbert and Susan Gubar claimed that male readers were flattered
by Austen's stories because they describe the submission of not just
any women, but women of quality, spirit, and intelligence. They saw
collusion on the author's part: "No less than the blotter held over the
manuscript on her writing desk, Austen's cover story of the necessity
for silence and submission reinforces women's subordinate position
in patriarchal culture."[68] A decade later, the desire to affix blame
somewhere in the formula had passed. In her earliest book on Austen,
Claudia Johnson allowed for accident and artfulness, with Austen
alert to the likely demands of posterity: "The precondition of Austen's
posthumous admittance into the canon was the apparent contentment
to work artfully within carefully constricted boundaries which have
been termed 'feminine.' "[69]

The Marxist-feminist critic Mary Poovey based her argument about
Austen on ideologies of gender that persuade women to accept and
validate ideas that perpetuate their own repression. "Romance" plots
very obviously do this, with their idealization of courtship: "By focusing on courtship, the myth of romantic love tends to freeze the relationship between a man and a woman at its moment of greatest
intensity . . . when women seem to exercise their greatest power."[70]
The promises of romance are obviously delusional, Poovey pointed
out, and the plot has to end well before they are tested; the woman
will never be so powerful, or so autonomous, or so desirable, again. But
the immediate gratification of this supreme moment is enough, in a
romance plot, to blot out the nagging thought of "And what happens
next?" The story ends with the triumphant feeling suspended, like a
diapason held down firmly at the end of the wedding march.

All through the '70s and '80s, individual Austen novels went in
and out of favor as the text of the moment in the academy. Oddly
enough, it was never *Pride and Prejudice*, the perennial "people's choice";
*Emma* was a favorite in the years when psychoanalytic criticism pre-

dominated, *Northanger Abbey* played right into the hands of the emerging discipline of history of the book, and *Mansfield Park* surged forward with the rise of postcolonial studies, sparked by the high-profile discussion of the book in Edward Said's *Culture and Imperialism* (1993). Elements in the novel that hardly seemed to be noticed before by critics—the overt acknowledgment of where Sir Thomas Bertram has derived his wealth (slave labor on his plantations in Antigua), the heroine Fanny Price's outburst about the treatment of slaves, and the "dead silence" her question is met with—have subsequently become, as Rajeswari Sunder Rajan has pointed out, the "locus of the novel's meanings."[71] The fact that this locus has shifted within recent memory from the aborted production of *Lovers' Vows*, or the trip to Sotherton (with all its transgressing of boundaries and metaphors of improvement), shows how flexible Austen can be in the hands of her interpreters. The character of Sir Thomas Bertram, for instance, has been represented in recent film dramatizations as at best a wholly compromised or complacent figure, at worst (as played by Harold Pinter in Patricia Rozema's 1996 film) a sadistic and ruthless colonial exploiter. But only forty years ago, even Trilling and Mudrick, who had generally revisionist views of so much else in the novels, saw Sir Thomas in an unequivocally generous light. Trilling thought him the personification of solidity, wholeness, and immutability, opposed to the "diversification of the self" threatened by the theatricals: "It is he . . . who makes of Mansfield Park the citadel that it is."[72]

Exponents of "heteronormativity" in Austen's work now vie with those who note its "queerness." Eve Sedgwick's provocatively titled essay "Jane Austen and the Masturbating Girl" caused debate and a certain amount of controversy when it appeared in an academic journal in 1993 but didn't reach the popular press, unlike a less sensational article by Terry Castle two years later in the *London Review of Books*. Castle was reviewing Deirdre Le Faye's new edition of *Jane Austen's Letters* and used the occasion to investigate the passionate nature of the Jane-Cassandra relationship. Noting the "whimsical yet fierce attachment" in Jane's earliest letters to Cassandra, the "intense psychic mirroring" of the older sister by the younger, and "a kind of homophilic fascination" in Austen's description of women generally,

Castle concluded that both sisters "found greater comfort and pleasure—more of that 'heartfelt felicity' that Emma Woodhouse finds with Mr Knightley, or Elizabeth Bennet with the handsome Darcy—in remaining with one another."[73]

When the editors of the magazine chose to headline the piece "Was Jane Austen Gay?" Castle's argument became fair game for the press, some members of which chose to interpret the headline (if not the article, which was not read with as much care) as suggesting that the Austen sisters indulged in incestuous lesbian sex. There was outrage from the broadsheets to the tabloids, so affronting was the idea that Austen may have had sexual feelings of any sort, never mind such unconventional ones. As David Nokes observed in the *Times Literary Supplement* soon after, "chief among Austen's traditionally English virtues is an instinctive reticence about sex . . . cherished notions of the integrity of Austen's art are intimately associated with a symbolic fetishization of the physical intactness of her body."

The outrage did not die down very quickly, as it was tempered with profound satisfaction at the spectacle of "Mr." Castle, American, academic, and obviously crazed, getting England's Jane so wrong. Castle's employers, Stanford University, issued a news release on August 16, 1995, in an attempt to calm the situation. Castle suggested politely that the depth of the reaction in Britain was in proportion to Austen's iconic status in her homeland: "I think there is a kind of fetishizing of Austen, not only among British academics, but among a lot of people who join Jane Austen societies, of which there are still a number in England. And [the press coverage] triggered off a very primitive reaction in people who use her to project their own fantasies about the past, and the purity of the past." Because Austen also has become "an icon of the early 19th-century spinster," Castle said, "people tend to view her as asexual, as not having had any sort of sensual life at all. But her novels, it seems to me, are about desire and eros and emotion. If they weren't, why would we care about them?"

ALONGSIDE ALL THE MINUTELY interpretative work done on Austen in the past three decades sit the achievements of three separate scholars working mostly outside the academy: David Gilson, Brian Southam, and Deirdre Le Faye. Gilson's bibliography of Austen, first published in 1982 and subsequently reissued, reflects decades of research into the original editions, translations, continuations, later editions, and thousands of critical essays and books; its very size and thoroughness make a powerful statement about Austen's achievement. In the 1960s Brian Southam's research on Austen's literary manuscripts opened up the study of the juvenilia and unfinished works, previously treated as ephemera, and his two Critical Heritage volumes—anthologies of criticism with detailed editorial commentary—spearheaded Austen reception studies, a new growth area. Deirdre Le Faye, like Gilson a professional librarian, has become a legendary figure in Austen scholarship, having written biographies of both Jane Austen and her cousin Eliza de Feuillide and the popular *Jane Austen: The World of Her Novels* among other books, edited *Jane Austen's Letters* (published in 1995), compiled a massive *Chronology of Jane Austen and Her Family*, and published innumerable articles in the *Book Collector*, *Review of English Studies*, *Notes & Queries*, and the *Collected Reports of the Jane Austen Society*. Le Faye's indefatigable hunting down of information about Austen and her circle, the work of a lifetime, has provided an unrivaled factual base for Austen studies, and she is the acknowledged super-authority on her subject. But insofar as she prides herself on offering definitive information, "hard facts," and little or (preferably) no interpretation, Le Faye's work stands in direct and somewhat combative opposition to almost all recent academic writing on Austen, where the very idea of a "definitive factual biography" would be dismissed by any postmodern or new-historicist critic as impossible, and by many others as undesirable.

The two main Jane Austen Societies, the original British-based one and JASNA, the Jane Austen Society of North America (founded in 1979, and now by far the biggest), have provided useful neutral zones that can be shared by fans, readers, and academics alike. Both the main societies feature lectures by leading scholars at their annual meetings and publish those papers and many other, unsolicited, contributions in professionally produced journals. JASNA has print and online versions of *Persuasions*, the Jane Austen Society of Australia (founded in 1988) publishes *Sensibilities*, and the Jane Austen Society UK's *Collected Reports* now runs to five volumes. The breadth of these resources is their great value, but the very lack of differentiation in them between kinds of Austen "knowledge" makes some scholars feel queasy, as do the junketing aspects of the Society's meetings and the unsophisticated pleasure many members take in Austen-themed readings, costumed performances, teas, games, and musical events—more pleasure perhaps than in the learned discourses that are meant to be the main event. Claudia Johnson has written amusingly of how badly Austen scholars do at JASNA quizzes ("We rarely recollect the colour of this character's dress or that servant's name") and how the boundaries between "interest" and "scholarly interest" get blurred: "We sometimes suffer the additional mortification of discovering our own papers becoming yet another relatively undifferentiated, unhierarchicalized item in the great repository of Austeniana assiduously collected by Janeites and compiled in newsletters and reports, printed somewhere between recipes for white soup and the latest word jumble."[74]

But Johnson acknowledges how self-serving the academic industry around Austen can be and how "some of our most basic assumptions about how to read her novels were calculated to consolidate the authority of a new professorate, with its distinctive programme and concomitant visions of class, gender, and national identity."[75] The academy's generation of texts, theories, and whole careers from one of the smallest oeuvres in the canon has indeed been phenomenal. Thirty or so years ago, it was still small enough to be parodied by David Lodge in his novel *Changing Places*, where Austen is the monolithic uber-subject chosen by Professor Morris Zapp as the target for his scholarly attention. Zapp's project, already some years advanced, is to work through the whole Austen canon, "saying absolutely everything that could possibly be said," with a view to closing the subject down:

The idea was to be utterly exhaustive, to examine the novels from every conceivable angle, historical, biographical, rhetorical, mythical, Freudian, Jungian, existentialist, Marxist, structuralist, Christianallegorical, ethical, exponential, linguistic, phenomenological, archetypal, you name it; so that when each commentary was written there would be simply *nothing further to say* about the novel in question. The object of the exercise, as he had often to explain with as much patience as he could muster, was not to enhance others' enjoyment and understanding of Jane Austen, still less to honour the novelist herself, but to put a definitive stop to the production of any further garbage on the subject. The commentaries would not be designed for the general reader but for the specialist, who, looking up Zapp, would find that the book, article or thesis he had been planning had already been anticipated and, more likely than not, invalidated. After Zapp, the rest would be silence. The thought gave him deep satisfaction. In Faustian moments he dreamed of going on, after fixing Jane Austen, to do the same job on the other major English novelists, then the poets and the dramatists, perhaps using computers and teams of trained graduate students, inexorably reducing the area of English literature available for free comment, spreading dismay through the whole industry, rendering scores of his colleagues redundant: periodicals would fall silent, famous English Departments be left deserted like ghost towns.[76]

Lodge's wonderful satire acknowledges a fear of proliferation; in criticism, as in life, in the 1970s, everything seemed to be getting out of hand. But the computers that Zapp imagined would help him eliminate Jane Austen have rather multiplied his problem, and the technological and cultural changes of the past thirty years have tended to embrace proliferation, encourage inclusiveness, and render all sorts of "discrimination" invalid. Zapp's worst nightmares have come true: Nowadays, a glance along the "A" shelf of any good bookshop will reveal a dizzying array of books on Jane Austen: study guides, biographies, sourcebooks, companions, books on Jane Austen and the theater, Jane Austen and food, and religion, and money, and the romantic poets . . . Jane Austen on film, in a social context, as a parson's daughter, as a sailor's sister, the historical Jane Austen, the postcolonial Jane Austen, Jane Austen's style. There is a whole book about the famous first sentence of *Pride and Prejudice*[77]—which of course reaches no conclusion about its meaning. All this in addition to the novels themselves; the letters, the juvenilia, the chronology, the bibliographies, the facsimiles. It's a vast industry to have arisen from a writer once thought of as an instinctive warbler about whom there was nothing to say, whose works, Anne Thackeray believed, resembled "the nest which some little bird builds of the materials nearest at hand . . . curiously constructed out of the simplest matters."

# CHAPTER 7

*Jane Austen*™

THE LATE-VICTORIAN CULT OF "DIVINE JANE" PERSISTED IN the popular imagination (albeit in widely differing forms) despite the many radically revisionist views of Austen and the significance and meaning of her writing that were put forward in the twentieth century. A genuinely popular author as well as a great one, she has come to exist, more obviously than any other English writer, in several mutually exclusive spheres at once. What appears to one reader as a biting satire on eighteenth-century provincial life is read by another purely for its nostalgia value; the feminist message of, say, *Pride and Prejudice* translates as a paean to sexual pragmatism and the virtues of the status quo, while the frustrations of the thwarted professional writer evident in Austen's letters strike some as marks of a delightfully unworldly amateurism. She has truly become all things to all men.

Austen didn't seem like an obvious candidate for mass popularity in the late nineteenth century or the late twentieth, before the public was whipped into a frenzy by Austen-Leigh's *Memoir* in the first instance and, in the second, a man in a wet shirt. As Margaret Oliphant observed, hers were not the kinds of books "which catch the popular fancy at once without pleasing the critic—a power sometimes possessed by very imperfect and unsatisfactory performances; neither do they belong to that highest class of all which takes every variety of imagination by storm, and steps into favour without any probation":

> They are rather of the class which attracts the connoisseur, which charms the critical and literary mind, and which, by dint of persistency and iteration, is carried by the superior rank of readers into a half-real half-fictitious universality of applause.... "The best judges" have here, for once, done the office of an Academy, and laureated a writer whom the populace would not have been likely to laureate, but whom it has learned to recognize.[1]

The public "learns to recognize" literary qualities, Mrs. Oliphant implies, that it is not able or inclined to appreciate through mere reading, and does so through the "persistency and iteration" of the opinion-forming class.

Austen's current success as a brand, or product, the name of which accrues interest from circulation alone, is a measure of "that ideological surplus value known as 'legitimacy' or 'authority'" that Linda Charnes has found in all "notorious" names.[2] A strong myth or "product legend" like Austen's depends upon separation from its origins; to quote Charnes again, it requires "the naturalizing or 'forgetting' of its own history" (a process that began for Austen even before her history was written). An opinion formed by a small group can in this way spread out and be held by a much larger group; its "half-real, half-fictitious" quality becomes not just the way it disseminates effectively, but the reason it does.

As Mrs. Oliphant said, Austen's novels are neither trash nor works of blinding genius, but lie somewhere—one could say *everywhere*—in between. An American reviewer in 1844 identified Austen's middlingness as the key to her effect, even at that early date: "Miss Austen—dear Miss Austen who never says a brilliant thing, nor paints a perfect character,— who is neither witty, nor passionate, nor eloquent, and is still minute, homelike, and true; and by these qualities alone, she twines about the inmost fibres of her readers' hearts."[3] The middle-aged, the middle class, and those who consider themselves slightly above the middlebrow are Austen's natural constituency. They (we!) love Austen—the idea as much as the books—because she comes from our own ranks and rocks no boats. With Austen, we know that we are never going to be taken to extremes.

Austen's narrowness has paradoxically been a major factor in her global mobility. Before the war, she was published in about a dozen languages, but in the following thirty years (propelled by film and other new media) she was translated into Japanese, Korean, Hebrew, Icelandic, Russian, Persian, Polish, Serbo-Croat, Bengali, Finnish, Chinese, Arabic, and Hungarian, as well as many minor tongues such as Marathi, Tamil, and Telugu. The "3 or 4 Families in a Country Village" formula, in plots dealing almost exclusively with money and marriage, speaks to millions the world over. As David Cecil wrote in 1948, "*Emma* is universal just because it is narrow."[4] The most empathetic readers of Austen may well be in modern-day Africa, where the Church of England is at its most traditional, and where family structures still resemble those familiar to the author. An article in the *Jane Austen Society Report* for 1962 showed that the pupils of a school in Nigeria had no trouble understanding the marital imperatives of *Pride and Prejudice* and the disposal problems connected with having five daughters.[5] *Bride and Prejudice*, Gurinder Chadha's 2004 Bollywood adaptation of the story, tapped into the same relevance to contemporary Sikhs—a relevance lost to contemporary Westerners.

It seems almost redundant to itemize aspects of Austen's appeal; there are the brilliantly constructed plots, the romance, the comedy, the pellucid language. She is one of the most accessible intellectuals among authors and the least didactic moralist. The interest of her books is "far more serious than their surface appearance would lead us to expect," as David Cecil said, rather ominously, but even the surface is entertainment enough. And there doesn't have to be a war on for the escapist element to appeal: "What a relief it is to come back to your witty volumes," Andrew Lang exclaimed in 1884, "and forget the follies of today in those of Mr Collins and Mrs Bennet!"[6] As G. K. Chesterton's clerihew has it, "The Novels of Jane Austen / Are the ones to get lost in."[7]

But the main reason for Austen's mass popularity is the one from which critics tend to avert their eyes: the love stories. The formula of girl meets boy, both meet obstacles but come together triumphantly in the end owes its neatness and directness to Austen and her streamlining of the romance plot she inherited. Just as great comedians have superb comic timing, Austen had an unerring instinct about where to place the romantic stimuli in her plots. It is especially effective in *Pride and Prejudice* and *Persuasion*, both of which keep readers in a delicious state of anxiety and expectation right up to the clinching proposal moments, regardless of how often you read the books. (The cinema trailer for the 1995 BBC film of *Persuasion* voiced-over: "The critics call *Persuasion* 'A Cinderella romance so delicious you want it never to end.'") *Emma* is more cryptic in its progress though ultimately most satisfying in its outcome. The hero and heroine are not so clearly made for each other as in the other two books, and Emma's realization that she is in love comes late on, delayed by the narrative viewpoint being almost exclusively her own. But when Knightley proposes, Austen writes a template for thousands of subsequent love scenes:

> "My dearest Emma," said he, "for dearest you will always be, whatever the event of this hour's conversation, my dearest, most beloved Emma—tell me at once. Say 'No,' if it is to be said."—She could really say nothing.—"You are silent," he cried, with great animation; "absolutely silent! at present I ask no more."
>
> Emma was almost ready to sink under the agitation of this moment. The dread of being awakened from the happiest dream, was perhaps the most prominent feeling.[8]

As Katherine Mansfield remarked with a sigh, "Mr Knightley in the shrubbery would be something!"[9]

More than half of all paperbacks published in 2004 were romances, and Jane Austen is the acknowledged mother of the genre; many of the books, like the works of Georgette Heyer and Barbara Cartland, return to Regency settings to get closer to their model. When the American imprint Silhouette Romances was being planned in the 1970s, everything in them was written to a formula developed by market research:

Even the name of the series (perhaps subconsciously evoking Austen) came from a consumer survey result. A group of women readers were asked what the ideal attributes of a romantic novel were, from the age of the heroine to the overall length of the book. The resulting tip sheet for writers could just as easily be applied to Austen's novels: the heroines were always to be "young and virginal," the heroes "strong and assertive," the plots utterly predictable, and the endings happy. There was to be no violence, blood, or pain; no slang language or obscenity, and no premarital sex. The heroine's age should be between nineteen and twenty-seven, and she should not be "beautiful in the high fashion sense." The hero should be eight to twelve years older than the heroine, "not necessarily handsome," but virile and not married, though he could be bereaved or divorced—as long as that wasn't his fault.[10] Austen's novels clearly contributed to this formula as well as shared the basic instincts behind it.

There are, of course, no raised heart rates, no touching, and certainly no kisses in any of Austen's novels, none of the thinly veiled or not-veiled-at-all orgasmic prose of the Gothic novelists that Austen herself enjoyed as rollicking good reads, not to mention the prurience that her literary hero Samuel Richardson indulged on his way to a moral. But the very absence of explicit eroticism leaves her books charged with sexual feeling, mostly of the young, virginal (therefore rather sex-obsessed) heroines, though the male characters' feelings are indicated too, through restlessness (Frank Churchill), meaningful looks (Wentworth), and agitated silences (Mr. Knightley). George Moore had noted in 1919 "that it was Miss Austen's spinsterhood that allowed her to discover the Venusberg in the modern drawing-room."[11] Her effectiveness in this regard seems only to increase with time. In a permissive age, the restraint and decorousness of her love scenes seem in themselves erotic, and the idea of the heroines attracting so much male attention by making so few sexual concessions becomes, for the modern woman, an unattainable fantasy of female empowerment.

Contemporary chick-lit follows Austen rather more closely than the Harlequin-style romance in its preference for pliable male characters: lovers for the heroines who promise to be helpmates rather than dominators. Austen's heroes (or men—for they aren't, in truth, very *heroic*) can be adapted easily to this model. They have often been complained of for being rather two-dimensional creatures: Even the manly ones, such as Captain Wentworth and Colonel Brandon, are shown in retirement or furlough; Darcy is too gentlemanly to be caught in the act of manliness, Edward Ferrars and Edmund Bertram are both young and pious, and Henry Tilney is downright girly, with his knowledge of muslins and chat about books. Such men are so non-threatening that a conscientious screenwriter such as Andrew Davies has felt it necessary to introduce scenes of "manly pursuits" in his adaptations, to inject into his scripts some of the testosterone that Austen always left out. In Davies's *Sense and Sensibility* (2007), Brandon does some shooting and falconry, Edward Ferrars swings his ax at the firewood, and they all gallop around furiously on steaming stallions when suffering from the disappointments of Austen's delayed-gratification plots.

Perhaps not surprisingly, the people who find Austen's treatment of sex and romance unconvincing tend to be men. A critic in 1924 complained that there was "no sex at all" in her work: "[She] is the feminine Peter Pan of letters. . . . In her world there is neither marrying nor giving in marriage but just the make-believe mating of dolls."[12] Sir Walter Raleigh, otherwise a great admirer of the novels, found the inferior vitality of the male characters completely laughable. "Her young men, my Gawd!" he wrote to Robert William Chapman in 1926:

> I will only take Darcy and Bingley. Of course they have no profession—they have money. But there is no scrap of evidence, no indication, that they can *do* anything, shoot a partridge, or add up figures, or swim or brush their hair. They never talk about anything except young women, a subject taboo among decent young men. (I find that women mostly don't know that men never talk intimately about them. Jane didn't know this.) Well, Darcy and Bingley have only one interest in life—getting married, and marrying their friends one to another. It is incredible, immense, yet it deludes you while you read.[13]

G. K. Chesterton tried to defend Austen's understanding of male psychology, even if her knowledge of male physicality seems a little limited. "[When Darcy says] 'I have been a selfish being all my life, in practice though not in theory' . . . he gets nearer to a complete confession of the intelligent male than was ever hinted by the Byronic lapses of the Brontës' heroes or the elaborate exculpations of George Eliot's."[14] But most male commentators agreed with Raleigh that Austen only "knew what she didn't know" about sex, and remained "concealed behind a fogbank of bourgeois morality" as Marvin Mudrick remarked, "routed by the sexual question she has raised."[15]

Wayne Booth in 1961 tried to reclaim Austen for normality (specifically, heterosexuality) by asserting that the author had no need to introduce actual "love scenes" into her novels, because all that a love scene would encompass was already encoded in (or on) the text and didn't need to be made explicit. And it is true that Austen does suggest a world of other thoughts in the slow, appreciative way that Emma suddenly "sees" Knightley at the Crown ball:

> There he was, among the standers-by, where he ought not to be; he ought to be dancing, . . . so young as he looked!—He could not have appeared to greater advantage perhaps any where, than where he had placed himself. His tall, firm, upright figure, among the bulky forms and stooping shoulders of the elderly men, was such as Emma felt must draw every body's eyes.[16]

Elizabeth Bennet indulges some similarly proprietary gazing in front of Darcy's portrait in the gallery at Pemberley. The fact that the subject is captured in oils makes him fair game for her imagination:

> At last it arrested her—and she beheld a striking resemblance of Mr. Darcy, with such a smile over the face, as she remembered to have sometimes seen, when he looked at her. . . . As she stood before the canvas, on which he was represented, and fixed his eyes upon herself, she thought of his regard with a deeper sentiment of gratitude than it had ever raised before; she remembered its warmth, and softened its impropriety of expression.[17]

The wild success of recent Austen films relies in great part on their visual realization of the erotic potential of the novels, on the dramatization of scandalous elements locked into some of Austen's backstories, and on the vision, generously lingered over by the camera, of a lot of handsome men in the flattering dress of the early 1800s. Several amateur compilations on YouTube cleverly rework the romantic highlights of the films: *Jane Austen Ladies* to Nellie Furtado's "Maneater"; *Juicy Period Drama Men* by "Elbenhexe" (to Better Than Ezra's "Juicy"), and *Period Drama Montage* by "DreamyViper." This last, setting clips of assorted hunks from recent TV and film adaptations (most of them Austen books) to the Weather Girls' "It's Raining Men," begins hilariously with JJ Feild, a charmingly twinkly Henry Tilney, saying to Catherine Morland, "I fear we may be about to get a little *damp*."

The YouTube compilations, comically compacting the stock elements we all respond to so readily in the films, provide an amusing catalog of them too: the hero turns his horse and rides off energetically, the hero enters a room and pierces the occupants with a look, the hero stares fixedly at the heroine across a crowded ballroom, the hero gallops through the rain, walks powerfully through the rain, dives into a lake, submerges his head under the bathwater, has a duel in the rain, chases after the heroine in the rain. Neither of them is wearing a hat. They search each other's eyes ("He looked the question," as Austen says so suggestively at the erotic crux in *Emma*). It is a truth universally acknowledged that this does it for the girls. Cue the kiss, the climax of every Jane Austen film. It is usually made as passionate as possible, but there is only ever the one. More than one kiss, or the sight of subsequent hero-heroine canoodling (which the 1999 *Mansfield Park* and the 2007 *Persuasion* attempted) would be, in these circumstances, like demanding a second communion wafer.

AUSTEN VERY OBVIOUSLY INSPIRED the boom in chick-lit books and romantic comedy films of the 1990s. Both emerged from and fed a new class of consumers: young unmarried women whose delayed search for a permanent mate had made the whole process seem urgent, even desperate. The hugely successful Bridget Jones books by the journalist Helen Fielding (which began as a newspaper column early in 1995) didn't just give this demographic a name, "singletons," but freely used Austen as a model. "Jane Austen's plots are very good and have been market researched over a number of centuries," Helen Fielding said in an interview, "so I decided simply to steal one of them. I thought she wouldn't mind and anyway she's dead."[18] Fielding made the link explicit by naming Bridget's dream man Mark Darcy, and, when the BBC dramatization of _Pride and Prejudice_ was broadcast later in the same year, incorporated Bridget's thoughts on the production into the column. When the resulting book was going to be filmed, the author "was emphatic" that Colin Firth should play her Mr. Darcy too. The scriptwriting team was the author, Fielding, Andrew Davies, and Richard Curtis: Bridget Jones, Jane Austen, and _Four Weddings and a Funeral_ all rolled together in one ball.

The association of Austen with highly successful books and films like the Bridget Jones series, or _Sex and the City_, described by Dana Stevens in the _New York Times_ as "a continual interrogation of Austen's 'universal truth,'"[19] has led to her novels being read as guides to Finding Mr. Right—read so literally that they spawn books such as _The Regency Rules_ (following the retrograde '90s bestseller on how to behave in ways men find attractive, _The Rules_) and _Jane Austen's Guide to Dating_, both "immense, incredible" applications. One of the horrible ironies of Austen's currency in contemporary popular culture is that she is referenced so freely and confidently in discussions of "empowerment," "girl power," and all the other travesties of womanly self-fashioning that stand in for feminism in the present day.

The success of chick-lit moved one British publisher, Hodder Headline, to cash in on the association in 2006 by rebranding Austen's novels in pastel-colored covers with swirly writing and butterflies, flowers, and bird emblems. The press release said: "Who is the fairy godmother of women's fiction? And who is still packaged like a dry, academic author, reaching only a tiny fraction of her potential audience? The answer, of course, is Jane Austen!"[20] Wordsworth Editions were also sensitive to the off-putting plainness of Austen's "packaging" and in 2005 commissioned a new picture of the author for their reprint of James Edward Austen-Leigh's _Memoir_. It was based on an engraving that first appeared in 1873 in an American publication, an ingenious riff on Lizars/Andrews's version of Cassandra's drawing, which is sometimes called "The Wedding-Ring Portrait," as the artist has added a ring to the subject's left hand. The hand doesn't appear in the Technicolor "Wordsworth Makeover" of 2005; there, Austen's face is rouged, her eyes enlivened, and her cap replaced by a strange plaited wig in a shade of gray-blue. Helen Trayler, the managing director of Wordsworth Editions, justified the move thus: "The poor old thing didn't have anything going for her in the way of looks. Her original portrait is very, very dowdy. It wouldn't be appealing to readers, so I took it upon myself to commission a new picture of her. We've given her a bit of a makeover, with make-up and some hair extensions and removed her nightcap. Now she looks great—as if she's just walked out of a salon."

Even with hair extensions and Botox, no image of Jane Austen is likely to become valued for its beauty alone, as is the uncharacteristically romantic photograph of Virginia Woolf by George Charles Beresford, which is the National Portrait Gallery's all-time best-selling postcard. "She's not a goddess. She has no copyright," the chairman of the Jane Austen Society told an interviewer. "It's just what happens when someone is so popular, and if it brings her to a different readership then that's good news." The literary agent Patrick Janson-Smith was equally philosophical about the "sexed-up" picture, pointing out that modern author photos "are airbrushed the whole time, especially American lady authors of a certain age. It's a shock to meet a writer when the reality falls a little short. We live in a shallow world where authors are increasingly sold on their appearance."

THE MOST REMARKABLE TURN in Austen's global fame has been the popularity of film and television versions of her works in the past fifteen years, beginning with the BBC's 1995 miniseries, *Pride and Prejudice*. There had been five previous TV adaptations of Austen's most famous novel, one as early as 1938, when the technology was in its infancy and the transmitter at Alexandra Palace had a guaranteed range of only twenty-five miles. The subject was always going to be popular with audiences, even with only thirty lines of resolution on a handkerchief-sized screen. In fact, its familiarity made Sue Birtwistle, the producer of the 1995 series, anxious that her project would not get the green light, so she pitched it to the financial executives without at first mentioning the title, relating the story as if it had just been written: "Well, there's five girls aged 15 to 22 years old and their mother is desperate to get them married to rich men because, though some are beautiful, they are poor." An executive was immediately excited by this and asked if the rights were available.[21]

When it was screened in the autumn of 1995, Birtwistle's *Pride and Prejudice* did not just get massive viewing figures but instantly assumed a sort of authority; it took up a lot of time (five and a half hours—not much less time than it would take to read the book), the production was lavish and at pains to look authentic, and it was filmed on film rather than video (which gave the whole thing a classy, "movie" look). The beloved story, reproduced in more detail than ever before in a witty and intelligent script by Andrew Davies, sprang to life with remarkable freshness: 40 percent of the United Kingdom's total viewing audience tuned in to witness its happy ending.

During the screening of the series, the actor playing Darcy, Colin Firth, became the nation's number one heartthrob, a position he—or rather, he-as-the-character—retains virtually unchallenged to this day. The chemistry between him and the actress playing Lizzie Bennet (Jennifer Ehle) was enhanced by a real-life, off-camera fling, but the scene that made him famous was the one, invented by Andrew Davies, in which Darcy is shown brooding by the lake at Pemberley, then stripping off his outer garments, diving into the water, and emerging with his clothes damp. Davies later said that the wet shirt hadn't been deliberate, and that in fact he had expected Firth to take his shirt off, but the actor's qualms led to a compromise. "I never thought a wet-shirt scene would be such a turn-on," Davies told the *Sunday Times* in 2007 of the sequence, which is now considered one of the most unforgettable moments in British TV history.[22] But the matrons of England went mad. "There was a period, which went on for a long time, when you would go to parties and whenever you went into the kitchen there would be a picture of Mr Darcy and his wet shirt, tacked up over the dishwasher," Davies recalled. "I'm very proud of that."

The man himself was cagey about the whole business. "It honestly doesn't mean anything to me," Firth told a reporter from the *Independent* in 2000. "I don't have anything to do with anything I did six years ago. I don't know if you remember how you spent your summer of '94, but that's how I spent my summer of '94, and that's about it."[23] Or, as Jane Austen herself would say, "Seven years I suppose are enough to change every pore of one's skin, & every feeling of one's mind."[24]

The series won several awards and sold immediately all around the world. When the video was released in the last week of transmission, the entire first run of twelve thousand copies sold out within two hours. Fifty-eight thousand more sold by the end of the week, astonishing the BBC merchandising department: "It is unheard of for a video to sell even half as well, especially when viewers are able to tape the episodes at home for free," a spokesman said.

If Austen's *Pride and Prejudice* is now regularly given away free with newspapers and voted Great Britain's favorite book and a literary treasure that "we can't do without," it is in great part because it is the book of the film. The superior popularity of the films has heartened some, who reasonably claim that it opens up the audience for all classic literature, but there are purists in odd places too. The ex-editor of the men's magazine *Nuts*, Phil Hilton, has objected strongly to the vulgarization of Austen's texts: "She is about more than romance, that's just the engine that drives the plot along," he told an interviewer from the BBC. "Unfortunately when adapted for film and TV the good stuff often ends up on the cutting room floor in favour of a handsome actor walking out of a lake."[25]

All previous surges of interest in Austen had been focused on publications—the *Memoir*, the *Letters*, *Love and Freindship*—but in the mid-1990s, without any newly discovered documents or pictures, without an anniversary even (which passed quietly in 1975), suddenly Jane Austen was everywhere. The eighteen months following *Pride and Prejudice* saw the release of Ang Lee's film of *Sense and Sensibility*; a Miramax *Emma*, starring Gwyneth Paltrow; a BBC production, released as an art-house film, of *Persuasion*; and the wittily parodic *Clueless* by Amy Heckerling, which set *Emma* in a modern-day Beverly Hills high school and mall. The *Wall Street Journal* spoke of "Austenmania" and *Entertainment Weekly* was moved to write up the phenomenon thus:

> She doesn't go to the see-and-be-seen parties. She's reticent with the press. There are nasty rumors that she engaged in an incestuous relationship with her sister, for God's sake. And frankly, she could use a makeover. But in this year alone, four of her novels have been adapted for the big and small screens. And with numerous World Wide Web sites devoted to her glory, she even holds her own with Internet pinup Brad Pitt. Not bad for a British broad who's been dead for 178 years.

The article was accompanied by a photo of Jane Austen poolside, complete with cell phone and movie scripts. The phone must have been ringing constantly, for in the subsequent years there were further big-screen versions of *Mansfield Park*, *Pride and Prejudice*, its vibrant Bollywood cousin, *Bride and Prejudice*, in which Austen's novel was transposed into contemporary Sikh culture, and *Kandukondain Kandukondain*, a Bollywood adaptation of *Sense and Sensibility*. The year 2007 saw an elaborate packaging of television adaptations, old and new, into a "Jane Austen season" on the United Kingdom's ITV, like a collected edition of books. It contained an excellent new *Northanger Abbey* (the least filmed of the titles) and *Sense and Sensibility*, both scripted by Andrew Davies; a new *Mansfield Park* and *Persuasion*; and an *Emma* from 1997, starring Kate Beckinsale. No one felt inclined to touch *Pride and Prejudice*, its previous small-screen version having attained an iconic status of its own, and when PBS screened the season as "The Complete Jane Austen" in the spring of 2007, they replayed the 1995 series in the empty slot, even though it was three times longer than any of the other films.

Douglas McGrath, a former scriptwriter for *Saturday Night Live* and writer and director of the 1996 *Emma*, was candid about the appeal of Austen to filmmakers: "I thought Jane Austen would be a good collaborator . . . because she writes, you know, superb dialogue, she creates memorable characters, she has an extremely clever skill for plotting—and she's dead."[26] Apart from being dead, and dead cheap (there are no copyright fees, of course, for any use of her texts), Austen was a great provider of compact story lines and crisp dialogue. " '90s sarcasm's got nothing on Austen's perfection of mean-it-with-a-sneer, say-it-with-a-smile dialogue," *Entertainment Weekly* concluded. "Yes, they're formulaic—the aging, clever, not too beautiful girl always gets the guy, eventually—but that only suits Hollywood all the more."

Ang Lee's *Sense and Sensibility*, which appeared in 1996, scripted by and starring Emma Thompson, linked arms with several other successful films of the time in ways that helped propel the idea of a "Jane Austen film" out of the "classic" ghetto and into the mainstream. Thompson, as Elinor Dashwood, was in some ways reprising her Oscar-winning performance as Margaret Schlegel in the 1992 Merchant Ivory production of *Howards End*, another role in which the elder sister, ostensibly less "feeling" and spontaneous than her vivacious sibling, has resources that are shown to be deeper, more tender, private, and, ultimately, more attractive. Thompson had herself in mind for the role when she wrote the screenplay (which also won her an Oscar for Best Adaptation), adding the completely un-Austenian (but utterly Forsterish) "dearest" to many of Elinor's speeches. It makes her first few appearances in the film sound as if Emma/Elinor has just walked off one set and on to the other.

The film also starred Hugh Grant as Edward Ferrars, acting the character as the same tongue-tied, minimal-eye-contact toff as his wildly successful role in *Four Weddings and a Funeral*, which was taking the British box office by storm just as *Sense and Sensibility* went into production. The casting followed the writer's wishes, for Thompson had had Grant in mind for Edward all along.[27] The production team was delighted at his acceptance of the role on grounds of crowd-pulling power, but there was another level of connection that was important structurally. Referencing *Four Weddings* so heavily, the audience could rest assured that Edward in *Sense and Sensibility* will, despite his "shyness" and preexisting engagement to Lucy Steele, end up married to the heroine.

Both Colin Firth and Hugh Grant later starred in *Bridget Jones* and *Bridget Jones: The Edge of Reason*, backing up the feeble claims of those films to Austen-likeness, and all the latest Jane Austen adaptations have drawn from the same small pool of familiar British actors: Victoria Hamilton, Sophie Thompson, Greg Hicks, Hugh Bonneville, Olivia Williams, Greta Scacchi, and Kate Beckinsale have all been double-cast in Austen adaptations. As Julian Barnes observed caustically in a review of the 1983 *Mansfield Park* on the BBC, such casting strategies are part of a winning formula: "lots of raked gravel, background music, mob-capped actors vaguely familiar from previous classic serials, and a deceptive deference to the surface of the text" are all part of "the National Trust approach to literature."[28]

As Barnes implied, the concept of overkill hardly applies in this arena. Twenty-five years on, you can switch on the television in Britain midway through any Sunday evening and almost certainly see a carriage jingling up or down a driveway, or a costumed dance, or a candle-lit dinner party. Thackeray, Austen, Dickens, Brontë, Eliot, Austen, Austen, Gaskell: the author is really the least important factor. They are popular products because they are seamlessly reliable and predictable. The *Mansfield Park* and *Northanger Abbey* commissioned by ITV for their 2007 "Jane Austen season" had almost identical "time passing" sequences in the titles, showing the heroine as a child laughing and playing ball games with her siblings/cousins, melting into the adult character doing the same thing a few years later. But the visual cliché hardly mattered; its repetition on two consecutive Sundays in March might indeed have been welcome to much of the audience. These were "Jane Austen films," and here was the latest dose.

For decades, Robert Z. Leonard's *Pride and Prejudice* was not the sole film adaptation of that novel but of any Austen novel, and it seemed totally sufficient. But there is a new tolerance for multiplication of treatments in the media that shows a degree of seepage from critical theory through to mass culture. No number of versions of a book, adaptations of a subject, or retellings of a popular story are too many to watch or sell, it seems, and few subjects get to the point of needing "revival" anymore, they are so constantly kept before our eyes. Sue Birtwistle felt it wise to conceal her desire to remake *Pride and Prejudice* in the 1980s, but she'd have no trouble pitching another Austen series, especially not the same one, again today. The technological advances that allow people to see films over and over again on their TVs and computers have fostered a totally different way of watching, to do with micro-knowledge, "special features," and a sort of super-familiarity (rather than overfamiliarity) with the material. Thus, you can buy a favorite movie almost as soon as it has left the theaters, only to find that you are just about ready for the next version. The back catalog can never get too crowded, as the author of *Confessions of an Austen Addict* has put it: 'If there were 50 adaptations of *Pride and Prejudice*, I'd see them all. I'd buy them all. I'd play them all till they started skipping and I had to buy a new one."[29]

In 2002 the BBC produced a low-budget biographical film about Austen called *The Real Jane Austen*, which interspersed actors in costume with a documentary narration, but this was a lone attempt to dramatize the author's life until the 2007 biopic, *Becoming Jane*. Based (very loosely) on Jon Spence's 2003 biography, *Becoming Jane Austen*, the film was a somewhat deranged mixture of actual facts about Austen's life, complete fictions about Austen's life, and references to Austen's novels, letters, and juvenilia that presented Austen's known flirtation with Tom Lefroy in 1796–97 as a life-changing event, not only the direct model for the plots of several of her novels (specifically *Pride and Prejudice*), but the trigger to "finding her voice."

No casual viewer of *Becoming Jane* would have the slightest idea how "true to facts" it is (although if enormous liberties were taken with, say, costumes or props, almost everyone would recognize that something was awry), and even viewers who know the main details of Austen's life would have no reason to suspect any particular part of the film of inaccuracy. Writers make poor subjects for biopics, as they lead, on the whole, pretty dull lives. And, of course, the whole concept of a truthful biopic is very questionable in the first place. The audience of a biopic has little choice but to treat everything they see with cqual credibility, and that, in time, affects how they visualize the subject, think of the life in question, and think of the books. One can imagine the student essays of the future that cite Austen's bête noire Lady Gresham (an invented character in *Becoming Jane*) as a model for Lady Catherine de Bourgh.

An entertaining shift of this kind was perceptible a couple of years ago in the long-running BBC radio soap *The Archers*, in which Nigel Pargetter (aristocratic owner of Lower Loxley Hall) tried to think up a romantic gesture with which to impress his parvenu wife Elizabeth on their wedding anniversary, choosing to give her a specially bound copy of *Pride and Prejudice* and "do a Mr. Darcy" by jumping into his own stately lake. Another character in the program, discussing the difficulties of the plan, says, "That's the trouble with books," implying that Austen, and not scriptwriter Andrew Davies, wrote the lake scene depicted in the 1995 film. On the program's message board, a thread called "Mr Darcy knowall alert" soon put members right on that score, prompting the following discussion:

> Does not knowing P+P backwards mean you are are [*sic*] Philistine? I did the tiresome thing for GCE about a thousand years ago. Although I passed, I have expunged the thing from my memory as far as possible—IIRC
>
> There were posh women in bonnets trying to force posh men to marry them, in order to buy more bonnets and ribbons. Is that about right? (czechmate67)
>
> Well, leaving aside the subtle observation of human affairs, the incisive examination of social mores and habits, the delicate portrait of British society which still resonates in many ways, the insight into the small details and domestic arrangements of a society of a period more usually studied against the grander and dramatic background of the Napoleonic wars, the perfectly-judged delineation of petty human misunderstandings, embarrassments, happinesses and unhappiness, and finally the very cleverly resolved love affairs which wind throughout to allow true emotion finally in the face of withering snobbery, judgement, bigotry and social constraints, I'd say yes, pretty much just bonnets and ribbons, czechmate.:-) (Bella Milbanke)

I've read P&P a couple of times, but it never occurred to me the lake scene wasn't in the book. Guess it just goes to show how a great movie scene (or a lot of hype) can leave an indelible impression on the mind, and change the perception of reality (or fiction). (Mile High Scotty)

To which another poster, "carrickbend," answered, "It was a Zeitgeist thing."[30]

Some academics professionally interested in keeping abreast of the Zeitgeist read the film versions of Austen books as texts themselves, applying the same sort of language and analysis to Andrew Davies's witty interpolations as they do to the novels he has adapted. Thus Cheryl L. Nixon has written about Darcy's dive as a revelation of his emotional capabilities and expression of a romantic bond with nature. On his own (he thinks) at Pemberley, Darcy can " 'strip down' to his essential self, a cleansing of social prejudices from his mind." The dive enacts a rebaptism, "a rebirth of his love for Elizabeth."[31] In the same book, the editors Linda Troost and Sayre Greenfield claim that "the image carves a new facet into the text,"[32] an unfortunate metaphor, perhaps, suggesting reduction, whittling away, and even defacement.

The line between one kind of fiction (Austen's texts) and another (things that have been designed to illustrate or evoke them) is, in cases like this, entirely erased. Like the 1890s vogue for Hugh Thomson's illustrations to *Pride and Prejudice*, it seems to place the center of attention in the wrong place. Deidre Lynch, a prolific writer on Austen, has complained that the Austen movies in the last decade "have almost overshadowed the books: Austenians touring country houses turned film sets that Jane Austen never saw inspect exhibits of costumes made for the movies, clothing that nineteenth-century people never wore. . . . In the construction of that imagined territory 'Jane Austen's world,' the balance between our authoring and her authoring may have gone off-kilter."[33]

Valérie Cossy, a student of literary translations of Austen, has likened the recent proliferation of film versions of Austen novels to the rough early translations in French in their relationships to the original texts: The film scripts "seem to take each novel as some raw material on the basis of which one can create a new artefact, better suited to the expectations of one's audience."[34] This is certainly true of the modernization of manners and language in the films, the high gloss of all the costumes and locations—even the supposedly squalid locations—and the transmission of a sufficiently impressive erotic charge. Some films have taken the license to translate much further, however. Patricia Rozema's 1999 version of *Mansfield Park* is, as Rachel Brownstein has pointed out,[35] a product of scholarship in some ways, alert to recent discourses about the book and to the increasing familiarity of readers with material such as Austen's letters and juvenilia. Rozema (who wrote the script of the film as well as directed it) entirely abandoned the author's characterization of Fanny Price and makes her into a fantasy version of the young Austen herself, a spirited, would-be writer. So spirited, in fact, that, played by the beautiful Frances O'Connor, she often appears angry and passionate, displays an energetically heaving bosom, and does a lot of galloping about—in the rain, naturally.

The 2007 ITV production of the same book for television followed this wholesale substitution of Austen's Fanny Price with a "feisty" contemporary girl, boldly and bizarrely casting TV favorite of that year, Billie Piper, as the supposedly tongue-tied and mousy heroine. Coproducer Suzan Harrison explained the disparity between the character in the book and the character in their film with wonderful circularity: "Once you've cast Billie, you could never pretend she's anything less than startling-looking, so we had to find other ways to emphasise her difference." Fanny Price's piety disappeared altogether, being "something people understand less well now"; similarly, Edmund was made "more playful, he's sillier, he drinks more. . . . All of us were keen not to be corseted by the decorum of the time."[36] Actual corsets of the time were, however, pivotal to the production, and Billie Piper's substantial embonpoint forever filling the shot was enough to distract any viewer from the peculiarities of the screenplay.

The fact is that people are no longer very particular about how or where they get their Austen or what Austen it is they get. Even the most faithful or sympathetic rendition on film of one of Austen's novels is charming in an entirely different way from the book's charm, and even the most authentic treatment can be appropriated inauthentically. The biographical drama made for television in 2007, *Miss Austen Regrets*, resembled every other "Austenmania" film in terms of its production values (an absolute necessity for the core audience) and quality cast from the "period drama pool," but worked from a highly intelligent and thoughtful script. The writer, Gwyneth Hughes, made better use of the available material (especially *Jane Austen's Letters*) than any biographer to date and subtly suggested a reading of Austen's mature character that included waspishness and frustration. By closely following the letters of 1815 in which Austen observes the flirtation between her niece Fanny Knight and Charles Haden, the doctor tending to Henry in London, Hughes came up with a revelatory scene that suggested the author's mixed, strong, and possibly slightly drunken feelings on this occasion. For once, a film version of "things Austen" made a contribution to interpretation, rather than simply wallowing in attractive costumes and props.

But the "Zeitgeist thing" has a tendency to make everything relax into a universally digestible form; not dumbing *down* so much as *out*. Gwyneth Hughes's script and Olivia Williams's intelligent impersonation of Jane Austen may have marked a high point in plausible drama about the author, but that isn't how the film has been represented subsequently. Posed photos of Williams in costume, 1) looking attractive, and 2) writing, are now on sale at the Jane Austen Centre in Bath, without acknowledgment that these are publicity shots connected to a film or that the subject is an actor, but as if they are pictures of "the real Jane."

THE FIRST SPIN-OFF PUBLICATION from the Austen "brand" was Sybil G. Brinton's novel of 1913, *Old Friends and New Fancies*, a frenziedly overpopulated book in which most of the major characters from all six novels by Jane Austen mill about, interact, and intermarry (Mary Crawford from *Mansfield Park* to Colonel Fitzwilliam from *Pride and Prejudice*, Georgiana Darcy from the latter to William Price from the former, etc.). Sequels and continuations of Austen appeared all through the last century, the most intelligent and successful being those by the novelist Emma Tennant, *Pemberley* (1993), *An Unequal Marriage* (1994), *Elinor and Marianne* (1996), and *Emma in Love* (1997). Latterly, Stephanie Barron has written a whole series of "Jane Austen Mysteries," in which the novelist, yes, solves crimes; other recent spin-offs show an obsession with time travel and parallel universes, including Amanda Elyot's *By a Lady*, in which a contemporary American woman time travels to Austen's England and meets the author, and *The Man Who Loved Jane Austen* by Sally Smith O'Rourke, in which a Victorian gentleman does the same, with romantic consequences. *Confessions of an Austen Addict* and *Lost in Austen* also feature contemporary women time traveling to Austen's day. The latter won out over obviously stiff competition when it was selected for a highly publicized TV adaptation in 2008.

The quote on the cover of *The Man Who Loved Jane Austen* says, "To be read with an expectation of pleasure," which surely goes for all books that include the words "Jane Austen" in their titles. The name generates a warm glow as readily as it generates cash. *The Jane Austen Book Club*, by Karen Joy Fowler, both fictionalizes the public appetite for Austen (the book is about six contemporary American suburbanites who explore "their own private Austens" by reading "all Jane Austen all the time") and, of course, feeds it at the same time. People truly can't get enough of Austen and talk of their cravings in terms of bingeing and unlicensed self-gratification. Deb Werksman, of publisher Sourcebooks, explained the public hunger for Austen this way: "I think Jane Austen simply didn't leave a big enough body of work. . . . You read them again and again. But after reading them fifteen times, you just begin to want more. Anything that will evoke the work of Jane Austen becomes very appealing."[37]

Once people are "getting their Austen" from secondary or tertiary sources, there are no limits to what can become of it. Her name turns up almost randomly in contemporary media: Mary Ann O'Farrell has noted the TV program *Survivor* described as "Jane Austen with monitor lizards," and Ang Lee's film *Crouching Tiger, Hidden Dragon* called "*Sense and Sensibility* with swords."[38] An episode of *Footballers' Wives* has a *Pride and Prejudice*–themed wedding (in which the groom gets stuck in his Darcy costume and is exposed as a bigamist), while the financier Michael Bloomberg is identified as "a single man in possession of a good fortune."[39] In February 2000, the FOX network transmitted a two-hour reality show, called *Who Wants to Marry a Multi-Millionaire?* which was inspired, apparently, by *Pride and Prejudice*. In the show, fifty women competed for the attention of a superrich bachelor called Rick Rockwell (appearing to them only in silhouette form), whom the winner then had to marry on the spot. In an interview later with Larry King, the groom expressed his feelings about the match: "If it works, imagine. I mean, this would be a storybook romance," but within days, he was exposed as a virtually penniless fraud, with a history of violence toward his previous girlfriend, and the marriage was quickly annulled. It makes one wonder which part of *Pride and Prejudice* the producers had been thinking of—the Darcy-Elizabeth plot or Wickham and Lydia's.

Arielle Eckstut's *Pride and Promiscuity: The Lost Sex Scenes of Jane Austen* (Edinburgh, 2003) catered jokily to a modern audience's expectations of passion between the heroine and hero (or, in the case of *Emma*, on her own). Catherine Morland discovers Henry Tilney's stash of fetish equipment; Jane Bennet is surprised by Miss Bingley and Mrs. Hirst getting into her bed at Netherfield. The book could be said to be more for the bibliophile audience than the soft-porn Janeite, however; its best joke is the letter purportedly from the publisher Crosby, rejecting "The Watsons" on grounds of obscenity and admitting to having destroyed all but the first fifty pages of the manuscript. Austen know-it-alls must have been more pleased with this than the general "Austen lover," several of whom in the Amazon comments columns showed remarkable ignorance of what was being sent up.

Austen's name can never have been so bizarrely evoked as during a conference at Durham University in March 2007, in a debate about proposed legislation to outlaw possession of extreme pornography. The images that the new law intended to target were ones of explicit bestiality, necrophilia, and "acts that appear to be life-threatening or are likely to result in serious, disabling injury." "Opposition among politicians to the new law is likely to be muted," Andrew Norfolk wrote in the *Times* of London, reporting the conference and the debate. "Brave or foolish would be the MP prepared to defend publicly the material shown on a website such as Necrobabes or Asphyxia. . . . What sane person could defend the rights of someone who gains arousal from the sight of women being humiliated, degraded, and—apparently—murdered?"[40] Jane Austen, it seems, for the remark from chapter 9 of *Emma*, by the heroine, that "one half of the world cannot understand the pleasures of the other," was cited in the debate in support of noncriminalization. "The argument went something like this," Norfolk continued. "I may not understand your sexuality, indeed I may find the images you like to view grotesque and repugnant, but is that sufficient reason to criminalise the act of viewing? All parties agreed that possessing internet footage of, for example, a genuine strangulation should be unlawful."[41] So, presumably, Jane Austen was on her own over that one.

The report was commented on by somebody called John Brownlee on the blog Wired, who thought "Emma's words were a minty fresh breath of common sense from the putrid air of ignorance that prevailed" at the proceedings. He quoted one delegate (described on another site as "a hysterical feminist") who had said, "Anyone turned on by the glorification of extreme violence is sick. It sends a message to abhorrent individuals that it is acceptable. . . . I will not get lost in a debate about human rights on this. There are some things that are just wrong." "The statement of an intelligent person giving themselves up to reactionary ignorance," Brownlee concluded. "Why can't more British women be like Emma?"[42]

THE ANONYMOUS REVIEWER IN *Blackwoods Magazine* who in 1818 predicted a time when the "familiar cabinet pictures" painted by Jane Austen would outstrip in interest "even . . . the great historical pieces of our more eminent modern masters"[43] seems to have understood that Austen would achieve far wider admiration in the future than she did in her own day. The way she was read by her contemporaries was often surprising; it strikes us as odd that the *Augustan Review*

complained of a "remarkable sameness in the productions of this author" (we want Austen to be consistent, in fact long for more of "the
same"), that Maria Edgeworth thought there was a lack of narrative
drive in *Emma*, and that Mary Russell Mitford found an "entire want
of taste" in the pertness of Elizabeth Bennet.[44] Sometimes it seems as
if they were reading quite different texts from ours: One early reviewer of *Emma* took John and Isabella Knightley at face value and
described them as the moral focus of the story, representing "unpre-
tending goodness,"[45] a bizarre construction in the opinion of most
modern readers. Austen herself seems to have anticipated being mis-
interpreted in this and many other ways: "I am going to take a heroine whom nobody but myself will much like," she said, setting out on
the creation of Miss Woodhouse. She seems to have been resigned to
being somewhat out of step with her time and its tastes.

The circumstances under which Jane Austen produced her books—
almost twenty years of being an unpublished author, followed by six
years of intense but localized recognition—meant she had time, almost her whole adult lifetime, to develop her characters, live with
them, and fantasize about them. Clearly she made a game of this with
her intimates, as when she looked out for portraits of Mrs. Bingley
and Mrs. Darcy at the 1813 watercolor exhibition or indulged her
nephews' and nieces' curiosity by telling them "many little particulars
about the subsequent career of some of her people," as James Edward
recalled. "She took a kind of parental interest in the beings whom she
had created, and did not dismiss them from her thoughts when she
had finished the last chapter."[46] While the novels remained unpublished, this kind of authorial "super-knowledge" kept them alive for
her, and once the stories were public property it allowed her to retain
a sense of control, an ultimate, print-defying capacity to keep creating
and re-creating, in trivial but highly possessive ways.

Austen had a puzzle-solving mind, concerned with construction
and timetables and detail. Robert William Chapman and later editors
have demonstrated how carefully she used calendars of specific years
against which to plot her fictions, and what importance she gave to
matters of fact (as shown by her inquiry "whether Northamptonshire
is a Country of Hedgerows" when writing *Mansfield Park*[47]). She

homed in on factual inconsistencies in her niece's draft novel; they clearly annoyed her ("Lyme will not do. Lyme is towards 40 miles from Dawlish and would not be talked of there. I have put Starcross instead"[48]). The apple blossom in June in *Emma* is an uncharacteristic slip of this kind in one of her own books (pointed out to her, too late, by her brother Edward), as is Pug's apparent sex change halfway through *Mansfield Park*. Perhaps she missed these errors in the proofs because they were "continuity" mistakes, the result of having revised her drafts so often that she couldn't keep in mind exactly what was and wasn't in the final one.

Austen's long-held control over her texts is one of the things that generates the unusual feeling of *life going on* in them, and which has helped make them so vivid and believable to generations of readers. That sense of Austen being for us and for our time is one of her most appealing attributes. Bloggers are wont to exclaim on the exact similarity between a situation in one of the novels and one in their own lives and the degree to which they can "relate" to them. "She's almost eerily contemporary despite the bonnets, the balls and the carriages, because she's so keen and hilarious an observer of human nature," Laurie Rigler, author of *Confessions of a Jane Austen Addict*, has said. Addressing the Jane Austen Society in 1963, Elizabeth Jenkins spoke for many when she said that the value of great artists (among whom she definitely placed Austen) "is that they inhabit the sphere outside time."[49]

One of the reasons that Austen is, without doubt, a "timeless classic" is that in her case the phrase is true in a literal sense as well as metaphorically. "Timelessness," so intimately connected to the processes of composition and revision that I described in chapters 1 and 2, is imprinted in the texts. Austen, the constant rewriter, keeping her juvenilia and old manuscripts at hand, going back over them and adding topical touches in the hope of making them come up to the present day, was obviously exercised by the problem of making her oeuvre look consistent. When she was correcting proof sheets of the first eight chapters of *Sense and Sensibility*, Jane wrote to her sister, in her characteristic shorthand style, "The *Incomes* remain as they were, but I will get them altered if I can."[50] The reference is to the discussions early in the novel between John and Fanny Dashwood about how much they are prepared to give widowed Mrs. Dashwood and her daughters from his father's estate. In the published version of this painfully believable scene, Fanny Dashwood reasons her husband down from his initial resolve to give the women £3,000 apiece to a vague intention of handing them the odd £50 every now and then. As the gradations involved are pivotal to the meaning of the scene, and £3,000 would have been a generous sum in 1811, it's extremely likely that Austen *did* subsequently update this figure on the proofs. But more importantly, she knew the sums were out of date and needed attention.

The fact is, the whole of *Sense and Sensibility* was out of date. The topic of "sensibility" itself was old news by 1811–12, a preoccupation of the previous decade (which was, of course, when the book had been conceived and most of it written). Austen's very first reviewer, in the *Critical Review* of February 1812, remarked on this exact "want of newness" in *Sense and Sensibility*. Later readers have the luxury of being able to read the book on its merits and judge it high accordingly, but to its contemporary audience *Sense and Sensibility* might have failed to impress in ways we cannot reconstruct.

I suspect that Austen took the remark in the *Critical Review* very much to heart. The problem was that all the material she was using, in her first years of publication, was old material. Anyone who has attempted to keep an unpublished novel of contemporary life current will know the surprising difficulties involved. I tried in 2006 to revise a novel written in 1996 and found it virtually impossible, not because of any desired changes to the plot or characterization, but because of small things, like the glaring obsolescence of the technology. Telephones seemed to be everywhere in the story, ringing quaintly for their absent owners; messages were written on notepaper, mail posted in boxes, and the flashier characters had use of a fax. Doling out cell phones and e-mail addresses did not, however, do the trick of modernizing the story sufficiently. Instead, it did a sort of violence to the flow of the book, from which the text couldn't recover.

I believe that Austen's familiarity with the hazards of updating made her study to avoid period-specific detail in new work when old and new began to appear side by side between 1811 and 1816. People often comment on the nonspecific nature of Austen's descriptions of persons, places, and things, the recourse to "regular features" or "fine eyes" as the indicators of beauty, the rooms and furniture which, like those at Pemberley, are merely "suitable to the fortune of their proprietor." More critically, she is held to be immune to, or ignorant of, signs of the times. Richard Simpson, writing about the *Memoir* in 1870,[51] began this persistent nagging about Austen's lack of topicality: "She was not wholly uninterested in politics ... but she lived and wrote through the period of the French Revolution and the European war without referring to them once, except as making the fortunes of some of her naval characters." She seemed detached from literary trends too, unlike Cassandra Cooke, whose *Battleridge: An Historical Tale* anticipates Scott, or Rev. James Stanier Clarke, whose suggestions may have been ill-conceived but, as Richard Cronin has pointed out, at least indicated "a man with up-to-date literary tastes."[52]

But Austen's novels, written and published during years of war, revolution, and massive social upheaval, deal quietly with their "3 or 4 Families in a Country Village" as if butter wouldn't melt in their mouths. Granted, *Mansfield Park* and *Persuasion* contain references to naval engagements and maneuvers, *Northanger Abbey* slips in a mention of Maria Edgeworth's 1801 novel *Belinda*, and there are those carefully inserted late references to Sir Walter Scott's *Marmion* and the new postage rates in *Sense and Sensibility*, but these are gestures—sometimes rather desperate seeming—toward contemporaneity, which if anything highlight how unfixed in time the novels are.

The "time" problem also arose in the characterization of the heroines, who range in age from seventeen to twenty-seven and were created at very different times in the author's life. Emma, for example, is a distinctly non-young woman. She's meant to be about twenty years old but is as fogeyish over rectitude (toward Mrs. Elton, for example) as someone of the next generation might be expected to be. This is what makes the match between her and Mr. Knightley credible: they do seem to be of an age, despite the author's information to the contrary. The book had a contemporary setting, and there was hardly any lapse of time between the writing and the publication of it, but Austen was not really able to invent a young heroine of 1815: Emma was a throwback, or rather, Emma was her own age in 1815, that is, approaching forty.

The result is that although Austen's novels were composed between 1792 and 1817, all six seem to take place in an imaginary 1801 or 1802, regardless of internal evidence to the contrary. The exception is "Sanditon," which is very much of 1817, but "Sanditon" is only a fragment, and who knows how much of its contemporary feel might have been ironed out by the author had she lived to finish it. It gives her oeuvre a remarkable coherence and consistency and has been a major factor in Austen's longevity and her appeal to generations disconnected from her own. The silver-fork novelists were quickly forgotten, not just because they were quite bad, but because they tended to be very topical, dealing with issues of the day such as Catholic emancipation and reform. Austen understood this; she knew that paring down detail would give her narratives more imaginative flexibility (she once warned her niece Anna against descriptions that are "more minute than will be liked. You give too many particulars of right hand & Left"[53]). She also knew that pinning her works to a particular time would date them; she had to "unpin" them, so she could use her disregarded early masterpieces.

The irony is that she has come to represent her period. "Jane Austen's Regency World" could as well have an equals sign instead of an apostrophe. She stopped the clock and now *is* her time.

Just as Jane Austen feels closer to our own time the further she recedes from it, so the sense of a personal connection being possible with the author has increased with the exponential growth of her fan base. Katherine Mansfield, clearly speaking personally, had remarked wryly in 1924 that "the true admirer of the novels cherishes the happy thought that he alone—reading between the lines—has become the secret friend of their author,"[54] but she was by no means the first to write about the friendship, even love, that many readers felt in their private communion with Jane Austen. Harriet Martineau, writing in her diary in 1837, identified a feeling that now pervades thousands of

Austen blogs on the Internet: that Austen's characters are "the unrivalled intimate friends of the whole public."[55] Constance Hill experienced similar feelings as a form of possession while writing her 1902 biography of Austen, an "intangible something" that had "exercised a sway of ever-increasing power over the writer and illustrator of these pages,"[56] while Anne Thackeray simply lost her heart; "as we turn from the story of Jane Austen's life to her books again," she wrote, reviewing the *Memoir of Jane Austen*, "we feel more than ever that she, too, was one of those true friends who belong to us inalienably—simple, wise, contented, living in others, one of those whom we seem to have a right to love."[57]

The Internet has made mass intimacy with Jane Austen available at the click of a mouse. Individual bloggers can see the whole of life through their reading and appropriation of the books; AustenProse, "a daily celebration of the brilliance of Jane Austen's writing," is particularly prolific and engaged: "My personal Austen tends toward appreciating her clever irony and wit; because I dearly love to laugh at life in defense of the serious reality. However, there will be some who disagree with me entirely and think that I have missed Austen's point. That's ok. There is room for many opinions, and like Jane Bennet, I will try to find the good in all of them!"[58] Following Austen, and the "blook" it relates to, *A Walk with Jane Austen*, both stem from the author Lori Smith's search "for a connection with the writer whose books (and the movies based on them) had become like literary comfort food for me." Other blogs, clearly run by extremely public-spirited individuals, seek to provide something like a service through their personal enthusiasm: Jane Austen Quote of the Day; Austentatious; AustenBlog, with its teacup logo, "one lump of snark or two?"; and the larger sites, Jane Austen's World (which takes a wholly materialist view of "food, dress, social customs and other nineteenth-century historical details" connected with Austen); and Jane Austen Today, which contains long posts about recent media events and running features, such as the online polls of "Worst Father" and "Longest-Suffering Heroine" in the novels.

One of many breakaway fan clubs (begun and almost entirely run on the Internet) is the archly self-mocking Republic of Pemberley, whose members ("Pemberleans" rather than "Janeites" or "Austenians") divide literature into two categories: Jane Austen books and non–Jane Austen books. Their online "Shoppe" sells Jane totes, T-shirts, and stamps ("I ♥ Mr Darcy") that parade a self-conscious irony, and on its home page, the Republic claims to be "Your haven in a world programmed to misunderstand obsession with things Austen," an interesting recasting of the Cheney test of a hundred years earlier, that it was a mark of ability "whether people could or could not appreciate Miss Austen's merits." Pemberlean irony has a nervous quality to it, as if it feels the chill breath of D. W. Harding at its back and worries, as Harding never did himself, about being taken for the wrong kind of admirer, the kind who doesn't appreciate that the author might be mocking him.

Other fans are much less self-conscious and not afraid to be seen wallowing. *Jane Austen's Regency World* is a magazine unashamedly devoted to the material construction of "all things Austen." It is produced in association with the Jane Austen Centre in Bath—not a study hub, as the name (and the example of the Shakespeare Centre in Stratford) might suggest, but a cheerfully populist exhibition of costumes, prints, period furniture, and enlarged stills from recent films. In their shop you can buy books; embroidery sets; pencils; an oil-painted image of Colin Firth as Darcy, printed on canvas, for £60; and reproduction pelisses, spencers, muslin dresses, and bonnets for those who like to look authentic at conventions. There is also a selection of gentlemen's cravats and a popular nightshirt range. No Darcy pillowcases yet, but that would be a logical extension of the franchise. The lady at the cash register seemed very sympathetic to her customers' needs and as I paid for a Darcy key fob said, "You'll be wanting to put your keys right on there."

What would Austen have made of all this? An impossible question, of course, but simply framing it hints at the enormity of our cumulative presumption, the vast distance our admiration has opened up between its object and the ways in which she is celebrated and consumed. Famous names "allow us to identify what's present with what's past," according to Leo Braudy; they are "vehicles of cultural memory and cohesion,"[59] but only vehicles, a method of transport, a means to an end. As it grows, a legend has to smooth itself out and disguise the diffuse and contradictory material from which it was formed, and if it is as well-traveled as Jane Austen's legend, it becomes very smooth indeed. There is no doubt that the historical Jane Austen would not recognize herself in any of it, even its grains of truth.

And what would she have thought of our interpretation of her work? This gave D. W. Harding the shudders, for he saw the risk of becoming (or being) one of the very "people whom she disliked," one of those benighted misreaders who fall headlong into the trap of the books and think them merely light, bright, and sparkling. According to Harding, this effect was "exactly as she meant [it] to be"; he credits Austen with a somewhat sinister, at best playfully malicious, disposition toward her audiences, contemporary and future, a view he would have found echoed in James Austen's unpublished poem about Jane's relish for people's foibles, "for ever on the watch / Some traits of ridicule to catch."

Lionel Trilling, in his essay "Emma and the Legend of Jane Austen," was easier on all of us when he suggested that the powerful personal emotions generated around this author and indulged grossly in Austenolatry may not be entirely the fault of people's lack of taste and "impulse to self-flattery," but perhaps triggered by the work itself, "in some unusual promise that it seems to make, in some hope that it holds out."[60] In other words, Trilling felt that Austen to some extent brought misreading, or overindulgent, personalized reading, on herself. If Trilling was right, perhaps the bumper stickers are right too and we should all "Blame Jane." Perhaps she simply succeeded too well at charming us: she knew what she liked in a novel, she labored to make her own novels as attractive as possible, and—it worked. Better than anyone could have imagined possible or desirable.

Henry James came near to saying the same as Trilling in 1914 when he wrote of the mass popularity of Austen as a form of presumption, but one that has been licensed from the inside: "Why shouldn't it be argued against her that where her testimony complacently ends the pressure of appetite within us presumes exactly to begin?" he asked. And, one could add, is illimitable. In the year that she died, Henry

Austen claimed that his sister would always be unknown to the public: "No accumulation of fame would have induced her, had she lived, to affix her name to any productions of her pen. In the bosom of her own family she talked of them freely, thankful for praise, open to remark, and submissive to criticism. But in public she turned away from any allusion to the character of an authoress."[61] This is clearly, forgivably, untrue. Austen was as motivated and ambitious as all possessors of great gifts are. When she joked with her sister in 1796, "I write only for Fame, and without any view to pecuniary Emolument," she was doing what she always did, making light of the things she felt most strongly about.[62] Aged twenty, utterly unknown and unpublished, and chary of making a fool of herself, Jane Austen still had every reason to feel secure at heart in her own talent and its eventual success. And though she had to wait another fifteen years till the publication of her first book, 1796 was the year when she wrote "First Impressions."

Austen is unlikely to have ever wanted a cap on her potential success, though, of course, she could never have imagined the farthest reaches of it. She was sufficiently philosophical (and cynical) to watch the early stages of its progress in her lifetime with unblinking interest at how little control remains to an author once a book is public property. Her recording of the "Opinions" of her friends and family shows these temperamental traits perfectly; she may have scorned the advice of Rev. James Stanier Clarke on how to improve her stories and inspired terror in Miss Mitford's friend with her satirical silences, but ultimately Jane Austen cared less about being misread than about not being read widely enough.

E. M. Forster recognized the truly transgressive aspects of the process when he remarked of *Jane Austen's Letters*[63] in 1932 that "they have reappeared exactly as she wrote them, but in a setting which makes them look strange to her, and we are part of the setting." It is not always a benign symbiosis, and certainly not controllable by any of the custodians of culture, but as Thomas Kebbel remarked in 1885, "While English society remains what it still is, with so much to remind us what it once was, and while the manners of one generation melt so imperceptibly into those of another that the continuity hardly seems broken, so long will the interest in Jane Austen continue to strengthen and expand."[64] The significance of Jane Austen is so personal and so universal, so intimately connected with our sense of ourselves and of our whole society, that it is impossible to imagine a time when she or her works could have delighted us long enough.

# *Abbreviations*

Bibliography—David Gilson, *A Bibliography of Jane Austen* (1982; reissued, with a new introduction and corrections, Winchester, 1997).

*CH*—Brian Southam, *Jane Austen: The Critical Heritage*, 2 vols. (London, 1968, reprinted 1987 and 1995).

*Complete Poems*—*The Complete Poems of James Austen*, ed. David Selwyn (Chawton, 2003).

*CR*—*Collected Reports of the Jane Austen Society*, 5 vols. (Bristol): vol. 1, *1949–65*; vol. 2, *1966–75*; vol. 3, *1976–85*; vol. 4, *1986–95*; vol. 5, *1996–2000*, with index 1949–2000. For the uncollected annual reports for individual years 2001–7, see below.

*Emma*—Jane Austen, *Emma*, ed. Richard Cronin and Dorothy McMillan (Cambridge, 2005).

*Juvenilia*—*Jane Austen, Juvenilia*, ed. Peter Sabor (Cambridge, 2006).

*Letters*—*Jane Austen's Letters*, ed. Deirdre Le Faye, 3rd edition (Oxford, 1995).

*Memoir*—James Edward Austen-Leigh, *A Memoir of Jane Austen and Other Family Recollections*, ed. Kathryn Sutherland (Oxford, 2002).

*MP*—Jane Austen, *Mansfield Park*, ed. John Wiltshire (Cambridge, 2006).

*MW*—Jane Austen, *Minor Works*, ed. R. W. Chapman (Oxford, 1954).

*NA*—Jane Austen, *Northanger Abbey*, ed. Barbara Benedict and Deirdre Le Faye (Cambridge, 2006).

*P&P*—Jane Austen, *Pride and Prejudice*, ed. John Wiltshire (Cambridge, 2006).

*Persuasion*—Jane Austen, *Persuasion*, ed. Janet Todd and Antje Blank (Cambridge, 2006).

*Record*—Deirdre Le Faye, *Jane Austen: A Family Record*, 2nd edition (Cambridge, 2004).

*Report*—Uncollected annual reports of the Jane Austen Society, 2001–7 (Bristol, 2001–7).

*S&S*—Jane Austen, *Sense and Sensibility*, ed. Edward Copeland (Cambridge, 2006).

## Notes

PREFACE

1. http://us.penguingroup.com/static/html/romance/janeaustenaddict.html.
2. *New York Times*, 30 January 1900.
3. *Independent*, 26 May 2007.
4. "The Jane Austen Syndrome," Garber, pp. 199–210.
5. "The Jottings of Sheikh Osama bin Austen," http://www.feedsfarm.com/article/ 872310db33673d1295a18f07ae323dfa91116b4b.html, and http://www.edsw.usyd.edu.au/ research/networks/aele/resources/BROCK_Rebutting_Andrew_Leigh.pdf.
6. *CH*, vol. 2, p. 19.
7. *Guardian*, 19 July 2007.
8. Copeland and McMaster, pp. 213 and 211.
9. By Sylvia Townsend Warner, in her *Diaries* (London, 1994), p. 250.
10. *CH*, vol. 2, p. 244.
11. Tomalin, p. 285.
12. http://thedelhiwalla.blogspot.com/2008/05/viewpoint-jane-austen-in-delhi.html.
13. Watt, p. 35.
14. *CH*, vol. 2, p. 41.
15. Trilling, p. 42.

CHAPTER 1: "AUTHORS TOO OURSELVES"

1. *Memoir*, pp. 81–82.
2. Braudy, p. 15.

3. 18–19 December 1798, *Letters*, p. 26.

4. Isobel Grundy, "Jane Austen and Literary Traditions," Copeland and McMaster, p. 190.

5. *Juvenilia*, p. 180.

6. *Record*, p. 64.

7. 29–30 November 1812, *Letters*, p. 197.

8. See the bibliography and notes to *Complete Poems*.

9. *Juvenilia*, p. 241.

10. *Record*, p. 89n.

11. "Lines Written at Steventon," *Complete Poems*, p. 73.

12. See her letter to her newly married granddaughter, Anna Lefroy, in 1814, *Record*, p. 218.

13. The works in question are the *Loiterer* by James and Henry Austen; Edward Cooper's *Sermons*; George Cooke's *Sermons*; Cassandra Cooke's *Battleridge: An Historical Romance*; James Henry Leigh's *The New Rosciad*; Cassandra, Lady Hawke's *Julia de Gramont*, and the works of Samuel Egerton Brydges.

14. *Memoir*, p. 90.

15. See her obituary in *Gentleman's Magazine*, vol. 74, pt. 2, pp. 1178–79.

16. Brydges (1834), p. 40.

17. "Sonnet XVI," Brydges (1785), n.p.

18. Brydges (1834), p. ix.

19. Ibid.

20. Ibid., pp. 40–41.

21. *Memoir*, p. 174.

22. *Complete Poems*, p. 4.

23. Ibid., p. 26.

24. Ibid., p. 20.

25. *Memoir*, p. 16.

26. Austen et al., no. 1, p. 4.

27. Ibid., p. 3.

28. Ibid., p. 4.

29. Ibid., no. 53, pp. 328–29.

30. Ibid., no. 9, p. 52

31. Peter Sabor gives a very useful summary of the various arguments for and against the identification of Austen as "Sophia Sentiment" in his edition of Austen's *Juvenilia*, pp. 356–62.

32. Austen et al., no. 60, p. 365.

33. Tucker, p. 99.

34. Austen et al., no. 1, p. 3.

35. Some critics believe that these two plays could have been by James himself, but Peter Sabor's noting of a manuscript change from "they" to "it" makes it much more likely that JA is referring to her own works. See *Juvenilia*, p. 61 and notes.

36. *Juvenilia*, p. 65.

37. Ibid., p. 71.

38. Ibid., p. 154.

39. Mary Leigh's "History of the Leigh Family" and her husband's note about her novel writing are in the Leigh MSS at the Shakespeare Birthplace Trust Records Office, DR 671/77a.

40. *Bibliography*, p. 89.

41. See, for example, Cassandra Cooke's unpublished letter to Fanny Burney d'Arblay of 22 November 1796, MS British Library, Egerton 3698, f. 127.

42. Burney, vol. 3, p. 137.

43. Ibid., p. 140.

44. For this and connections between *Camilla* and other Austen works, see Harman, pp. 268–70.

45. *Critical Review*, n.d., quoted in Raven et al., p. 778.

46. Farnell Parsons, "Jane Austen's Passage to Derbyshire," *Report* 2002, pp. 34–39.

47. Brydges, preface to *Mary de Clifford*, p. iv.

48. Brydges (1834), vol. 1, p. 6.

49. Brydges, *Mary de Clifford*, p. 208.

50. *P&P*, p. 403.

51. *Letters*, p. 22.

52. Brydges (1834), vol. 1, p. 10.

53. *Letters*, p. 22.

54. Morgan, MA2911.

55. *Record*, p. 104.

56. *P&P*, p. 41; *NA*, pp. 107–8.

57. *Letters*, p. 26.

58. St. Clair, p. 249.

59. *Letters*, p. 199.

60. Cassandra Austen to Mary Lloyd, 30 November 1796, *Record*, p. 99.

61. L'Estrange, vol. 2, p. 305.

62. *Record*, p. 50.

63. 8–9 January 1799, *Letters*, p. 35.

64. *Letters*, p. 44.

65. *Bibliography*, p. 24.

66. *NA*, p. 30.

67. *CH*, vol. 2, pp. 228–29.

CHAPTER 2: PRAISE AND PEWTER

1. *Memoir*, p. 106.

2. *Letters*, p. 289.

3. Morgan, MA2911.

4. For details of the 1800 pamphlet, see *Bibliography*, item L3, and Ragg.

5. See *Memoir*, p. 105 and n., and *Bibliography*, p. 83.

6. *Letters*, p. 174, and *CR*, vol. 5, pp. 78–83.

7. *Letters*, p. 182.

8. 24 January 1809, *Letters*, p. 169.

9. *Letters*, p. 174.

10. Ibid., p. 175.

11. Sutherland, p. 147.

12. *Memoir*, p. 149.

13. *Letters*, p. 202.

14. Ibid., p. 182.

15. Ibid., p. 186.

16. *Record*, p. 188.

17. *CH*, vol. 1, p. 35.

18. Aspinall, p. 26.

19. "Opinions of *Mansfield Park*: Collected and Transcribed by Jane Austen," *CH*, vol. 1, p. 51.

20. *Record*, p. 191.

21. *Letters*, p. 217.

22. *Complete Poems*, p. 39.

23. "Lines written at Steventon in the Autumn of 1814, after refusing to exchange that Living for Marsh Gibbon in the borders of Buckinghamshire & Oxfordshire," *Complete Poems*, p. 71.

24. *Letters*, p. 121.

25. Ibid., p. 76.

26. Cooper (1815), pp. 262–63.

27. *Letters*, p. 322.

28. *Memoir*, p. 27.

29. 29 January 1813, *Letters*, p. 202.

30. 29–30 November 1812, *Letters*, p. 179.

31. *Letters*, p. 217.

32. 29 January 1813, *Letters*, p. 201.

33. For data here, see St. Clair, appendix 1, and Jan Fergus, "The Professional Woman Writer," in Copeland and McMaster.

34. *Letters*, p. 201.

35. Le Faye, *Fanny Knight's Diaries*, p. 25.

36. 24 May 1813, *Letters*, pp. 212–13.

37. MS British Library, add. ms 41253, f. 17.

38. *CH*, vol. 1, p. 8.

39. Ibid., pp. 42, 46–47.

40. *Letters*, p. 213.

41. Tomalin, p. 238.

42. MS British Library, add. ms 41253, f. 19.

43. 25 September 1813, *Letters*, p. 231.

44. Ibid., p. 250.

45. 3–6 July 1813, *Letters*, p. 217.

46. "Opinions of *Mansfield Park*," *CH*, vol. 1, p. 50.

47. See Jan Fergus, in Copeland and McMaster, p. 23.

48. *Letters*, pp. 281 and 282.

49. Austen-Leigh, *Fugitive Pieces*, p. 27.

50. *Letters*, p. 281.

51. Fairweather, p. 419.

52. Ibid., p. 420.

53. Miss Mitford's grandfather Dr. Russell was vicar of Ashe until his death in 1783.

54. Mary Russell Mitford to Sir William Elford, 3 April 1815, L'Estrange, pp. 305–6.

55. Miss Mitford doesn't specify who the mutual friend who visited Austen was. Her mother's testimony about the "husband-hunting butterfly" is often called into doubt because she moved away from Ashe in 1783, but as she went only ten or twelve miles away from Steventon to Alresford, which is about eight miles from Chawton, it seems likely Mrs. Mitford heard almost as much of the Austens as before.

56. There is a reference in a letter of 11–12 October 1813 to naming a heroine after an acquaintance called Charlotte, the name of the heroine of "Sanditon," and the month before, JA had been describing the hypochondriac Mrs. Bridges in terms very redolent of Diana Parker in "Sanditon" (*Letters*, p. 231).

57. Smiles, pp. 281–83.

58. *Letters*, pp. 293–94.

59. Ibid., p. 291.

60. Ibid., p. 297.

61. Ibid., p. 306.

62. Ibid., p. 307.

63. "Plan of a Novel," *MW*, p. 430.

64. *CH*, vol. 1, p. 56.

65. *Letters*, p. 302.

66. *CR*, vol. 4, p. 407.

67. *CH*, vol. 1, p. 63.

68. *Letters*, p. 313.

69. Ibid., p. 312.

70. 31 December 1815, *Letters*, p. 309.

71. *Letters*, p. 313.

72. *Letters*, p. 333.

73. Southam (2001), p. 86.

74. *Letters*, p. 166.

75. Ibid., p. 333.

76. Cecil (1978), p. 183.

77. James Austen to James Edward Austen, Tucker, p. 111.

78. Berg MS 209715B, as quoted in Doody, p. 246, with textual note on p. 282.

79. It has been amended to "dead" in the tidied-up version, written out later by James Austen. See Margaret Anne Doody's discussion of this manuscript in the introduction to *Catharine and Other Writings*, p. xxi; see also David Selwyn's textual and explanatory notes in *Collected Poems and Verse of the Austen Family*.

## CHAPTER 3: MOULDERING IN THE GRAVE

1. L'Estrange, vol. 2, p. 13.
2. *Bibliography*, M5 iii, p. 470.
3. *Complete Poems*, p. xi.
4. Ibid., p. 87.
5. "To the Memory of Miss Jane Austen," Austen-Leigh (2006), pp. 58–60.
6. Austen-Leigh (1942), p. 265.
7. *Letters*, p. 339.
8. 9 September 1817, Nicholson, p. 246.
9. *Letters*, p. 231.
10. *CH*, vol. 1, p. 87.
11. Ibid.
12. Ibid., p. 102.
13. Ibid., pp. 100–101.
14. *P&P*, p. 414.
15. *Retrospective Review*, 1823, quoted in *CH*, vol. 1, p. 111.
16. *CH*, vol. 1, pp. 80 and 83.
17. Ibid., p. 267.
18. Lamb, p. 177.
19. Hazlitt.
20. See Gilson, "Jane Austen, the aristocracy and T. H. Lister," pp. 56–65.
21. Lister, vol. 1, p. 148.
22. Quoted in John Gore, "*Pride and Prejudice* and Miss Eden," *CR*, vol. 1, p. 134.
23. See Mandal and Southam, p. 5.
24. See Catharine Nepomnyashchy's essay "Jane Austen in Russia: Hidden Presence and Belated Boom" in Mandal and Southam.
25. Hastings, p. 20.
26. Ibid., p. 21.
27. Ibid., p. 23.
28. Henry Austen to Charles Austen, 24 November 1822, Morgan, MA4500.
29. Ibid.
30. British Library, add. ms 41253, f. 16.
31. Austen-Leigh (1942), p. 283.
32. Ibid., p. 271.
33. Gilson, "Jane Austen and John Murray," p. 520.
34. Dowden et al., vol. 5, p. 2003.

35. Henry Austen to Richard Bentley, British Library, add. ms 46611, f. 311–12.

36. Anna wrote to her half brother James Edward Austen-Leigh in a letter postmarked 8 August 1862, "I would give a good deal, that is as much as I could afford, for a sketch which Aunt Cassandra made of her in one of their expeditions—sitting down out of doors on a hot day, with her bonnet strings untied." Chapman (1948), p. 213.

37. *Memoir*, p. 154.

38. Sadleir, unpaginated.

39. Richard Bentley to Fanny Burney d'Arblay, 12 October 1835; Burney, vol. 12, p. 879n.

40. Macaulay, p. 694.

41. 14 March 1826, Scott, p. 135.

42. Clark, pp. 176 and 420. It is just as well that Sarah Harriet Burney never heard Austen's view of her own novel, *Clarentine*, published in 1798. "We are reading Clarentine, & are surprised to find how foolish it is. I remember liking it much less on a $2^d$ reading than at the $1^{st}$ & it does not bear a $3^d$ at all," *Letters*, p. 120.

43. *S&S*, p. 298.

44. Watt, p. 3.

45. Brydges (1834), vol. 2, p. 269.

46. *Letters*, p. 252.

47. Ibid., p. 5.

48. *Record*, p. 101.

49. *S&S*, p. 299.

50. *Letters*, p. 344.

51. *Memoir*, p. 198.

52. *Record*, p. 241.

53. British Library, add. ms 41253, ff. 15, 16, 17, and 19.

54. *CH*, vol. 1, p. 120.

55. Cassandra Elizabeth Austen to Charles Austen, 9 May 1843, Morgan MA4500.

56. *Juvenilia*, p. xxv.

57. Austen (1952), p. 10.

58. Chapman (1948), p. 67.

59. *Memoir*, p. 184.

60. *Letters*, p. 93.

61. Unpublished letter in the collection of Mr. Robert H. Taylor, quoted in *Bibliography*, M66.

62. "Recollections of John White," Austen (1952), p. 20.

63. Ibid.

64. Proudman, p. 8.

65. Austen-Leigh (1942), p. 294.

CHAPTER 4: A VEXED QUESTION

1. *CH*, vol. 1, p. 2.

2. Ibid., p. 148.

3. *Bibliography*, M121.

4. Austen-Leigh (1920), p. 2.

5. Queen Victoria's diary, 7 March 1858, quoted in *CH*, vol. 2, p. 141; *CR*, vol. 1, p. 120.

6. Taylor, vol. 2, p. 193.

7. *Memoir*, p. 186.

8. *Letters*, p. 44.

9. National Portrait Gallery, 20 May? 1869, and Hampshire Record Office 23M93/86/3c. Anna Lefroy made her own continuation of "Sanditon," not published in her lifetime, so may have felt personally thwarted by her cousin. She also used the designation "a Niece of the late Miss Austen," for the publication of a short novel called *Mary Hamilton* in Alaric Alexander Watts's *Literary Souvenir*, 1834.

10. Austen-Leigh (1942), p. 300.

11. Ibid., p. 315.

12. Austen-Leigh (1920), p. 2.

13. Gaskell, pp. 336–37.

14. Ibid., pp. 337–38.

15. *MW*, pp. 397–98.

16. Gaskell, p. 338.

17. *CH*, vol. 1, p. 150.

18. Ibid., p. 200.

19. Ibid., p. 213.

20. Ibid., p. 196.

21. Caroline Austen to James Edward Austen-Leigh, 1 April? 1869, *Memoir*, p. 186.

22. Trevelyan, vol. 2, pp. 379 and 466.

23. Her daughter reported watching Anna burning a manuscript, which she took to be this novel, "Which Is the Heroine?" though a novel of that—very unusual—title was published anonymously in 1826, and could have been Anna's.

24. *Memoir*, p. 162.

25. Ibid., p. 166.

26. Ibid., p. 8.

27. Ibid., p. 184.

28. Ibid., p. 221n.

29. Ibid., p. 173.

30. Ibid., p. 189.

31. Ibid., pp. 186–87.

32. Ibid., p. 186.

33. Ibid., p. 188.

34. Ibid., p. 158.

35. *Letters*, p. 144.

36. Le Faye (2000), pp. 38–39.

37. Ibid.

38. *Memoir*, p. 158.

39. Ibid., p. 10.

40. Ibid., p. 132.

41. Ibid., p. 73.

42. Ibid., pp. 9–10.

43. Ibid., p. 79.

44. *CH*, vol. 1, p. 64.

45. Morgan MA3610, and *Memoir*, p. 23.

46. *Memoir*, p. 21.

47. Ibid., p. 51.

48. Ibid., p. 82.

49. Ibid., p. 173.

50. 16–17 December 1816, *Letters*, p. 323.

51. *Memoir*, p. 18.

52. Ibid., p. 90.

53. Quoted in Miller, pp. 7–8. Brontë had sent him an embarrassingly confessional letter about her ambitions.

54. *Memoir*, p. 112.

55. Ibid., p. 192.

56. *CH*, vol. 2, p. 163.

57. Austen-Leigh (1920), p. 64.

58. *Record*, p. 282.

59. Austen-Leigh (1920), p. 65.

60. *Memoir*, p. 43.

61. "Written at Winchester on Tuesday the 15th July 1817," Selwyn, p. 17.

62. *Memoir*, p. 190.

63. Ibid.

64. *CH*, vol. 2, p. 163.

65. Ibid., pp. 168 and 170.

66. Ibid., p. 5.

67. Ibid., p. 181.

68. Morgan Library; letter included with MS of "Lady Susan."

69. The artist is now thought to have been Ozias Humphry (1742–1810), whose monogram on the painting was documented in the 1980s, but which is no longer visible. For more on the intricacies of the Rice Portrait debate, see my article "Who's That Girl?" 14 April 2007, http://www.guardian.co.uk.

70. Anon., "Jane Austen and Her Biographers," p. 360.

## Chapter 5: Divine Jane

1. "Her Life's One Romance," Malden, p. 33.

2. Adams, preface.

3. Austen-Leigh (1920), pp. 80–81.

4. *Memoir*, p. 104.

5. Ibid., pp. 104–5.

6. *CH*, vol. 2, p. 215.

7. Anon., "Jane Austen and Her Biographers," *Church Quarterly Review*, p. 356.

8. Beside his £500 fee, Thomson received a royalty of 7d a copy; see *Bibliography*, p. 267.

9. *CH*, vol. 2, p. 218.

10. Ibid., p. 215.

11. Ibid., p. 174.

12. Ibid., p. 62.

13. Ibid., p. 227.

14. Ibid., p. 271.

15. Ibid., p. 202.

16. Ibid., pp. 233–34.

17. Ibid., p. 65.

18. *CR*, vol. 1, p. 111.

19. Bussby, no page numbers.

20. Carrington, p. 545.

21. Rhydderch, p. 240.

22. Emerson, p. 336.

23. *CH*, vol. 2, p. 232.

24. Twain, p. 262.

25. Ibid., p. 266.

26. *Following the Equator*, ch. 62, quoted in *CH*, vol. 2, p. 232.

27. Twain, p. 280.

28. *CH*, vol. 2, p. 232.

29. Ibid., p. 233.

30. Watt, pp. 10–11.

31. *CH*, vol. 2, p. 179.

32. James, p. 168.

33. Ibid.

34. *CH*, vol. 2, p. 189.

35. Ibid., p. 195.

36. Ibid., p. 218.

37. Ibid., p. 39.

38. Ibid., p. 77.

39. Ibid., p. 39.

40. Showalter, p. 41.

41. *CH*, vol. 2, p. 10.

42. Edlmann, pp. 343–50.

43. Hill, p. 53.

44. Mandal and Southam, p. 5.
45. Halperin, p. 284.
46. Ibid., pp. 289–90.
47. Ibid., p. 307.
48. 6 April 1897, quoted in the notes to Claudia Johnson's essay "The Divine Miss Jane," in Lynch.
49. Translated by René Varin, *CR*, vol. 1, p. 143.
50. Originally a D.Litt. thesis, Sorbonne, Paris, 1915.
51. Austen-Leigh (1920), p. 96.
52. *CH*, vol. 2, p. 79.
53. Fussell, p. 162.
54. *CR*, vol. 4, p. 267.
55. Lane, "Dr. Robert W. Chapman," 6 August 1954.
56. Chapman (1920), pp. 22–23.
57. Ibid., preface and p. 24.
58. These notes are in Chapman's "Jane Austen Files" in the Bodleian Library, Oxford.
59. See Martin Jarrett-Kerr, letter to *Times Literary Supplement*, 3 February 1984, p. 111.
60. Kipling, p. 335.
61. Ibid., p. 337.
62. Ibid., p. 348.
63. Ibid., p. 340.
64. *CR*, vol. 1, p. 299.
65. Bien, p. 43.
66. Constance Hill to Mrs. Robert Mills, 20 May? 1918, Hampshire Record Office, 71M82/PW2/1.
67. Hill, p. vi.
68. *Daily Telegraph*, 19 July 1917.
69. Ibid.
70. *Emma*, p. 391.
71. *Daily Telegraph*, 19 July 1917.
72. Cecil (1978), p. 23.
73. *CH*, vol. 2, p. 31.
74. *CR*, vol. 1, p. 141.
75. Chapman (1950), p. 11.
76. Ibid.
77. It may also be worth recording here that the Cambridge classical scholar A. W. Verrall had considered just such an edition of Austen in the 1880s but never made one.
78. Lane, "Dr. Robert W. Chapman," 6 August 1954.
79. I can only guess that there was some sort of preexisting agreement for her to do this book.
80. Chapman (1953), p. 6.
81. Morgan, MA1034, item 3.

82. *Juvenilia*, p. xlviii.

83. *Times Literary Supplement*, 15 June 1922, quoted in *Juvenilia*, p. l.

84. *CR*, vol. 1, p. 171.

85. Gilson, "Jane Austen's Text," p. 62.

86. "Jane Austen: Poetry and Anti-Poetry," Howard, p. 295.

87. See *Juvenilia*, p. xxxvii.

88. Chapman (1953), p. 44.

89. Chapman (1932), vol. 1, p. xi.

CHAPTER 6: CANON AND CANONIZATION

1. *CH*, vol. 2, p. 190.

2. Ibid., p. 193.

3. *Bibliography*, M84, p. 486.

4. *Daily Telegraph*, 18 July 1917.

5. James, p. 167.

6. *CH*, vol. 2, p. 290.

7. Ibid., p. 174.

8. Raleigh, p. 471.

9. James, p. 168.

10. Macaulay, p. 694.

11. *CH*, vol. 2, pp. 287–88.

12. Ibid., p. 301.

13. Chapman (1953), p. 46.

14. *CH*, vol. 2, p. 97.

15. Woolf, p. 169.

16. Watt, p. 9.

17. Forster, p. 145.

18. Ibid., pp. 154–55.

19. Lascelles (1961), p. 368.

20. RWC to Henry Hake, 26 October 1932, National Portrait Gallery.

21. Ibid.

22. J. H. Hubback to Henry Hake, 13 October 1932, National Portrait Gallery.

23. Her cousin William Austen-Leigh, coauthor of *Jane Austen: Her Life and Letters*, *A Family Record*, lived at "Hartfield" in Roehampton.

24. RWC to Henry Hake, 26 October 1932, National Portrait Gallery.

25. Ibid., 22 April 1948. The writer Patrick O'Connor owns another copy of the same silhouette, obviously of nineteenth-century manufacture. It seems possible that they are both remnants of a small-issue souvenir.

26. Chapman (1948), p. 214.

27. *CR*, vol. 2, p. 174.

28. *Letters*, pp. 42 and 77.

29. Ibid., p. 24.
30. Dunaway, p. 128.
31. Huxley, p. 447.
32. Dunaway, pp. 138 and 154.
33. Linklater, p. 122.
34. Churchill, pp. 376–77, 20 December 1943.
35. *CH*, vol. 2, p. 196.
36. Viveash, p. 338.
37. Neagle, p. 146.
38. Ibid., p. 148.
39. *CR*, vol. 1, p. 112.
40. Ibid., p. 18.
41. Ibid., p. ix.
42. Ibid., vol. 2, p. 174.
43. He contributed to PMLA in 1930 and published an article on JA's early reading public in *Review of English Studies*.
44. *CR*, vol. 2, p. 214.
45. Ibid., vol. 1, p. 108.
46. Lascelles (1939), p. v.
47. Leavis (1948), p. 17.
48. *Tribune*, 28 May 1948.
49. Auden, pp. 83–84.
50. Gorer, pp. 203–4.
51. Watt, p. 170.
52. Ibid., p. 167.
53. *CH*, vol. 2, p. 288.
54. Leavis (1968), vol. 2, p. 73.
55. Ibid., p. 1.
56. Watt, p. 118.
57. Ibid., p. 119.
58. Cecil (1948), p. 99.
59. Cecil (1978), pp. 10–11.
60. Ibid., p. 13.
61. Ibid., p. 8.
62. *CR*, vol. 4, p. 285.
63. "Jane and All That," Coleman, p. 247.
64. *CR*, vol. 5, p. 205.
65. Ibid., vol. 4, p. 170.
66. Ibid.
67. Terry Eagleton, "Irony and Commitment," *Stand* 20, no. 3 (1978).
68. Gilbert and Gubar, pp. 154–55.

69. Johnson, p. xiv.

70. Poovey, p. 237.

71. Todd (2005), p. 105.

72. Watt, p. 136.

73. Castle, p. 130.

74. "Austen Cults and Cultures," Copeland and McMaster, p. 223.

75. Ibid., p. 213.

76. Lodge, p. 34.

77. Per Serritslev Petersen (ed.), *On the First Sentence of* Pride and Prejudice: *A Critical Discussion of the Theory and Practice of Literary Interpretation* (1979).

CHAPTER 7: JANE AUSTEN™

1. *CH*, vol. 1, p. 225.

2. Charnes, p. 2.

3. *CR*, vol. 5, p. 105.

4. Cecil (1948), p. 121.

5. *CR*, vol. 1, p. 214.

6. *CH*, vol. 2, p. 41.

7. Included in E. C. Bentley's *Biography for Beginners* (London, 1905), no page numbers.

8. *Emma*, p. 468.

9. Mansfield, vol. 4, p. 339.

10. Michiko Kakutani, "New Romance Novels Are Just What Their Readers Ordered," *New York Times*, 11 August 1980, C13.

11. *CH*, vol. 2, p. 277.

12. George Sampson in the *Bookman*, quoted in *CH*, vol. 2, p. 101.

13. Raleigh, p. 471.

14. *CH*, vol. 2, p. 240.

15. Watt, p. 92.

16. *Emma*, p. 352.

17. *P&P*, p. 277.

18. Sleeve notes, *Bridget Jones's Diary* DVD, Miramax, 2001.

19. *New York Times*, 23 February 2004.

20. Quoted by Zoe Williams in her article "Keep Jane Plain," *Guardian Weekend*, 27 May 2006.

21. Quoted in Garber, pp. 206–7.

22. Rosie Millard, "Sex and Sensibility Work Wonders, Dear Jane," *Sunday Times*, 30 December 2007.

23. Carol McDaid interviewing Colin Firth, *Independent*, 9 June 2000.

24. Letter to Cassandra Austen, 8–11 April 1805, *Letters*, p. 99.

25. Denise Winterman, "Jane Austen: Why the Fuss?" http:// news.bbc.co.uk/1/hi/ magazine/6426195.stm.

26. Quoted in Parrill, p. 3.

27. Thompson, p. 210.

28. Julian Barnes, *Observer*, 13 November 1983.

29. Laurie Rigler, interviewed on a publisher's Web site: http://us.penguingroup.com/static/html/romance/janeaustenaddict.html.

30. Thread on *The Archers* Message Board, September 2006, http://www.bbc.co.uk/dna/marchers.

31. "Balancing the Courtship Hero: Masculine Emotional Display in Film Adaptations of Austen's Novels," in Troost and Greenfield, p. 24.

32. Ibid., p. 6.

33. Todd (2005), p. 117.

34. Cossy, p. 17.

35. At the "Austen and Contemporary Literature and Culture" conference, Chawton House, June 2007.

36. "Revved-up Austen," *Radio Times*, 17–23 March 2007.

37. "Austen's Power: Jane Addiction Sweeps Theaters, Bookstores," *USA Today*, 2 August 2007.

38. Mary Ann O'Farrell, "Austen and Contemporary Literature and Culture" conference, Chawton House, June 2007.

39. Quoted by Garber, p. 205.

40. Andrew Norfolk, *Times*, 17 March 2007, http:// www.timesonline.co.uk/tol/news/uk/article1527806.ece.

41. Ibid.

42. http://blog/wired.com/tableofmalcontents/2007/03/jane_austens_em.html.

43. *CH*, vol. 2, p. 67.

44. *Record*, pp. 232, 231, and 220.

45. Todd (2005), p. 87.

46. *Memoir*, pp. 188–89.

47. *Letters*, p. 202.

48. Ibid., p. 268.

49. *CR*, vol. 1, p. 258.

50. April 1811, *Letters*, p. 182.

51. *CH*, vol. 1, p. 242.

52. Todd (2005), p. 290.

53. *Letters*, p. 275.

54. Todd (2005), p. 118.

55. Harriet Martineau's diary, October 1837, quoted in *CH*, vol. 2, p. 136.

56. Hill, p. viii.

57. *CH*, vol. 2, p. 168.

58. http://austenprose.wordpress.com/2008/05/30/my-personal-austen-does-reading-austen-make-me-a-better-person/.

59.  Braudy, p. 15

60.  Trilling, p. 44.

61.  *Memoir*, p. 162.

62.  14–15 January 1796, *Letters*, p. 3.

63.  Forster, p. 153.

64.  *CH*, vol. 2, p. 41.

# Manuscript Sources

Bodleian Library, Oxford: Jane Austen, "Volume the First," MS Don.e.7; Robert William Chapman, "Jane Austen Files," MS Eng. Misc. c. 924; notes, MS Don.d.81; letter to Ethel Sidgwick, MSS Eng.Lett. c. 471, f. 143; letter to Bertram Dobell, MS Dobell c. 6, ff. 221–24.

British Library, London: Jane Austen, Letters and Papers (including letters by Jane Austen, Henry Austen, Richard Crosby, "Opinions" of *Mansfield Park* and *Emma*), add. 41253; correspondence of the Cooke and Leigh families, add. 38457, add. 38233; Bentley Papers, add. 46611, add. 46618, add. 46626; Hastings Papers, add. 29174; Letters to Frances Burney (d'Arblay), Egerton 3698.

Chawton House Library, Chawton, Hampshire: Jane Austen, manuscript of "Sir Charles Grandison," item 792.

Hampshire Record Office, Winchester: correspondence about the Jane Austen Library Fund 1918–52, 71M82/PW2/1; Austen and Austen-Leigh Papers, 23M93.

Morgan Library, New York: letters by Jane Austen, Cassandra Austen, Charles Austen, James Austen, Henry Austen, Augustus Austen-Leigh, William Austen-Leigh, Robert William Chapman et al., MA1034, MA1958, MA2911, MA3610, MA4500; manuscript pages of "The Watsons," MA1034.

National Portrait Gallery, London, Heinz Archive: file of correspondence between Robert William Chapman and Henry Hake, 1932–48.

New York Public Library, New York, Berg Collection: a collection of 271 letters to various members of the Burney family, etc., MS m.b. (Arblay).

Shakespeare Birthplace Trust Records Office, Stratford: Mary Leigh, "History of the Leigh Family" with a note on the author by the Reverend Thomas Leigh, manuscript and typescript copy. DR 671/77 and 77a.

# Selected Bibliography

Adams, Oscar Fay, *The Story of Jane Austen's Life* (Chicago, 1891).

Anon., "Jane Austen and Her Biographers," *Church Quarterly Review* 56 (1903), pp. 344–68.

Aspinall, A. (ed.), *Letters of the Princess Charlotte 1811–1817* (London, 1949).

Auden, W. H., *Collected Poems*, ed. Edward Mendelson (New York, 2007).

Austen, Caroline, *My Aunt Jane Austen: A Memoir* (Winchester, 1952).

[Austen, James, et al.], *The "Loiterer": A Periodical Work First Published at Oxford in the Years 1789 and 1790* (Dublin, 1792).

Austen, Jane, *Catharine and Other Writings*, ed. Margaret Anne Doody and Douglas Murray (Oxford, 1993).

Austen, Jane, *Pride and Prejudice*, edited with an introduction, etc. by K. M. Metcalfe (Oxford, 1912).

Austen, Jane, *Sanditon: An Unfinished Novel by Jane Austen, Reproduced in Facsimile from the Manuscript in the Possession of King's College, Cambridge*. Introduction by B. C. Southam (Oxford and London, 1975).

Austen-Leigh, James Edward, *Fugitive Pieces: Trifles Light as Air: The Poems of James Edward Austen-Leigh*, ed. David Selwyn (Winchester, 2006).

Austen-Leigh, Mary Augusta, *Personal Aspects of Jane Austen* (London, 1920).

Austen-Leigh, R. A. (ed.), *Austen Papers 1704–1856* (London, 1942).

Austen-Leigh, William and Richard A., *Life and Letters of Jane Austen* (London, 1913).

Austen-Leigh, William, and Knight, Montagu, *Chawton Manor and Its Owners* (London, 1911).

Bautz, Annika, *The Reception of Jane Austen and Walter Scott: A Comparative Longitudinal Study* (London, 2007).

Bien, Peter, *L. P. Hartley* (London, 1963).

Brabourne, Edward Knatchbull-Hugessen (ed.), *Letters of Jane Austen*, edited with an introduction by Edward Brabourne, with a new introduction by David Gilson (London, 1994).

Braudy, Leo, *The Frenzy of Renown: Fame and Its History* (Oxford, 1986).

Brinton, Sybil G., *Old Friends and New Fancies: An Imaginary Sequel to the Novels of Jane Austen* (London, 1913).

Brydges, Sir Samuel Egerton, Bt., *Sonnets and Other Poems; with a Versification of The Six Bards of Ossian* (London, 1785).

Brydges, Sir Samuel Egerton, Bt., *Arthur Fitz-Albini: A Novel*, 2 vols. (London, 1798).

Brydges, Sir Samuel Egerton, Bt., *Mary de Clifford: A Story, Interspersed with Many Poems*, 2nd edition (London, 1811).

Brydges, Sir Samuel Egerton, Bt., *The Autobiography, Times, Opinions and Contemporaries of Sir Egerton Brydges*, 2 vols. (London, 1834).

Burney, Frances, *The Journals and Letters of Fanny Burney (Madame d'Arblay) 1791–1840*, ed. Joyce Hemlow et al., 12 vols. (Oxford, 1972–84).

Bussby, Frederick, *Jane Austen in Winchester* (Winchester, 1975).

Butler, Marilyn, *Jane Austen and the War of Ideas* (Oxford, 1975).

Byrne, Sandie, *Jane Austen—"Mansfield Park": A Reader's Guide to Essential Criticism* (Basingstoke, 2004).

Carrington, Charles, *Rudyard Kipling: His Life and Work* (London, 1955).

Castle, Terry, *Boss Ladies, Watch Out!: Essays on Women, Sex and Writing* (London, 2002).

Cecil, Lord David, *Poets and Storytellers* (London, 1948).

Cecil, Lord David, *A Portrait of Jane Austen* (London, 1978).

Chapman, R. W., *Portrait of a Scholar and Other Essays Written in Macedonia 1916–18* (Oxford, 1920).

Chapman, R. W., "A Jane Austen Collection," *Times Literary Supplement*, 14 January 1926.

Chapman, R. W., "Jane Austen and Her Publishers," *London Mercury* 22 (1930), pp. 337–42.

Chapman, R. W. (ed.), *Jane Austen's Letters to Her Sister Cassandra and Others*, 2 vols. (Oxford, 1932).

Chapman, R. W., *Jane Austen: Facts and Problems* (Oxford, 1948).

Chapman, R. W., *Jane Austen: A Critical Bibliography* (Oxford, 1953).

Chapman, R. W., et al., *Book Collecting: Four Broadcast Talks* (Cambridge, 1950).

Charnes, Linda, *Notorious Identity: Materializing the Subject in Shakespeare* (Cambridge, Mass., 1993).

Churchill, W. S., *The Second World War*, vol. 5: *Closing the Ring* (London, 1952).

Clark, Lorna J. (ed.), *The Letters of Sarah Harriet Burney* (Athens and London, 1997).

Coleman, Terry, *The Only True History: Collected Interviews and Other Pieces* (London, 1969).

Coleridge, Sara, *Memoirs and Letters of Sara Coleridge*, 2 vols. (London, 1873).

[Cooke, Cassandra], *Battleridge: An Historical Tale, Founded on Facts, by a Lady of Quality* (London, 1799).

Cooper, Rev. Edward, *Practical and Familiar Sermons, Designed for Parochial and Domestic Instruction*, 3rd edition, 1815.

Cooper, Rev. Edward, *The Crisis; or, An Attempt to Shew from Prophecy; Illustrated by the Signs of the Times, the Prospects and the Duties of the Church of Christ at the Present Period. With an Inquiry into the Probable Destiny of England During the Predicted Desolations of the Papal Kingdoms* (London and Edinburgh, 1825).

Cooper, James Fenimore, *Precaution*, new revised edition, Bentley's Standard Novels no. 74 (London, 1838).

Copeland, Edward, and McMaster, Juliet, *The Cambridge Companion to Jane Austen* (Cambridge, 1997).

Cossy, Valérie, *Jane Austen in Switzerland: A Study of the Early French Translations* (Geneva, 2006).

Dowden, Wilfred S., et al. (eds.), *The Journal of Thomas Moore*, 6 vols. (New Jersey, 1983–91).

Dunaway, David King, *Huxley in Hollywood* (London, 1989).

Edlmann, Edith, "A Girl's Opinion on Jane Austen," *Temple Bar* 94 (1892), pp. 343–50.

Emerson, Ralph Waldo, *Journals of Ralph Waldo Emerson*, ed. E. W. Emerson and W. E. Forbes (Boston, 1909).

Fairweather, Maria, *Madame de Staël* (London, 2005).

Fawcett, Millicent Garrett, *Some Eminent Women of Our Times* (London, 1899).

Fénéon, Félix (trans.), *Catherine Morland* (Paris, 1899).

Fergus, Jan, *Jane Austen: A Literary Life* (Basingstoke, 1991).

Forster, E. M., *Abinger Harvest* (London, 1936).

Fussell, Paul, *The Great War and Modern Memory* (Oxford, 1975).

Galperin, William H., *The Historical Austen* (Philadelphia, 2003).

Garber, Marjorie, "The Jane Austen Syndrome," *Quotation Marks* (London, 2003).

Gaskell, Elizabeth, *Life of Charlotte Brontë*, ed. Alan Shelston (Harmondsworth, 1975).

Gilbert, Sandra M., and Gubar, Susan, *The Madwoman in the Attic: The Woman Writer and the Nineteenth-Century Literary Imagination* (New Haven and London, 1979).

Gilson, David, "The Early American Editions of Jane Austen," *Book Collector* 18 (1969), pp. 340–52.

Gilson, David, "Jane Austen's Books," *Book Collector* 23 (1974), pp. 27–39.

Gilson, David, "Serial Publication of Jane Austen in French," *Book Collector* 23 (1974), pp. 547–50.

Gilson, David, "Jane Austen and John Murray," *Book Collector* 34 (1985), pp. 520–21.

Gilson, David, "Henry Austen's 'Memoir of Miss Austen,'" *Persuasions* 19 (1997), pp. 12–19.

Gilson, David, "Jane Austen, the Aristocracy and T. H. Lister," *CR* 2002, pp. 56–65.

Gilson, David, "Jane Austen's Text: A Survey of Editions," *Review of English Studies*, NS 53 (2002), pp. 61–85.

Gore, John, *"Pride and Prejudice* and Miss Eden," *CR*, vol. 1, pp. 134–36.

Gorer, Geoffrey, "The Myth in Jane Austen," *American Imago* 2 (1941), pp. 197–204.

Halperin, Joan Ungersma, *Félix Fénéon: Aesthete and Anarchist in Fin-de-Siècle Paris* (New Haven, 1988).

Handley, Graham, *Criticism in Focus: Jane Austen* (New York, 1992).

Harman, Claire, *Fanny Burney: A Biography* (London, 2000).

Hastings, George E., "How Cooper Became a Novelist," *American Literature*, vol. 12, *1940–41*, pp. 20–51.

[Hawke, Cassandra], *Julia de Gramont*, 2 vols. (London, 1788).

Hazlitt, William, "The Dandy School," *Examiner*, 18 November 1827.

Hill, Constance, *Jane Austen, Her Homes and Her Friends* (London, 1902).

Hogan, Charles Beecher, "Jane Austen and Her Early Public," *Review of English Studies*, NS 1 (1950), pp. 39–54.

Honan, Park, *Jane Austen: Her Life* (London, 1987).

Howard, Richard, *Paper Trail: Selected Prose 1965–2003* (New York, 2004).

Hubback, Catherine Anne, *The Younger Sister* (London, 1850).

Hubback, J. H. and Edith C., *Jane Austen's Sailor Brothers* (London, 1906).

Huxley, Aldous, *Letters of Aldous Huxley*, ed. G. Smith (London, 1969).

James, Henry, "The Lesson of Balzac," *Atlantic Monthly* 96 (1905), pp. 166–80.

Jane Austen Memorial Trust, *Jane Austen's House, Chawton, Hants, Foreword and Guide* (n.d.).

"Jane Austen Number," *Bookman* 21 (January 1902).

Jenkins, Elizabeth, *Jane Austen* (London, 1938).

Johnson, Claudia L., *Jane Austen: Women, Politics and the Novel* (Chicago and London, 1988).

Kipling, Rudyard, *The Wish House and Other Stories* (New York, 2002).

Knapp, Samuel L., *Female Biography: Containing Notices of Distinguished Women, in Different Ages and Nations* (Philadelphia [1834]).

Lamb, Lady Caroline, *The Whole Disgraceful Truth: Selected Letters of Lady Caroline Lamb*, ed. Paul Douglass (New York, 2006).

Lane, Maggie, *Jane Austen's Family, Through Five Generations* (London, 1984).

Lane, Margaret, "Dr. Robert W. Chapman," *Times Literary Supplement*, 6 August 1954.

Lascelles, Mary, *Jane Austen and Her Art* (Oxford, 1939).

Lascelles, Mary, "Robert William Chapman, 1881–1960," *Proceedings of the British Academy*, 47 (1961), pp. 361–70.

Le Faye, Deirdre, *Fanny Knight's Diaries: Jane Austen Through Her Niece's Eyes* (Winchester, 2000).

Le Faye, Deirdre, "New Marginalia in Jane Austen's Books," *Book Collector* 49, no. 2 (2000), pp. 222–26.

Le Faye, Deirdre, *A Chronology of Jane Austen and Her Family* (Cambridge, 2006).

Leavis, F. R., *The Great Tradition* (London, 1948).

Leavis, F. R. (ed.), *A Selection from "Scrutiny,"* 2 vols. (Cambridge, 1968).

[Lefroy, Anna], *Mary Hamilton, By a Niece of the Late Miss Austen* (London, 1927).

Leigh, Agnes, "An Old Family History," *National Review* 49 (1907), pp. 277–86.

L'Estrange, Rev. A. G., *The Life of Mary Russell Mitford, Related in a Selection from Her Letters to Her Friends*, 3 vols. (London, 1870).

Linklater, Eric, *The Impregnable Women* (London, 1938).

[Lister, Thomas Henry], *Granby: A Novel*, 3 vols. (London, 1826).

Litz, A. Walton, " 'The Loiterer': A Reflection of Jane Austen's Early Environment," *Review of English Studies*, NS 12 (1961), pp. 251–61.

Lodge, David, *Changing Places: A Tale of Two Campuses* (London, 1975).

Lynch, Deidre (ed.), *Janeites: Austen's Disciples and Devotees* (Princeton, 2000).

Macaulay, Thomas Babington, *Essays and Lays of Ancient Rome*, new impression (London, 1899).

Macdonald, Gina and Andrew (eds.), *Jane Austen on Screen* (Cambridge, 2003).

Mack, Robert L. (ed.), *The "Loiterer": A Periodical Work in Two Volumes. Published at Oxford in the Years 1789 and 1790 by the Austen Family, with Critical Notes and an Introduction by Robert L. Mack* (Lewiston, 2006).

Malden, Sarah Fanny, *Jane Austen* (London, 1889).

Mandal, A., and Southam, B. C. (eds.), *The Reception of Jane Austen in Europe* (London and New York, 2007).

Mansfield, Katherine, *The Collected Letters of Katherine Mansfield*, ed. Vincent O'Sullivan and Margaret Scott, 5 vols. (Oxford, 1984–2008).

Marshall, Mary Gaither (ed.), *Jane Austen's "Sanditon": A Continuation by Her Niece, Together with "Reminiscences of Aunt Jane" by Anna Austen Lefroy* (Chicago, 1983).

McMaster, Juliet, and Stovel, Bruce (eds.), *Jane Austen's Business: Her World and Her Profession* (1996).

Miller, Lucasta, *The Brontë Myth* (London, 2001).

Mudrick, Marvin, *Jane Austen: Irony as Defense and Discovery* (Princeton, 1952).

Neagle, Anna, *There's Always Tomorrow* (London, 1982).

Nicholson, Andrew (ed.), *The Letters of John Murray to Lord Byron* (Liverpool, 2007).

Oliphant, Margaret, "Miss Austen and Miss Mitford," *Blackwood's Magazine* 107 (March 1870).

Parrill, Sue, *Jane Austen on Film and Television: A Critical Study of the Adaptations* (North Carolina, 2002).

Parsons, Farnell, "Jane Austen's Passage to Derbyshire," *CR* 2002, pp. 34–39.

Poovey, Mary, *The Proper Lady and the Woman Writer: Ideology as Style in the Works of Mary Wollstonecraft, Mary Shelley and Jane Austen* (Chicago, 1984).

Proudman, Elizabeth, "The Essential Guide to Finding Jane Austen in Chawton." Publication of the Jane Austen Society of North America (2003).

Ragg, Laura M., *Jane Austen in Bath* (London, 1938).

Raleigh, Sir Walter Alexander, *The Letters of Sir Walter Raleigh* (1879–1922), ed. Lady Raleigh, with a preface by David Nichol Smith, 2nd edition (London, 1926).

Raven, James, Forster, Antonia, and Bending, Stephen, *The English Novel 1770–1829: A Bibliographical Survey of Prose Fiction Published in the British Isles*, vol. 1, *1770–1799* (Oxford, 2000).

Rhydderch, David, *Jane Austen: Her Life and Art* (London, 1932).

Rogers, Pat, "Sposi in Surrey," *Times Literary Supplement*, 23 August 1996.

Sadleir, Michael, "Bentley's Standard Novel Series: Its History and Achievement," *Colophon*, pt. 10 (1932).

Said, Edward, *Culture and Imperialism* (London, 1993).

Scott, Walter, *Journal of Walter Scott*, ed. J. G. Tait (1939).

Selwyn, David (ed.), *Collected Poems and Verse of the Austen Family* (Manchester, 1996).

Seymour, Beatrice Kean, *Jane Austen: Study for a Portrait* (London, 1937).

Shields, Carol, *Jane Austen* (London, 2001).

Showalter, Elaine, *Sexual Anarchy: Gender and Culture at the Fin de Siècle* (London, 1992).

Smiles, Samuel, *A Publisher and His Friends: Memoir and Correspondence of the Late John Murray*, 2 vols. (London, 1891).

Smith, Grover (ed.), *Letters of Aldous Huxley* (London, 1969).

Southam, Brian (ed.), *Critical Essays on Jane Austen* (London, 1968).

Southam, Brian (ed.), *Jane Austen's "Sir Charles Grandison"* (Oxford, 1980).

Southam, Brian, *Jane Austen's Literary Manuscripts: A Study of the Novelist's Development Through the Surviving Papers*, new edition (London, 2001).

St. Clair, William, *The Reading Nation in the Romantic Period* (Cambridge, 2004).

Stephen, Leslie, "Humour," *Cornhill* 33 (1876), pp. 324–25.

Sutherland, Kathryn, *Jane Austen's Textual Lives: From Aeschylus to Bollywood* (Oxford, 2005).

Taylor, Henry, *Autobiography of Henry Taylor, 1800–1875* (London, 1885).

Thompson, Emma, *Jane Austen's "Sense & Sensibility": The Screenplay and Diaries* (London, 1995).

Todd, Janet (ed.), *Jane Austen in Context* (Cambridge, 2005).

Todd, Janet (ed.), *The Cambridge Introduction to Jane Austen* (Cambridge, 2006).

Tomalin, Claire, *Jane Austen: A Life* (London, 1997).

Trevelyan, G. O., *Life and Letters of Lord Macaulay*, 2 vols. (London, 1876).

Trilling, Lionel, *Beyond Culture: Essays on Literature and Learning* (New York, 1965).

Troost, Linda, and Greenfield, Sayre (eds.), *Jane Austen in Hollywood* (Kentucky, 1998).

Tucker, George Holbert, *A History of Jane Austen's Family* (Stroud, 1998).

Tuite, Clara, *Romantic Austen: Sexual Politics and the Literary Canon* (Cambridge, 2002).

Twain, Mark, *Mark Twain's Notebook*, ed. Albert Bigelow Paine (New York and London, 1935).

Villard, Léonie, *Jane Austen: A French Appreciation, Translated by Veronica Lucas from "Jane Austen: sa vie et son œuvre," with a New Study of Jane Austen by R. Brimley Johnson* (London, 1924).

Viveash, Chris, "*Emma* and Robert Donat," *CR*, vol. 5, pp. 338–41.

Waldron, Mary, *Jane Austen and the Fiction of Her Time* (Cambridge, 1999).

Ward, William S., "Three Hitherto Unnoticed Contemporary Reviews of Jane Austen," *Nineteenth Century Fiction* 26 (1971–72), pp. 469–77.

Warner, Sylvia Townsend, *Jane Austen* (London, 1951).

Warre Cornish, Francis, *Jane Austen* (London, 1913).

Watt, Ian (ed.), *Jane Austen: A Collection of Critical Essays* (Englewood Cliffs, 1963).

Williams, Merryn, "Finishing 'The Watsons,'" *Report of the Jane Austen Society*, 2002, pp. 14–20.

Woodworth, Mary Katherine, *The Literary Career of Sir Samuel Egerton Brydges* (Oxford, 1935).

Woolf, Virginia, *The Common Reader* (London, 1925).

# Acknowledgments

For the use of copyright materials and illustrations, and kind permission to quote from manuscripts in their collections, I would like to thank the National Portrait Gallery, London; Heinz Archive and Library (correspondence between Robert William Chapman and Henry Hake); Shakespeare Birthplace Trust, Stratford-on-Avon (Leigh family manuscripts); the British Library, London (Austen and Bentley papers); the Morgan Library, New York City (Austen collections); Hampshire Record Office, Winchester (Austen-Leigh papers); the Bodleian Library, Oxford (Robert William Chapman notes); the National Library of Scotland (John Murray archive); the Victoria and Albert Museum; the Berg Collection of the New York Public Library; and Columbia University Library. I am particularly grateful to the president and scholars of Saint John Baptist College in the University of Oxford for granting permission to reproduce George Austen's letter to Thomas Cadell, and to the college librarian, Catherine Hilliard, for showing me the manuscript and facilitating my request. I am also deeply indebted to Patrick O'Connor for his permission to let me use a previously unpublished image from his collection.

Many individual members of staff at libraries, galleries, and other institutions have been very generous with their time and expertise, and I would like to thank in particular David McClay, curator of the John Murray Archive in the National Library of Scotland; David Busby, Samantha Townsend, James Allen, and Clive Hurst of the Bodleian Library; Emma Butterfield of the National Portrait Gallery; Elaine Lucas of the Victoria and Albert Museum; Emma Mee of the Design and Artists Copyright Society; David Abbott of IPC publications; Maria Molestina of the Morgan Library; and Tim Moreton of the Heinz Archive at the National Portrait Gallery, who very kindly showed me the silhouette in the collection labeled, "L'Aimable Jane."

The Jane Austen Memorial Trust, which does so much for Janeites everywhere, has been extremely kind in making material available to view and giving permission to reproduce several images. I am especially grateful to three members of staff at Jane Austen's House Museum in Chawton, Ann Channon, Tom Carpenter, and Louise West, who answered my queries at various times in the writing of this book with great cheerfulness and courtesy.

Anyone writing about Jane Austen will owe a huge debt of gratitude to scholars past and present, and I am particularly indebted to David Gilson, Deirdre Le Faye, and Brian Southam, and to the current generation of editors and critics, led by Kathryn Sutherland, Claudia Johnson, Peter Sabor, and Janet Todd. For their various helpful leads, contributions of information, hospitality, and general encouragement I would like to thank John Carey, Terry Castle, Lindsay Duguid, Lyndall Gordon, Georgina Hammick, Helen Lefroy, Patrick O'Connor, Liza Picard, Henry and Anne Rice, Emmett and Pat Schlueter, Roger Swearingen, Ian Thomson, and Marion Turner. Blakey Vermeule's impersonation of Louisa Musgrave at Lyme Regis was a highlight of "research," as was the very entertaining day I spent with Claudia Johnson, Clara Tuite, and the rest of the Janeite party who attended the auction of the Rice Portrait at Christie's in New York in April 2007.

I am more grateful than I can say to the trustees of Chawton House Library who awarded me a fellowship in 2008 and enabled me to spend several delightful weeks in that beautiful and highly evocative Austen location. Librarian Jacqui Grainger was a wonderful guide to the treasures of the collection, and research fellow Gillian Dow could not have been a better-informed, more lively, or more genial overseer. I would also like to thank Sandy Lerner, the inspired patron of the whole Chawton House project, and members of staff, past and present: Helen Scott, Emma Heywood, Sarah Cross, Steve Lawrence, and Corinne Saint. Alan Bird and Sally Hughes and my charming fellow fellows Pauline Morris and Olivia Murphy made my sojourn at the Stables very happy.

At Henry Holt, I have been privileged to work with a legendary editor, Jack Macrae, whose input was invaluable in shaping the final draft of this book. My great thanks go also to Supurna Banerjee of Henry Holt for all her work on the U.S. edition and to my agent, Geri Thoma, for her unerring wisdom, friendship, and support on this as on every other project.

I would also like to thank three dear young people, Charles, Isabel, and Benedict Schmidt, and my mother, Pat Harman, who kept a sharp eye out for Austen-related cuttings and very helpfully taped what seemed like dozens of TV adaptations of Austen novels. Love and thanks go to Paul Strohm, whose methods of composition are so different from my own but who waited patiently for a glimpse of the manuscript and proved such an invaluable reader of it in the end. I also owe a huge debt of gratitude as well as of friendship to Mark Bostridge, whose idea this was in the first place; and to the most ardent and knowledgeable Janeites among my friends, Sandie Byrne, Jacob Strohm, and Marion Turner, whom I would most like to please.

# Index

## A

Adams, Oscar Fay, 124, 129–30
*Agnes Grey* (Brontë, A.), 99
Alton, Hampshire, 22, 56, 92, 178
Andrews, James, 115–16, 117, 142, 169, 206
*The Archers* (BBC Radio), 213–14
Arlington (Lister, T.), 72
Arnold, Matthew, 183
*Arthur Fitz-Albini* (Brydges, S. E.), 19
Ashe, Hampshire, 7, 19, 237n53, 237n55
Ashford, Daisy, 156
Asquith, Lady Cynthia, 187
*Atlantic Monthly*, 132
Auden, W. H., 183
*Augustan Review*, 219–20
Austen, Anna, *see* Lefroy, Jane Anna
    Elizabeth
Austen, Caroline Mary Craven (JA's niece),
    6, 8, 48, 90
  on Andrews's portrait of JA, 116
  death of, 120
  invaluable biographical assistant, 105–6,
    110
  and literary reputation of JA, 101–2, 103,
    118
  manuscript items in possession of, 95–96
  on publication of Austen-Leigh's
    biography, 117
Austen, Cassandra (JA's mother), 1, 3, 5, 6,
    29, 42, 77, 89, 91
  agitation about Leigh Perrot money, 40
  death of, 89
  family finances, difficulties with, 34,
    79–80
  Jane first child to die, 61
  *Mansfield Park*, opinion on, 47
  view of Jane's literary gifts, 65
Austen, Cassandra Elizabeth (JA's sister),
    1, 4–5, 8, 31, 79–80, 81–82, 143, 180
  annuity from Tom Fowle, 34
  collaboration with JA on *Mansfield Park*,
    47
  correspondence from JA, 45, 46
  death of, 98
  early years with JA, 3–4
  on "Elinor and Marianne," 19–20

Austen, Cassandra Elizabeth (*cont'd*)
  engagement and tragedy for, 23–24
  Fanny Knight and, 32
  inheritance from JA, 65–66
  JA's last writing, 59–60
  memo on timescale of JA's compositions,
    28
  pious commemoration of JA, 106
  posterity of JA, control over, 87–93
  praises passed on by, 43
  manuscripts left by, 95–108
  *Pride and Prejudice*, on publication of, 41
  publishing losses, burden of, 77
  *Sense and Sensibility*, on publication of, 37
  sketches of JA, 115, 116, 168, 169, 170,
    206
  watercolor vignettes for JA's "History of
    England," 5, 156
Austen, Cassandra (Cassy) Esten (JA's
    niece), 101, 115, 116, 169
Austen, Charles John (JA's brother), 3, 4, 5,
    34, 78
  active and successful life at sea, 40
  death of, 98
  executor for Cassandra, 89–90, 91
  naval career, 143
  *Pride and Prejudice*, surprise at success of,
    45
  salary, lowish nature of, 79
  treasures descended through, 168, 180
Austen, Colonel Thomas, 121
Austen, Edward. *See* Knight, Edward (JA's
    brother)
Austen, Fanny Sophia (Frank's daughter),
    105
Austen, Francis (Frank) William (JA's
    brother), 3, 4, 6, 31, 40, 93, 143
  attendance at JA's funeral, 61
  collaboration with JA on *Mansfield Park*,
    47
  death of, 98, 104
  generosity with memorabilia of JA, 97–98
  knighthood for, 89
  marriage to Martha Lloyd, 80, 89
  reports from JA to, 42, 45–46

  resourcefulness of, 97
  settlement for, 79
Austen, George (JA's brother), 3, 30, 79, 98
Austen, Rev. George (JA's father), 3, 4, 5–6,
    11, 19–21, 34, 61
  death of, 31, 34
  encouragement for JA from, 20–21, 29
  letter to publisher Cadell, 105
Austen, Henry Thomas (JA's brother), xv,
    11, 28, 34, 51, 54, 87, 89, 227–28
  agent for JA, 36–37, 41–42
  attendance at Jane's funeral, 61
  and Bentley, negotiations for JA's
    copyrights, 80–82, 89
  "Biographical Notice" (1818), 82–83, 84,
    101, 109, 113, 118, 171
  business slump, 56–57, 77–79
  collaboration with JA on *Mansfield Park*,
    47
  death of, 98
  graduate of Oxford, 3, 12
  and identification of JA's authorship,
    43, 45
  illness, 50
  inheritance from JA, 65–66, 89
  intimately knowledgeable, 104
  JA's closeness to, 4
  marriage to Eliza de Feuillide, 22
  maximization of Jane's celebrity, efforts
    in, 48
Austen, Rev. James (JA's brother), 3, 5, 6, 14,
    77, 79, 82, 227
  ambition and talent of, 8–9
  JA's identity guarded by, 43
  literary accomplishments and the *Loiterer*,
    10–13
  marriages of, 22, 23
  memorial poem for JA, 62–63, 67
  middle-aged melancholy and stasis, 40
  morbid sensibility, plagued by, 109
  poem in celebration of publication of
    *Sense and Sensibility*, 37
Austen, Jane
  academic study of, 124, 132–33, 160–62,
    190–91, 194–96, 214–16

accidental artist, promotion as, 161

American collections of memorabilia, 180–82

anonymity, 37, 38–39, 43, 45

appeal of, aspects of, xviii–xix, 135–36, 199

appropriation of "Austenlike" qualities by other writers, 71–73

assertiveness, 33–34

audience, prose affected by consciousness of, 32

audience widening for novels of, 123

"Austen mania," surges in, xx, 208

as biographical subject, 108–16

biographies, 123–25, 182, 186, 187, 188–89, 221

birth and early life, 3–4

booksellers and publishers, access to, 29–30

Brydges reminiscence of, 84–85

businesswoman, 50–51

Cassandra's sketches of, 115, 116, 168, 169, 170, 206

centenary of death, 149–51

Chapman, Robert W., and works of, 145–46, 153–55, 156–59, 162, 166–70, 187, 202, 220

Charlotte Brontë's criticism of, 99–100

charm of, reflected in characters, 110, 128, 176

chick-lit appeal of writing, xx, 201–2, 205–7

Churchill and, 175–76

collaborative composition, 47

composition, timescales for, 28

confidence in works, 22

copyright concerns, 33, 39, 41–42, 46, 51, 77, 80–81, 89, 94

criticisms of early reviewers, 73

"critic's novelist—highly spoken of and little read," 94

cult status, 129–31, 197

death of, 60, 61

death of, 150th anniversary commemoration, 188

deference toward Cassandra, 87

*Dictionary of National Biography (DNB)*, 124, 136, 165

domestic humor, 166

drafting habit, 36

*Emma*, theatrical presentation of, 177

Englishness of, 139, 144, 152–53, 186–87

ephemera of, public interest in, 119

estate, dispersal of, 65–66

estate of, 95–96, 97–98, 100, 101–8

experimentalism, 25–26

fame, effects of, 48–49, elements of, 2–3 temporary and localized, 65

family finances, difficulties with, 34

fans of, 44, 89, 225–26

fashionable interest in *Sense and Sensibility*, 38

father, death of, 31

feminism and, 136, 189, 197, 205

Fénéon and French appreciation, 139–42

film treatments of novels, 151, 172–75, 204–5, 208–9, 211, 214–15

funeral, 61

global phenomenon (and global brand), xvi–xviii, 198

Great War and popularity of writing, 144–49

half-forgotten niche writer, 94

Harding on, 184, 188–89, 226, 227

Hartley's negativity on, 149

Henry James on, 133–34, 166, 227

"heteronormativity" in works of, 191–92, 203–4

"husband-hunting butterfly," 115

identity as author, revelation of, 45–46

ideologies and disciplines, alternative approaches to work of, 183–85, 190–91

illness, 59

illustrations in works of, 126–27, 157–58, 172, 214

images of, 81–82, 168–72, 206, 209

influence in America, *Precaution* and, 74–76

inspiration, doubts on, 49

Austen, Jane (*cont'd*)
  Internet and mass intimacy, 225–26
  juvenilia, 5–6, 11, 13–15, 32, 97, 104, 106,
    155, 156, 193, 196, 221
  last writing, 59–60, 118
  literary reputation, defenses of, 98–102
  love stories and mass appeal, 200–205
  manuscripts, control over, 57–58, 220
  manuscripts, publishing frustrations,
    25–26
  market worth, fall in, 80–81
  marriage proposal from Harris
    Bigg-Wither, 30
  mass market for, 126, 197–99
  memorabilia, 167–68, 180
  memorial poems for, 62–65
  memorial tablet in Winchester Cathedral,
    122
  modernity of, 86, 165
  mother of romance, 200–201
  "New Woman" and writing of, 135–36
  obscurity, period of, 76–77, 94–95
  "overwriting," fear of, 56
  perseverance of, 28
  physical description of, 67
  "Plan of a Novel," 52–53
  popularity with romantic contemporaries,
    86–87
  portraits of, 121–22, 142, 168–69, 241n69
  posterity of, Cassandra's control over, 87,
    88–91
  praise and appreciation from Sir Walter
    Scott for, 54–55, 85
  *Pride and Prejudice*, triumph in
    publication of, 41–43, 44–45
  prince regent "a great admirer," 51, 55–56
  profession, attitude toward, 27–28
  public acknowledgment of authorship, 61
  publication of work, early solicitation,
    20–21, 29
  readership, small expansion of, 32, 71
  reading and early writing, 3–4, 21–22
  Regency revival and, 165
  republication by Bentley of novels, 81–83
  reviews of *Pride and Prejudice*, 44–45

  revision, method of, 35–36
  revisionism on, 183–85
  Russian success of novels of, 74
  sales of *Sense and Sensibility*, 39
  scale and boundaries in works of, 113–14,
    160–61
  secrecy, myth of, 1–2
  self-regulation as writer, 32–33, 56, 62–63,
    113
  *Sense and Sensibility*, publication of, 36
  sex and romance, criticism of treatment
    of, 202
  television treatments of works, 205,
    206–8, 209, 211, 212–14, 215–16
  Tennyson's admiration for, 95
  therapeutic potential of writing, 146–48
  timelessness of work, 221–24
  vigilance over traits of others, 63
  wasting of titles by, 77
  working milieu, home context and, 1–3,
    112, 220
  worldliness of, 189–90
  writing, early encouragement in, 5–6
  writing circles, access to, 29
  YouTube compilations, 204
  Zeitgeist thing of, 137, 214, 216
Austen, Mary (Lloyd, wife of Frank), 24,
    31, 104
Austen-Leigh, Rev. James Edward (JA's
    nephew), xx, 27–28, 46, 125–26, 135,
    142–43, 155, 161
  attendance at JA's funeral, 61, 93
  biography of JA, 102–6, 108–14, 116–17;
    second edition, 117, 119
  on boundaries and scale, 114–15
  on character of JA, 107
  criticism of biographical portrait, 119–20
  death of, 120
  draftsmanship of, 82
  on James Austen and the *Loiterer*, 12–13
  on JA's "parental" interest in characters,
    220
  and literary reputation of JA, 101–2
  memorial tablet to Jane, erection of, 122
  memories of youth, 41

on scale and Jane's "little bit of Ivory," 113–14

writing and corresponding with JA, 48

Austen-Leigh, L. A., 155

Austen-Leigh, Lois, 169

Austen-Leigh, Mary Augusta, 57, 95, 98, 102, 143

Austen-Leigh, Richard Arthur, 143–44, 169

Austen-Leigh, William, 143, 155

*Austen Papers* (Austen-Leigh, R. A.), 144

Austenolatry, 227

Austin, Alfred, 145

## B

Bailey, John, 165

Baillie, Isobel, 188

Barnes, Julian, 211

Barron, Stephanie, 217

Basingstoke, 22, 30

Bath, Somerset, 24
family move to, 29

*Battleridge: An Historical Tale* (Cooke, C.), 15, 17–18, 223

Beckinsale, Kate, 209, 211

*Becoming Jane Austen* (Spence, J.), 212

*Becoming Jane* (Julian Jarrold film), 212–13

*Belinda* (Edgeworth, M.), 223

Benn, Mary, 42

Bennett, Arnold, 164

Bentley, Richard, 76, 80–82, 82–84, 89, 94, 118, 119, 120, 139

Beresford, Charles, 206

Bessborough, Henrietta Spencer, Countess of, 38

*Bibliography of Jane Austen* (Chapman, R. W.), 157

*Bibliography of Samuel Johnson* (Courtney, W. P., and Smith, D. N.), 145

Bigg, Catherine and Alethea, 30, 86

Bigg, Elizabeth, 145

Bigg-Wither, Harris, 30, 86, 106, 145

Birrell, Augustine, 156

Birtwistle, Sue, 207, 212

Blackall, Rev. Dr. Samuel, 23

*Blackwoods Magazine*, 70–71, 219

Blessington, Marguerite, Countess of, 72

Bloomberg, Michael, 218

Blunden, Edmund, 145

Bonneville, Hugh, 211

Booth, Wayne, 203

Boringdon, Lady Frances. *See* Morley, Frances, Countess of

Boswell, James, 145–46

Brabourne, Lord. *See* Knatchbull-Hugessen, Edward, Lord Brabourne

Bradley, A. C., 129, 144, 162, 163

Bramstone, Mrs. Augusta, 47

Braudy, Leo, 2, 227

Brett-Smith, H. F., 146, 148

*Bride and Prejudice* (Gurinder Chadha film), 209

Bridges, Elizabeth (Mrs. Edward Austen), 22

*Bridget Jones's Diary* (Fielding, H.), xvi, 204–5

*Bridget Jones's Diary* (Sharon Maguire film), 205, 211, 246n18

Brinton, Sybil G., 216

*British Critic*, 38, 44, 53, 70

Brock, C. E. and H. M., 127

Brontë, Charlotte, xix, 98, 99–100, 101, 110, 114–15, 132, 183, 211

Brontë sisters, 98–99, 101, 133, 150, 151, 173, 203

Brown, John, 95

Brownlee, John, 219

Brownstein, Rachel, 215

Brunton, Mary, 37

Brydges, Charlotte, 7

Brydges, Mrs. Elizabeth, 7

Brydges, Samuel Egerton, 7–8, 18–19, 40, 58, 84–85, 86

Bulwer-Lytton, Edward G. E. L., 72, 84, 85

Burke, Henry Gershon, and Alberta Hirschheimer, 180–81

Burney, Fanny (later Madame d'Arblay), 3, 15–17, 20, 39, 52, 76, 84, 101, 138, 162

Burney, Sarah Harriet, 85

Burns, Robert, 100

Bury, Lady Charlotte, 72

Butler, Marilyn, 189
*By a Lady* (Elyot, A.), 217
Byron, George Gordon, Lord, 39, 44, 50,
    54, 65, 66, 71
Bywater, Ingram, 156

## *C*

Cadell, Thomas (publisher), 16, 20–21, 24,
    25, 29, 41, 105
*Camilla* (Burney, F.), 16, 17, 20, 84
Campbell, Thomas, 81
Carlisle, George Howard, Earl of, 89
Carlyle, Thomas, xix, 161
Carpenter, Lieutenant John Philip, 179
Carpenter, T. Edward, 179, 181, 182
Carrington, Dora, 165
Cartland, Barbara, 200
Castle, Terry, 191–92
"Catharine, or The Bower" (Austen, J.), 4,
    5, 19, 21, 35, 59
"Catherine Morland" (Fénéon, F.), 141
Cecil, Lord David, 132, 148–49, 152,
    186–87, 188, 199
*Cecilia* (Burney, F.), 16, 17, 84
Chadha, Gurinder, 199
*Changing Places* (Lodge, D.), 194–95
Chapman, Robert William, 145–46, 153–55,
    156–59, 162, 166–70, 187, 202, 220
Charlotte Augusta, Princess of Wales, 38
Charnes, Linda, 198
Chatel, Charles, 140
Chatto and Windus (publisher), 156
Chawton, 22, 34–35, 42–43, 77
    Cassandra's later life in, 92–93
Chawton Cottage, 129, 149–51, 178,
    179–80, 181
    tenancy doubts, 58
Cheney, R. H., 126, 135
Chesterton, G. K., 156, 199, 203
*Chronology of Jane Austen* (Le Faye, D.), 193
*Church Quarterly Review*, 122
Churchill, Winston S., 175–76
Clarendon Press (and Chapman's edition of
    Austen's works), 153, 155, 156, 166,
    170, 182

Clarke, Rev. James Stanier, 51–53, 56, 114,
    170, 223, 228
Clavel, Maurice, 75
*Clueless* (Amy Heckerling film), 209
Cobbett, William, 78
*Coelebs in Search of a Wife* (More, H.), 35
Colburn, Henry (publisher), 48, 72, 80
Coleridge, Samuel Taylor, 85–86
Coleridge, Sara, 86
*Collected Poems and Verse of the Austen
    Family* (Selwyn, D., ed.), 116
Collins, Wilkie, 94
*Confessions of an Austen Addict* (Rigler,
    L. V.), 212, 217, 221
Conrad, Joseph, xv
Cooke, Rev. George, 15
Cooke, Mary, 52
Cooke, Cassandra, 15–16
    *Battleridge: An Historical Romance*, 15,
        223
    and *Camilla*, 16–17
Cooper, Edward, 11, 40–41
Cooper, James Fenimore, 75–76, 83–84
Cooper, Jane, 5
Cooper, Susan, 75
Cossy, Valérie, 214
*The Country and the City* (Williams, R.),
    189
*Country Life*, 164
Cowper, William, 9
*Critical Heritage* (Southam, B.), 193
*Critical Review*, 16, 38, 44, 222
Cronin, Richard, 223
Crosby, Benjamin (publisher), 29, 30,
    33–34, 58
Crosby, Richard (publisher), 34
Cruttwell (Bath bookseller), 29
*Culture and Imperialism* (Said, E.), 191
Curtis, Hugh, 178
Curtis, Richard, 205

## *D*

Daiches, David, 183
*Daily Telegraph*, 152
d'Arblay, Madame. *See* Burney, Fanny

Darnell, Dorothy, 178, 180

Davies, Andrew, 202, 205, 207–8, 209, 213, 214

Deane, Hampshire, 7–8, 18, 19

*Debits and Credits* (Kipling, R.), 146

Dent (publisher), 127

*Diary and Letters* (Burney, F.), 84, 101

Dickens, Charles, 81, 94, 158, 173, 182, 211

*Dictionary of National Biography* (*DNB*), 124, 136, 165

Disraeli, Benjamin, 85

Dobson, Austen, 128

Donat, Robert, 176–77

Doody, Margaret Anne, 59

Dorset, Catherine Ann, 38, 66

Dostoyevsky, Fyodor, 182

Doyle, Sir Francis, 124

Duckworth, Alistair, 189

Duret, Theodore, 141–42

### *E*

Eagleton, Terry, 189

Eckstut, Arielle, 218

Eden, Emily, 72

Edgeworth, Maria, 3, 54, 71, 72, 76, 85, 138, 220, 223

Edlmann, Edith, 137

Egerton, Thomas, 11, 36, 37, 41–42, 46, 48, 50, 51, 77, 80

Ehle, Jennifer, 207

Elford, Sir William, 61

"Elinor and Marianne" (Austen, J.), 29, 217
  *see also Sense and Sensibility*

*Elinor and Marianne* (Tennant, E.), 217

Eliot, George, 203, 211

"The Elliots" (Austen, J.), 57, 58, 59, 66, 74
  *see also Persuasion*

Elyot, Amanda, 217

Emerson, Ralph Waldo, 131

*Emma* (Austen, J.), 81, 190, 199–200
  copyright expiry on, 94
  distribution of, 54
  French translation of, 74

notice in literary press, 54
  pirated edition of, 74
  publication of, 50–51
  relegation to servant's library, 95
  sale of, negotiations on, 50–51
  theatrical presentation of, 177
  wasting of, 77

*Emma* (Douglas McGrath film), 208

*Emma in Love* (Tennant, E.), 217

*Emma* (ITV), 209

*Encyclopedia Britannica*, 136

*Englishwoman's Domestic Magazine*, 101, 136

*English Women of Letters* (Kavanagh, J.), 102

*Entertainment Weekly*, 209, 210

*Eugene Onegin* (Pushkin, A.), xvi, 74

*Evelina* (Burney, F.), 16, 20, 84

###  *F*

Farrer, Reginald, 184

Fawcett, Millicent, 136

Fénéon, Félix, 139–40, 141, 142

Feuillide, Comtesse Eliza de (JA's cousin), 5, 10, 14, 22, 37, 40, 41, 77, 87

Fielding, Helen, 205

Fielding, Henry, 9

*First Impressions* (Holford, M.), 24–25

Firth, Colin, 205, 207–8, 211, 226

*Footballers' Wives* (Shed Productions), 217–18

*Foreign and Colonial Review*, 91

Forster, E. M., xvi, 127, 166, 280

*Four Weddings and a Funeral* (Mike Newell film), 205, 210

Fowle, Elizabeth Caroline, 90

Fowle, Fulwar Craven, 8, 90

Fowle, Tom, 23, 34, 88

Fowle family, 59, 79

Fowler, Karen Joy, xviii, 217

Fox, Charles James, 45

Frederick, Duke of York and Albany, 38

Freud, Sigmund, 136
Freudian analysis, 183
Fulford, Roger, 95
Fussell, Paul, 144–45

*G*

Gable, Clark, 173
Galignani (Parisian publisher), 139
Garber, Marjorie, xvii
Garrett, Edmund H., 127
Garrick, David, 164
Garrod, H. W., 164
Garson, Greer, 174, 175
Gaskell, Elizabeth, 98–99, 101, 110, 114, 211
*Gentleman's Magazine*, 53, 73
George, Prince Regent (later George IV), 46, 51, 53, 55, 95, 114, 170
George III, xvi
Gibson, Mary, 105
Gide, André, 142
Gifford, William, 53, 55–56
Gilbert, Sandra, 190
Gilpin, William, 18
Gilson, David, 72, 155, 157, 193
Gissing, George, 137, 183
*Glenarvon* (Lamb, C.), 71
Godmersham, Kent, 3, 32, 37, 40, 43, 47, 138
Godwin, William, 71
Goldsmith, Oliver, 4, 143
*Gone with the Wind* (Victor Fleming film), 174
Gore, Catherine, 73
Gore, John, 157
Gorer, Geoffrey, 183
Gower, Lord Granville, 38
*Granby* (Lister, T.), 72, 73
Grant, Hugh, 210–11
Gray, John, 141
Gray, Thomas, 9, 186
Great Bookham, Surrey, 15
*The Great War and Modern Memory* (Fussell, P.), 144
Greenfield, Sayre, 214

Grundy, Isobel, 3–4
Gubar, Susan, 190

*H*

Hake, Henry, 168–70
Hamilton, Elizabeth, 38, 66
Hamilton, Victoria, 211
Hammond, Christopher, 127
Hancock, Philadelphia, 179
Harding, D. W., 184, 188–89, 226, 227
*Harper's Monthly*, 132
Harrison, Suzan, 215
Hartley, L. P., 148–49
Hastings, George E., 75, 76
Hawke, Lady Cassandra, 15
Hazlitt, William, 71
Head, Edith, 174
Heath, Edward, 188
Heckerling, Amy, 209
Henry, Emile, 139
Henry VIII, 4
*Herbert Lacy* (Lister, T.), 72
Heyer, Georgette, 200
Hicks, Greg, 211
Hill, Constance, 137–38, 149–50, 225
Hill, Ellen, 137–39, 149–51
Hill, Rev. Herbert, 86
Hill, Walter M., 168
Hilton, Phil, 208
"History of England" (Austen, J.), 4, 5, 18, 156
*History of England* (Goldsmith, O.), 4, 143
Hitler, Adolf, 175, 176
Hodder Headline (publisher), 205
Hogan, Charles Beecher, 168, 180, 181
Holbert, George, 13
Holford, Margaret, 25
Hook, Theodore, 84
Howard, Richard, 157
*Howards End* (James Ivory film), 210
Howells, W. D., 26, 128–29, 132, 150
Hubback, Catherine Anne, 90, 96, 142
Hubback, John, and daughter Edith, 142–43, 168–69
Hubble, Grace, 174

Hughes, Gwyneth, 216

Huntingdon, Margaret Lane, Countess of, 154, 187

Hutton, R. H., 119, 134–35

Huxley, Aldous, 148, 173–74

Hythe, Kent, 56

*Ida of Athens* (Owenson, S.), 58

Iddesleigh, Stanford Northcote, Earl of, 129

*Idler*, 11

*The Impregnable Women* (Linklater, E.), 175

*The Improvement of the Estate* (Duckworth, A.), 189

Inchbald, Mrs. Elizabeth, 3, 28, 124

*Independent*, 208

*The Irish Guards in the Great War* (Kipling, R.), 148

J

Jackson, Eleanor (Mrs. Henry Austen), 77, 79

Jacobinism, 189

James, Henry, xv, xvii, 133–34, 161, 163, 166, 182, 227

*Jane Austen, Facts and Problems* (Chapman, R. W.), 170

*Jane Austen, Her Homes and Her Friends* (Hill, C.), 138–39, 151

*Jane Austen: Her Life and Letters* (Austen-Leigh, W. and R. A.), 143

*Jane Austen: Irony as Defense and Discovery* (Mudrick, M.), 188–89

*Jane Austen, sa vie et son oeuvre* (Villard, L.), 143

*Jane Austen: The World of Her Novels* (Le Faye, D.), 193

*Jane Austen and Her Art* (Lascelles, M.), 182

*Jane Austen and the War of Ideas* (Butler, M.), 189

*The Jane Austen Book Club* (Fowler, K. J.), xviii, 217

Jane Austen Festival, Bath, xviii

*Jane Austen in Hollywood* (Troost, L., and Greenfield, S.), 214, 247n31

*Jane Austen* (Jenkins, E.), 182

*Jane Austen's Guide to Dating* (Henderson, L.), 205

*Jane Austen's Letters to Her Sister Cassandra and Others* (Chapman, R. W.), 159, 166, 169, 171, 216, 228

Jane Austen Society, 181, 182, 194
  Cecil as president, 186
  demographics of committee, 187–88
  formation of, 177–79

*Jane Austen Society Collected Reports*, 193, 194

Jane Austen Society of Australia, 193–94

Jane Austen Society of North America (JASNA), 193–94

*Jane Austen's Regency World*, 226

*Jane Austen's Sailor Brothers* (Hubback, J. H. and E. C.), 142–43, 169

*Jane Eyre* (Brontë, C.), 99

"Janeism," xvii, 129–31, 145, 146–48, 153, 158, 162–64, 186
  spread of, 164, 165
  term "Janeite," coining of, 128

Janson-Smith, Patrick, 206

Jay, John, 75

Jefferies, Richard, 183

Jenkins, Elizabeth, 156, 170, 178, 180, 187, 221

Johnson, Claudia, xviii, 190, 194

Johnson, Dr. Samuel, 84, 146

Johnson, Richard Brimley, 128

Joyce, James, 142

*Julia de Gramont* (Hawke, C.), 15

K

Kafka, Franz, 149

*Kandukondian Kandukondian* (Rajiv Menon film), 209

Karup, Carl, 139

Kavanagh, Julia, 102

Kebbel, Thomas E., xx, 228–29

Kempe, C. E., 129–30

Kerr, Lady Robert, 45

Kettle, Arnold, 185

Keynes, Geoffrey, 145

King, B. B., xvi
King, Larry, 218
Kipling, Rudyard, 130, 146–48, 163
Knatchbull-Hugessen, Edward, Lord
    Brabourne, 120–21, 166–67, 168
Knight, Rev. Charles, 93
Knight, Edward (JA's brother), 3, 5, 32, 34,
    37, 40, 45, 58, 78, 79–80
  attendance at JA's funeral, 61
  death of, 98
  financial help from, 34
  landed gentleman in Kent, 22
Knight, Fanny (later Lady Knatchbull), 37,
    45, 47, 52–53, 57, 58, 111, 180, 187
  Cassandra's empathy with, 32, 88
  inheritance of Jane's letters, 90, 95
  publication of letters Cassandra left to, 120
  reluctance to divulge letters, 104, 107–8,
    118
Knight, Major Edward, 178
Koenigstein, François Claudius (known as
    Ravachol), 139

L

Lamb, Lady Caroline, 71
Lang, Andrew, 199
Lascelles, Mary, 167, 182
*The Last of the Mohicans* (Cooper, J. F.), 76
Lawrence, D. H., 152–53
Le Croix, Octavius, 129
Le Faye, Deirdre, 172, 191, 193
Leavis, F. R., 132, 182
Leavis, Q. D., 185
Lee, Ang, 208, 209–10, 217
Lefroy, Anne, 7, 18, 19
Lefroy, Fanny Caroline, 88
Lefroy, Jane Anna Elizabeth ("Anna," JA's
    niece), 22, 28, 38–39, 47–48, 81, 85, 88,
    90–91, 95
  on Catherine Anne Hubback's purloining
    JA's work, 96–97
  and literary reputation of JA, 101, 103,
    104–5
  manuscript items in possession of, 95
  on portrait of JA, 115

Lefroy, Sophia, 47
Lefroy, Tom (chief justice of Ireland), 23,
    105, 106, 109
Lefroy, Tom (nephew of Tom Sr.), 105
Leigh, Augusta, 54
Leigh, James Henry, 15
Leigh, Mary, 15
Leigh, Dr. Theophilus, 15
Leigh, Rev. Thomas, 15
Leigh Perrot, James, 78
Leigh Perrot, Jane, 29, 40, 79
Leigh Perrot family, 40, 56, 65, 79, 80
Leonard, Robert Z., 173, 174
*Letters of Jane Austen* (Knatchbull-
    Hugesson, E., ed.), 120–22, 166–67,
    168
Lewes, G. H., xix, 94, 99–100, 101, 132, 161,
    163
Liddell, Alvar, 188
*Life of Byron* (Moore, T.), 102
*Life of Charlotte Brontë* (Gaskell, E.), 99,
    110
*Life of Scott* (Lockhart, J. G.), 76, 85, 88,
    102
Linklater, Eric, 175
*Lionel Lincoln* (Cooper, J. F.), 84
Lister, Thomas, 72–73, 83
Littleworth, William, 92
Litz, A. Walton, 184
Lizars, engraver of JA's portrait, 116–17,
    142, 169, 206
Lloyd, Martha (later Lady Francis Austen),
    1, 5, 25, 42, 53, 77
  Cassandra's intended executrix, 89
  collaboration with Jane on *Mansfield Park*,
    47
  marriage to Frank Austen, 80
  and reading of "First Impressions," 24, 96
Lloyd, Mary (later Mrs. James Austen), 5,
    105, 111
Lockhart, John Gibson, 76, 85, 88, 102
Lodge, David, 194–95
*Loiterer*, 11–13, 36, 39, 40
London, 37, 43, 176
London Bridge, 182

*London Review of Books*, 191

*Lost in Austen* (ITV), 217

Lothian, Philip Kerr, Marquess of, 173

"Love and Freindship" (Austen, J.), 12, 156, 165, 208

Lovering, Frederick, 170, 180

Lowell, James Russell, 124

Lowndes, Thomas (publisher), 21

Lucas, E. V., 128, 136

Ludlow, Lady Alice, 155

Lyford, Dr. Giles King, 59

Lynch, Deidre, 214

## M

Macaulay, Thomas Babington, xix, 84, 94, 102, 163

MacCarthy, Rachel, 149

Macmillan (publisher), 127

*Macmillan's Magazine*, 120

*The Madwoman in the Attic* (Gilbert, S., and Gubar, S.), 190

Malden, Sarah Fanny, 124, 134

Mallarmé, Stephane, 140, 141, 142

Malthus, Thomas, 71

Mansfield, Katherine, 165, 200, 224

*Mansfield Park* (Austen, J.), 21, 81, 191
    beginnings of, 36, 41
    copyright expiry on, 94
    criticism of, 47
    economies in production of, 46–47
    French translation of, 74
    publication of, 46–47, 50, 51
    success of, 46, 47–48
    themes of, 46
    wartime references in, 223
    wasting of, 77

*Mansfield Park* (BBC TV), 211

*Mansfield Park* (ITV), 209, 211, 215

*Mansfield Park* (Patricia Rozema film), 191, 209, 215

*The Man Who Loved Jane Austen* (O'Rourke, S. S.), 217

Manydown House, Basingstoke, 30

Marivaux, Pierre, 69

*Marmion* (Scott, W.), 37

Martin, Mrs., of Maidenhead Inn, 21–22

Martineau, Harriet, 224

Marx, Groucho, 126

*Mary de Clifford* (Brydges, S. E.), 18–19

*Mary Hamilton* (Austen, A.), 103

Mathew, Anne (Mrs. James Austen), 13

McGrath, Douglas, 209–10

*Memoir of Jane Austen* (Austen-Leigh, J. E.), xx, 27, 104, 105, 155–56, 161, 205, 208, 225
    family reading favorites, 137
    portrait of Jane in, 116–17
    public interest, stirring of, 117, 118, 122, 197
    reviews and derivatives, 123–24, 125–26, 142–43

*Memoirs of Dr. Burney* (Burney, F.), 84

Merrill, Stuart, 140

Metcalfe, Katherine, 154–55, 162

Milbanke, Annabella, 44, 54

Milne, A. A., 173

*Miss Austen Regrets* (BBC TV), 216

Mitford, Mary Russell, 23, 48–49, 61, 115, 220, 228, 237n55

Montolieu, Isabelle de, 74

Moore, George, 201

Moore, Tom, 102

More, Hannah, 35

Morgan, Lady, 72

Morgan, J. Pierpont, 158, 168, 180

Morier, James Justinian, 84

Morley, Frances, Countess of, 54, 56, 72

Morley, Karen, 175

Mudrick, Marvin, 184, 188, 191, 203

Murfin, Jane, 174

Murray, John (publisher), 50–51, 53, 54, 55, 57, 66, 68, 76–77, 80

## N

National Trust, xvi, 179, 211

Neagle, Anna, 177

Newman, Thomas Harding, 121

*The New Rosciad* (Leigh, J. H.), 15

*New York Times*, xvi, 170, 205

Nicolson, Harold, 167
*Night Thoughts* (Young, E.), 144
Nixon, Cheryl L., 214
Nokes, David, 192
Norfolk, Andrew, 218–19
*Northanger Abbey* (Austen, J.), xv, 16, 21, 81,
    191
  copyright expiry on, 94
  Metcalfe edition, 154–55
  posthumous publication with
    "Biographical Notice," 68–69
  Queen Victoria's reading of, 95
  remaindering of, 77
  "Susan," first version, 21, 24–26, 29, 33
*Northanger Abbey* (ITV), 209, 211
*Notes & Queries*, 94, 164, 193
*Nouvelle revue française*, 142
*Novels of Jane Austen* (Chapman, R. W.),
    155, 157–58, 166
*Nuts*, 208

O'Connor, Frances, 215
*The Odd Women* (Gissing, G.), 137
O'Farrell, Mary Ann, 217
*Old Friends and New Fancies* (Brinton,
    S. G.), 216
Oliphant, Margaret, xvii, 119–20, 123, 126,
    184, 197–98
Olivier, Laurence, 175
Opie, Mrs. Amelia, 75–76
O'Rourke, Sally Smith, 217
Oxenden, Mary, 43

&#x1D4AB;

Paget, Lady Augusta, 38, 66
Palmer, Harriet, 180
Paltrow, Gwyneth, 208
Payne and Cadell (publisher), 16, 20–21
*Pelham, or The Adventures of a Gentleman*
    (Bulwer-Lytton, E. G. E. L.), 72
Pellew, George, 133
Pemberley, Republic of, 225–26
*Pemberley* (Tennant, E.), 217
Penney, Christine, 54

*Personal Aspects of Jane Austen* (Austen-
    Leigh, M. A.), 57, 143
*Persuasion* (Austen, J.), xv, 21, 81, 200
  beginnings of, 57
  copyright expiry on, 94
  posthumous publication with
    "Biographical Notice," 68–69
  remaindering of, 77
  wartime references in, 223
*Persuasion* (BBC TV), 208–9
*Persuasion* (ITV), 209
*The Pilot* (Cooper, J. F.), 83
Pinter, Harold, 191
*The Pioneers* (Cooper, J. F.), 76
Piper, Billie, 215
Plunkett, Walter, 174
Poe, Edgar Allan, 132
*Poems of the North* (Brett-Smith, H. F.),
    146
*The Poetical Register*, 7
Pollock, Sir Frederick, 150
Poovey, Mary, 190
*A Portrait of Jane Austen* (Cecil, D.), 186
Potter, Beatrix, 179
*Precaution* (Cooper, J. F.), 74–76
*Pride and Prejudice* (Austen, J.), 81, 190, 199,
    214
  "book the United Kingdom can't do
    without," xvii
  copyright expiry on, 94
  "Darcy-philia," 44
  "First Impressions," first version, 17,
    20–21, 24–25, 35, 36
  Metcalfe edition, 154–55
  opening sentence, xvi–xvii
  referred to as best of Austen's writing,
    55
  remaindering of, 77
  rights to, 80
  second edition published, 50
*Pride and Prejudice* (BBC TV), 206–7,
    212
*Pride and Prejudice* (Joe Wright film), 209
*Pride and Prejudice* (Robert Z. Leonard
    film), 173–75, 211

*Pride and Promiscuity: The Lost Sex Scenes of Jane Austen* (Eckstut, A.), 218

Prior, Matthew, 144

Proust, Marcel, 166

Pushkin, Alexander, 74

## Q

*Quarterly Review*, 54, 68

Queen Victoria. *See* Victoria, Queen

Quincy, Eliza, 97, 106, 117

## R

Radcliffe, Anne Ward, 3, 21, 28

Rajan, Rajeswari Sunder, 191

Raleigh, Sir Walter, 154, 162, 202, 203

*Rambler*, 11

*The Real Jane Austen* (BBC TV), 212

*The Regency Rules* (Henderson, L.), 205

*Retrospective Review*, 70

*Review of English Studies*, 193

*La Revue blanche*, 141, 142

Rhydderch, David, 130

Rice, Elizabeth, 107

Rice, Rev. John Morland, 121

Rice Portrait, 121–22, 142, 168–69, 241n69

Richardson, Samuel, 16, 28, 69, 201

Rickword, Edgell, 182–83

Rigler, Laurie, 221

Robinson, Henry Crabbe, 85

Robinson, John Mackinnon, 160

Robson of Bond Street (publisher), 16

Roosevelt, Franklin D., 176

Rosebery, Archibald Philip Primrose, Earl, 168

Routledge (publisher), 126

Royal Academy, 46

Rozema, Patricia, 191, 215

## S

Said, Edward, 191

Saintsbury, George, 126, 127–28, 129, 135–36, 162

Sand, George, 140

Sandford, Henry, 86–87

"Sanditon" (Austen, J.), 1, 36, 90, 97, 100, 117, 164, 224

beginnings of as "The Brothers," 49–50, 59

Chapman and, 155

James Edward and access to, 104

Sassoon, Siegfried, 145, 180

*Saturday Night Live* (NBC TV), 209

Saxton, Eugene, 173

Scacchi, Greta, 211

*School for Scandal* (Sheridan, R. B.), 14

Scott, Sir Walter, 37, 45, 54–55, 65, 71, 85, 111, 139, 162, 223

*Scrutiny*, 185

Sedgwick, Eve, 191

*Self-Control* (Brunton, M.), 37

*The Semi-Attached Couple* (Eden, E.), 72

*Sense and Sensibility* (Ang Lee film), 208, 210–11

*Sense and Sensibility* (Austen, J.), 31, 81, 221–22

copyright expiry on, 94

"Elinor and Marianne," first version, 17, 19–20, 25, 35

French translation of, 74

remaindering of, 77

rewrites and first publication of, 36–37

second edition published, 50

*Sense and Sensibility* (ITV), 209

Seurat, Georges, 142

*Sex and the City* (HBO TV), 205

Seymour, Beatrice Kean, 176

Shakespeare, William, xix, 44, 84, 95, 100, 108, 163–64, 175

Sharp, Anne, 180

Shearer, Norma, 173

Sheridan, Richard Brinsley, 14, 43, 82–83, 89

Shervington, Diana, 172

Shields, Carol, 23

Shirreff, Miss (ardent fan of JA's writing), 43–44, 88

Sibleys, Misses, of West Meon, 22

Silhouette Romances, 200

Simpson, Richard, 119, 163, 223

*Sir Charles Grandison* (Richardson, S.), 16, 28, 35

Smiles, Samuel, 50

Smiley, Sir Hugh and Lady, 188

Smith, Charlotte, 3, 124

Smith, Goldwin, 160

Smith, Lori, 225

Smith, Sidney, 85

*Sonnets and Other Poems* (Brydges, S. E.), 7–8

Soofi, Mayank Austen, xviii–xix

Sotheby's, 168, 180

Sourcebooks, 217

Southam, Brian, 57–58, 162, 193

Southey, Robert, 85, 86–87, 88, 114

*Spectator*, 11, 116, 119

Spence, Jon, 212

*The Spy* (Cooper, J. F.), 83

Staël, Anne Louise, Madame de, 48, 83

Stalin, Joseph, 176

Stanhope, Philip Henry, Lord, 118

St. Clair, William, 22

Stephen, Leslie, 124–25, 128, 136, 162, 163, 165

Stevens, Dana, 205

Stevenson, Robert Louis, 141

Steventon, Hampshire, 43, 62, 77–78, 103, 129, 138, 143, 150, 236n23, 237n55
    Jane's birth and life in, 3, 5, 9–10, 11, 14, 18, 21, 24, 30, 39
    rectory at, 22, 106, 109, 112, 158

Steventon & Manydown Reading Society, 22

Strachey, Lytton, 165

*Studies on Hysteria* (Freud, S.), 136

*Sunday Times*, 207

*Survivor* (CBS TV), 217

"Susan" (Austen, J.), 21, 24, 33, 35, 36, 50, 66
    manuscript of, changes in, 58
    publication problems, 29–31
    *see also Northanger Abbey*

Sutherland, Kathryn, 35, 155

### *T*

Tailhade, Laurent, 139–40

Tanner, Tony, 184

*Tatler*, 11

Tauchnitz (German publisher), 139

Temple Bar, 137

Tennant, Emma, 217

Tennyson, Alfred, 95

Thackeray, Anne, 119, 196, 225

Thackeray, William Makepeace, 94, 141, 211

Thalberg, Irving, 173

Thompson, Emma, 210

Thompson, Sophie, 211

Thomson, Hugh, 127, 214

Thrale, Hester Lynch (later Mrs. Piozzi), 84

*Times*, 156, 219

*Times Literary Supplement* (*TLS*), 156, 164, 192

Tomalin, Claire, xviii

*Topographer*, 18

Toulouse-Lautrec, Henri de, 142

Trayler, Helen, 206

Trilling, Lionel, xx, 177, 184, 189, 191, 227

Trollope, Anthony, 183

Troost, Linda, 214

Twain, Mark, 131–32

Twitchell, Joseph, 132

Tytler, Sarah, 124

### *U*

*An Unequal Marriage* (Tennant, E.), 217

### *V*

Vallotton, Félix, 142

*The Vicar of Wakefield* (Goldsmith, O.), 131

Victoria, Queen, xvi, 95, 120

Villard, Léonie, 143

Vuillard, Édouard, 142

### *W*

*A Walk with Jane Austen* (Smith, L.), 225

Walkley, A. B., 152

*Wall Street Journal*, 209

*The Wanderer* (Burney, F.), 39, 52, 84

Ward, Mrs. Humphrey, 120

"The Watsons" (Austen, J.), 28, 31, 35, 59, 90, 96, 97, 104, 117, 155, 164, 167
  beginnings of, 31
  manuscript, 35
Watt, Ian, 132, 184
Waugh, Alec, 144
*Waverley* (Scott, W.), 45
Webster & Co. (publisher), 131
Wellington, Gerald Wellesley, Duke of, 188
Werksman, Deb, 217
West, Rebecca, 161–62
Whately, Richard, Archbishop of Dublin, 68–69
Whitbread, Samuel, 43
White, John, 92
Wilde, Oscar, 141
Williams, Olivia, 211, 216
Williams, Raymond, 184, 189
Wilson, Edmund, xix, 184–85
Winchester, Hampshire, 59, 61, 62, 129–31

Winchester Cathedral
  Jane Austen's tomb, questions on whereabouts of, 63, 122
  memorial tablet in, 122, 130
Wired (blog), 219
Wollstonecraft, Mary, 28
*Women as They Are* (Gore, C.), 73
Woolf, Virginia, xviii, xx, 4, 83, 158–59, 164, 165, 206
Wordsworth, William, 86, 100
Wordsworth editions, 205–6
*Wuthering Heights* (Brontë, E.), 99
*Wuthering Heights* (William Wyler film), 173
Wyler, William, 175

Yellow Book, 136, 142
Young, Edward, 144
*The Young Visiters* (Ashford, D.), 156
*The Younger Sister* (Hubback, C.-A.), 96–97

Zidane, Zinedine, xvi

# About the Author

CLAIRE HARMAN is the author of a biography of the novelist Sylvia Townsend Warner that won the John Llewellyn Rhys prize. Her subsequent biography of the eighteenth-century novelist Fanny Burney was shortlisted for the Whitbread Prize. Her last book, *Myself and the Other Fellow: A Life of Robert Louis Stevenson*, was published in hardcover in 2005 to great critical acclaim on both sides of the Atlantic. Harman has taught English at the universities of Manchester and Oxford in England and creative writing at Columbia University in New York City. She writes regularly for the literary press, reviewing books, films, plays, and exhibitions. Harman was elected a Fellow of the Royal Society of Literature in 2006.